WEAPONS FOR VICTORY

WEAPONS FOR VICTORY

THE HIROSHIMA DECISION FIFTY YEARS LATER

Robert James Maddox

University of Missouri Press   Columbia and London

Library of Congress Cataloging-in-Publication Data

Maddox, Robert James.

   Weapons for victory : the Hiroshima decision fifty years later /
Robert James Maddox.

     p.   cm.

   Includes bibliographical references and index.

   ISBN 0-8262-1037-6 (alk. paper)

   1. Hiroshima-shi (Japan)—History—Bombardment, 1945. 2. Nagasaki-shi
(Japan)—History—Bombardment, 1945. 3. Atomic bomb—History. 4. United
States—Military policy. 5. Nuclear warfare—Moral and ethical aspects.
6. United States—Foreign relations—Soviet Union. 7. Soviet Union—Foreign
relations—United States. I. Title.

D767.25.H6M23   1995

940.54'25—dc20   95-20129

                                                   CIP

Designer: Stephanie Foley

Typesetter: BOOKCOMP

Printer and Binder: Thomson-Shore, Inc.

Typefaces: Franklin Gothic and Palatino

CONTENTS

ACKNOWLEDGMENTS

A grant from the Nuclear History Program and a sabbatical leave from the Pennsylvania State University enabled me to complete the research for this volume. The staffs at archives and libraries were unfailingly helpful, but I owe special thanks to Edward J. Drea at The Center of Military History, Larry Bland at the George C. Marshall Library, and to Will Mahoney at the National Archives. I am indebted to John Lukacs and Robert H. Ferrell for their advice and help, and to my colleague Christine A. White for sanding down some of the rough spots in my prose.

WEAPONS FOR VICTORY

When one considers the possibility that the Japanese military would have sacrificed the entire nation if it were not for the atomic bomb attack, then this bomb might be described as having saved Japan.

—Dr. Taro Takemi,
former president of the Japan Medical Association

On the morning of August 6, 1945, the American B-29 *Enola Gay* released an atomic bomb over the Japanese city of Hiroshima. The explosion caused enormous physical destruction, killed at least seventy thousand inhabitants outright, and wounded many thousands more. On August 9 another bomb was dropped on Nagasaki. These two catastrophic events have remained controversial ever since, as shown by the furor over the National Air and Space Museum's *Enola Gay* exhibit and over the gruesome mushroom cloud postage stamp in the autumn of 1994. The official justification for using the bombs was that they saved enormous losses on both sides by avoiding an invasion of Japan. Critics have disputed this explanation as simplistic, or worse. They have accused President Harry S. Truman and his advisers of everything from failing to explore alternatives to engaging in a monstrous conspiracy to slaughter all those people for no more compelling reason than to employ "atomic diplomacy" against the Soviet Union.

Although some individuals earlier had condemned using the bombs, criticism mounted during the tumultuous 1960s when growing opposition to the Vietnam war spawned slashing attacks on all aspects of recent American foreign policy. Books by William Appleman Williams and D. F. Fleming echoed the charge originally levied by British scientist P. M. S. Blackett that Hiroshima and Nagasaki may more accurately be seen as the first chapter of the cold war than as the last chapter of World War II. Neither Williams nor Fleming, however, offered much in the way of substantiation for this provocative assertion.[1]

In 1965, Gar Alperovitz's *Atomic Diplomacy: Hiroshima and Potsdam, the Use of the Atomic Bomb and the American Confrontation with Soviet Power* appeared. Here was an entire volume devoted to the issue, heavily freighted with academic paraphernalia (every chapter contained more than one hundred footnotes, some more than two hundred), purporting to show that Truman and the men around him all along regarded the bombs primarily for their value in making the Soviets "more manageable" rather than for their merit in defeating an already beaten Japan. Indeed, according to Alperovitz, Truman deliberately refrained from seeking Japan's surrender until the bombs could be used to impress the Soviets with the enormous power the United States had at its disposal.[2]

The book had an enormous impact in the field. Those favorably inclined toward what was known as "New Left revisionism" greeted it as a pathbreaking exposure of a plot the Truman administration had taken great pains to conceal from the American people. One reviewer hailed it as "A daring and elaborate work of historical reconstruction." *Atomic Diplomacy*, Christopher Lasch later proclaimed, "made it difficult for conscientious scholars any longer to avoid the challenge of revisionist historians."[3] Even those who did not accept Alperovitz's conclusions for the most part treated the book as a scholarly enterprise. What reviewers did not know, or neglected to point out, was that despite the appearance of meticulous documentation it was based on pervasive misrepresentations of the historical record.

Atomic Diplomacy went on to become a staple in revisionist literature. It was frequently cited, if not always with total approval, and excerpts from it began appearing in numerous anthologies. It has since been revised and expanded twice. Of the 1985 version, Yale diplomatic historian Gaddis Smith wrote that despite a few "relatively minor errors" the "preponderance of new evidence since 1965 sustains the original argument."[4] The thesis that Truman wanted to use the bomb to make the Soviets "more manageable" now appears in some of the most popular diplomatic history textbooks used by thousands of students. Walter LaFeber's *The American Age: U.S. Foreign Policy at Home and Abroad*, for instance, has Truman practicing "atomic diplomacy" by "waving the bomb without making overt threats and hoping the Soviets would give in."[5]

Over the past decade a new wrinkle has been introduced to cast suspicion on the claim that Truman used the bombs to prevent heavy losses. In "A Postwar Myth: 500,000 U.S. Lives Saved" (1986), Stanford historian Barton J. Bernstein compared that figure—which is what Truman claimed that General George C. Marshall had told him—with casualty projections made by military planners in mid-June 1945 for the proposed two-stage invasion of Japan. The planners' report estimated that approximately 40,000 soldiers would be killed, and another 153,500 men would be wounded or missing in action. Although Bernstein limited himself to suggesting ominously that the "myth" had helped deter Americans from asking "troubling questions" and that its destruction "should reopen these questions," Alperovitz and others have since used the lower figures to support the conspiracy thesis.[6]

This is writing history backward. That Truman and those of his advisers who participated in the decision to use the bombs later would defend themselves against criticism by exaggerating (if such they did) the cost of invasion tells us nothing about their thinking at the time. Even if Truman had been informed of the planners' estimates—he was not— the notion that he would have considered the sacrifice of forty thousand (or twenty thousand or ten thousand) American lives acceptable had it not been for the opportunity to awe the Soviets is droll. As he put it to an individual who tried to persuade him not to use the bombs: "The question was whether we wanted to save many American lives and Japanese lives or whether we wanted . . . to win the war by killing all our young men."[7]

Alperovitz, Bernstein, and others have given wide publicity to the "low" casualty estimates in numerous magazine articles and in Op Ed pieces in newspapers such as the *Washington Post* and the *New York Times*. The text that would have accompanied the *Enola Gay* exhibit as originally written also relied on the same document. A revised version used instead an estimate of sixty-three thousand casualties for the first stage of the invasion, scheduled for November 1. This number Bernstein had "found" (other scholars have known about it for years) in a June 18 diary entry of Admiral William D. Leahy, Truman's personal chief of staff and a member of the Joint Chiefs of Staff.[8]

Citing casualty estimates made in June from any source presents a glaringly misleading picture of what the military situation looked like by the time orders went out to use atomic bombs. These figures were based on the assumption that the Japanese had about 350,000 defenders at the initial landing sites and that American air and naval power would prevent large-scale augmentation. As early as 1982, Australian scholars Dennis and Peggy Warner showed that the planners' report was based on "singularly poor intelligence," and that by late July new data placed the number of defenders at 545,000 with three months left to continue pouring in reinforcements before the invasion began. Recent books by Edward J. Drea (1992) and John Ray Skates (1994) provide more detailed accounts of this massive, unanticipated buildup. The Warners also pointed out that the casualty figures "tossed about" in mid-June "might have been surpassed in a single day" by kamikaze attacks on packed troop transports.[9]

The conclusion is inescapable. Those who still cite either the planners' report or Leahy's June 18 diary entry as relevant to the actual circumstances either remain unaware of the literature on the subject, in which case they are incompetent to write about it, or they know the figures had become meaningless but nonetheless continue to employ them to promote their own agendas.

Other revisionist fictions were included in the original *Enola Gay* text. Visitors to the Smithsonian Institution would have learned that Admiral Leahy "said in 1950 that he had denounced the bombing as adopting 'ethical standards common to barbarians in the dark ages' " and that in 1948 General Dwight D. Eisenhower claimed "to have opposed the use of the bomb in conversations with President Truman." This information supports the view that Truman knew the bombs were militarily unnecessary (as well as morally repugnant to at least two of his highest-ranking officers) but used them anyway to awe the Soviets. In an apparent gesture toward fairness, the text admitted that "corroborating evidence for these assertions is weak." The truth is that corroborating evidence is nonexistent for the simple reason that neither Leahy nor Eisenhower made the assertions attributed to them.

The Leahy quotation appears in the final pages of his memoirs, published in 1950. He made clear that these passages represented his attitude at the time of writing, but nowhere in the book did he even suggest that he had voiced such objections before Hiroshima. Eisenhower in 1948 wrote that he had expressed misgivings about the bombs to Secretary of War Henry L. Stimson. He said nothing about mentioning them "in conversations with President Truman."[10]

The present volume offers interpretations of the events leading up to Hiroshima and Nagasaki. Along the way I have pointed out some of the more blatant revisionist distortions such as those already mentioned. I have done so not merely to be argumentative, but in the probably vain hope that such myths no longer will be treated seriously in the discourse about using atomic bombs against Japan.

CHAPTER 1

The Legacy of Unconditional Surrender

President Franklin D. Roosevelt and British Prime Minister Winston S. Churchill met at Casablanca, French Morocco, in January 1943. They and their staffs discussed matters such as the administration of North Africa and future operations against the Axis powers. The meeting concluded on January 24 with an outdoor press conference. In his opening remarks, Roosevelt stated, "The elimination of German, Japanese and Italian war power means the unconditional surrender by Germany, Italy, and Japan." This did not imply the "destruction" of the populations of these nations, he continued, but rather of the "philosophies . . . based on conquest and the subjugation of other people." He went on to say that the conference should be called "the 'Unconditional Surrender' meeting," to which Churchill at his side responded "Hear! Hear!" Thus was launched one of the most controversial policies of the war.[1]

Roosevelt later explained that the phrase had occurred to him just a few minutes earlier when he had persuaded two rival French leaders to shake hands in front of photographers. "We had so much trouble getting these two French generals together that I thought to myself that this was as difficult as arranging the meeting of [Ulysses S.] Grant and [Robert E.] Lee," he said, "and then suddenly the press conference was on, and Winston and I had no time to prepare for it, and the thought popped into my mind that they had called Grant 'Old Unconditional Surrender' and the next thing I knew, I had said it."[2]

Why Roosevelt felt compelled to pretend that the idea had just "popped" into his mind can only be guessed. Eight months earlier he had indicated his agreement with a State Department advisory group's conclusion that the war against Germany and Japan should be waged until they surrendered unconditionally. "We are fighting this war," as one of the group members put it, "because we did not have an unconditional surrender at the end of the last one."[3] Shortly before he left for Casablanca, Roosevelt had informed the Joint Chiefs of Staff that he intended to discuss with Churchill the advisability of notifying Stalin that the United States and Great Britain meant to fight "until they reached Berlin, and that their only terms would be unconditional surrender." At the press conference, moreover, he spoke from notes that referred to unconditional surrender three times.[4] He did ad lib mention of Grant's nickname, which appears to be the only accurate part of his recollection.

Churchill's memory proved equally faulty—or self-serving—when he said after the war that Roosevelt had made the statement "without consultation with me," and that he had supported it only because "working with great, loyal, and powerful friends from across the ocean, we had to accommodate ourselves."[5] That is false. On January 19 Churchill had cabled the British War Cabinet for its view on announcing Anglo-American determination to prosecute the war against Germany and Japan until unconditional surrender was achieved. The cabinet not only responded favorably, but recommended the inclusion of Italy.[6]

When reminded of this exchange of cables, Churchill admitted his error but then claimed that he *had* been surprised by Roosevelt's decision to reveal the policy at the press conference. Actually, Churchill himself had suggested to FDR at a meeting with the Combined Chiefs of Staff that they include a statement on unconditional surrender in the official press release. And he had added the word "Italy" in his own hand to the original draft of the release.[7] Possibly Roosevelt made the announcement orally because he thought it would receive more attention that way, but this was a matter of procedure only. And Churchill, at the end of his own remarks to the press, had defined the Allied goal as "the unconditional surrender of the criminal forces that have plunged the world in sorrow and ruin."[8] Churchill's postwar efforts to distance himself from the doctrine should not be permitted to conceal the fact that at the time Roosevelt with good reason believed the British supported it.

Critics have denounced unconditional surrender as a colossal error; one referred to it as "perhaps the biggest political mistake of the war."[9] German and Japanese propagandists used it to promote the belief that the Allies meant to destroy their societies, some have pointed out, thereby bolstering the will to persevere. Failure to hold out prospects of a negotiated peace also undermined those Germans who otherwise would have been encouraged to overthrow Hitler. This, in turn, might have resulted in German capitulation before Soviet armies penetrated into the heart of Europe. The formula also weakened the position of Japanese peace advocates, who might have ended the Pacific conflict months earlier had assurances been given that their emperor could be retained.

Defenders of unconditional surrender emphasize how speculative such criticisms necessarily are. Propagandists in the Axis powers controlled the media, and unconditional surrender merely provided them with additional grist for their contention that national survival was at stake. Besides, through countless radio broadcasts and other means, the Allies repeatedly declared—as FDR had in his original announcement—that the formula did *not* mean social destruction and enslavement. Potential conspirators against Hitler and the Japanese moderates most certainly were aware of these promises.

Even more important, the armies of both nations held effective power and without their support no group could have entered negotiations for peace. Not only were the militarists' own hands stained by complicity in bringing on the war and in the commission of widespread atrocities, but also the terms they would have insisted on to salvage their own status would have been unacceptable. In short, there is no way of telling whether the doctrine prolonged the war in any way.

The value of the unconditional surrender formula, advocates argue, far outweighed any drawbacks. It offered an uncomplicated, inspirational slogan for popular consumption. It served as a pledge to suspicious Soviet leaders that the United States and Great Britain would make no separate peace. Most important, it provided the lowest common denominator of war aims among the Allies, thereby preventing divisive disputes before victory was attained. "Frankly, I do not like the idea of [tripartite] conversations to define the term 'unconditional surrender,' " Roosevelt wrote on one occasion. "Whatever words we might agree on would probably have to be modified or changed the first time some nation wanted to surrender."[10]

No doubt Roosevelt did value the phrase as a slogan, by which he often set great store. Throughout the war he considered American morale a delicate commodity and often made significant concessions to it. He had agreed to the invasion of North Africa against the advice of his top military advisers in part because he believed it was imperative for public opinion that the United States go on the offensive against Germany as quickly as possible. "It is of the highest importance," he told his advisers, "that U.S. ground troops be brought into action against the enemy in 1942."[11]

Events surrounding the North African landings in November of that year provided additional reasons for promulgating the doctrine. French officials and troops in Morocco, Tunisia, and Algeria were at least nominally loyal to the so-called Vichy government, a quasi-fascist, collaborationist regime established after German victory in 1940. Resistance by some 120,000 French soldiers in North Africa might imperil operations being carried out by mostly inexperienced invasion forces. To avoid this potential catastrophe, Allied commander Dwight D. Eisenhower negotiated an armistice with a high-level Vichy official, Admiral Jean Darlan, who happened to be in Algiers at the time. Eisenhower also had Darlan installed as commander in chief of French military forces and as head of the civil government in North Africa. What became known as the "Darlan Deal" aroused great furor in the United States because it struck many as a perversion of what the war was supposed to be about.

Roosevelt, intimidated by the public outcry, for several days refused to support what Eisenhower had done. Only strong protests by FDR's personal chief of staff, Admiral William D. Leahy; Army Chief of Staff George C. Marshall; and Secretary of War Henry L. Stimson prodded him into defending Eisenhower's actions. He tried to placate critics by announcing that negotiations for an armistice had been motivated by the understandable desire to save lives, and that military and civil arrangements were temporary expedients "justified by the stress of battle." Darlan's assassination in December and the subsequent inclusion of Free French leader General Charles De Gaulle in the North African government helped to defuse the situation, but doubts remained. Unconditional surrender served notice that there would be no more such questionable "deals" in the future.[12]

The Darlan episode also had bearing on relations with the Soviet Union. Numerous reports had reached Washington and London of Soviet-German contacts in Sweden and elsewhere. If Joseph Stalin believed that the United States and Great Britain might be willing to strike a bargain with Germany, as they had with Darlan, would this not influence him to seek his own accommodation? Anglo-American failure to meet Soviet demands for a second front in Europe made this scenario more plausible. Roosevelt rashly had led Stalin to believe that such an operation would be mounted in 1942. The decision at Casablanca to postpone an invasion yet another year could only deepen the latter's suspicions that his allies were willing to see the Soviets and Germans tear each other apart while they waited to make advantageous settlements at little cost to themselves. Words were poor substitutes for action, but Roosevelt hoped to prevent a separate Nazi-Soviet peace by committing the United States and Great Britain to total victory.

FDR's devotion to the formula went well beyond such tactical considerations, important though they were. Noted for his vacillation on many issues, he rejected numerous subsequent requests to "clarify" the doctrine, thereby rendering it less ominous to the enemy in hopes of weakening resistance. Such requests, at various times, came from the British, the Combined Chiefs of Staff, the American Joint Chiefs of Staff, and the State, Navy, and War departments. Roosevelt occasionally wavered, but in the end spurned such pleas because he believed unconditional surrender was a prerequisite for achieving a lasting peace.

His familiarity with the concept had more recent application than General Grant's nickname. Toward the end of World War I, a heated debate had arisen in the press and in Congress over the terms that should be extended to Germany. "Unconditional surrender" became a popular phrase. Several Senate resolutions employed it as the only acceptable basis on which the war should end. War hero General John J. Pershing, commander of the Allied Expeditionary Force in France, supported it, as did Theodore Roosevelt. Franklin, in his capacity as Assistant Secretary of the Navy, could not speak to the issue openly but his conduct suggests that he was closer to his cousin's point of view than to President Woodrow Wilson's "Peace Without Victory." In a debate over disposition of the German navy, FDR as acting secretary urged the president to demand surrender rather than internment of the fleet, despite protests that the Germans would balk at such harsh treatment.[13]

Roosevelt later became well aware of the use Adolf Hitler and others had made of the "stab in the back" thesis: that Germany had not lost the war militarily but had been betrayed by Jews and marxists at home. He was determined that there be no repetition. When asked at a press conference in July 1944 whether unconditional surrender "still stands," he replied: "Yes. Practically all Germans deny the fact that they surrendered during the last war, but this time they are going to know it. And so are the Japs." Two weeks later he told reporters that the peace he envisioned would be "nothing like last time. That is out. That was a gift from God and General Foch."[14]

Reluctant to be specific about the formula, FDR often relied on a story about General Grant's conduct at Appomattox Courthouse at the end of the Civil War. There, he said, Grant refused to discuss Lee's repeated appeals for conditions. Finally, only *after* Lee agreed to unconditional surrender, Grant showed himself generous in providing food to hungry soldiers and permitting officers to keep their horses for the spring planting.[15] No one, apparently, informed Roosevelt that his version of history was fictitious. Grant had acquired his nickname years earlier during a campaign in the western theater. No exchange such as Roosevelt imagined ever took place between the two generals.

FDR wrote and spoke more often about his intentions toward the Germans than the Japanese. He regarded Germany as by far the greater threat, which is why he gave the European theater highest priority. As time went on, particularly after the successful Allied invasion of France in June 1944, it became obvious that Germany would be defeated long before Japan. Finally, treatment of Germany involved issues requiring agreement with the Soviet Union, which had not yet gone to war with Japan by the time of Roosevelt's death.

He was less benign toward the German people in private than his public allusions to Grant's generosity suggested. "We have got to be tough with Germany," he told Secretary of the Treasury Henry J. Morgenthau in August 1944, "and I mean the German people not just the Nazis. We either have to castrate the German people or you have got to treat them in such manner so they can't just go on reproducing people who want to continue the way they have in the past." A few weeks later he spoke in the same vein to Secretary of War Stimson. Too many Americans and British believed that "only a few Nazi leaders" were responsible for what had happened, he said, and that "is not based on fact. The German people as a whole must have it driven home to them that the whole nation had been engaged in an unlawful conspiracy."[16] His subsequent flirtation with Morgenthau's drastic plan to convert Germany into an agrarian nation provides another example of his attitude.

There is little reason to suppose that he felt much differently about how Japan should be treated, as indicated by his "And so are the Japs" statement cited above. That would have been implausible considering Japanese atrocities in China during the 1930s and their attack on Pearl Harbor. In April 1943, when he learned that the Japanese had executed several American aviators captured after an air raid on Tokyo a year earlier, he wrote Secretary of State Cordell Hull that he was "deeply stirred and horrified," and approved a note to the Japanese government stating that the United States intended to punish those officials responsible for "such uncivilized and inhuman acts."[17] As the Americans had been sentenced at public trials held in Tokyo, it was obvious that approval had come from the highest levels of government. Reports of the Bataan Death March reached Washington a few months later. Roosevelt withheld announcement until early 1944, at which time he told newsmen he thought the affair "gives us a pretty good slant . . . on the mentality of the Japanese."[18]

Roosevelt had provided no intimation of relenting on unconditional surrender for Japan by the time of his death on April 12, 1945. Churchill had made such a suggestion at the Yalta Conference in February. Why not invite the Soviet Union to join the United States, Great Britain, and China in issuing a declaration calling upon Japan to surrender unconditionally? Confronted with such great-power unity, Churchill went on, the Japanese might ask "what mitigation of the full rigor of unconditional surrender would be extended to her if she accepted the ultimatum." He said it would be up to the United States to decide, but "there was no doubt that some mitigation would be worth while if it led to the saving of a year or a year and a half of a war in which so much blood and treasures would be poured out."

FDR was unenthusiastic. He said the matter might be discussed with Stalin, but doubted an ultimatum would have much effect on the Japanese "who still seemed to think that they might get a satisfactory compromise." He told Churchill he doubted that they would "wake up" until all their islands had "felt the full weight of air attack."[19] Instead of suggesting a four-power declaration, Roosevelt negotiated an agreement with Stalin to join in the war against Japan after the defeat of Germany in return for concessions in Manchuria and elsewhere.

Roosevelt reported on the Yalta meeting before a joint session of Congress on March 1. Agreements reached with Stalin and Churchill, already published in the conference communiqué, enabled him to be more specific than before as to what would be done with Germany:

occupation, destruction of Nazism and militarism, punishment of war criminals, disarmament, and the extraction of reparations. Further along in his speech he indicated that something resembling such treatment awaited the Japanese, whose unconditional surrender "is as essential as the defeat of Germany." This "is especially true if our plans for world peace are to succeed. For Japanese militarism must be wiped out as thoroughly as German militarism."[20]

The Cairo Declaration of November 1943 already had committed the United States to severe treatment of Japan with regard to territorial possessions. At their meeting in Egypt, FDR, Churchill, and Chinese leader Chiang Kai-shek had agreed to force Japan to return Manchuria and Formosa (Taiwan) to China, evacuate Korea as a prelude to its eventual independence, relinquish all Pacific islands acquired since World War I, and "be expelled from all other territories which she has taken by violence and greed." In short, as one historian put it, the goal of the Cairo Declaration was "to squeeze the Japanese genie back into the pre-Perry bottle." To secure these objectives, the declaration concluded, the signatories would prosecute the war until "the unconditional surrender of Japan."[21]

Four days after Roosevelt's death, new president Harry S. Truman addressed a joint session of Congress. He called upon all Americans to support him in carrying out the ideals "for which Franklin Delano Roosevelt lived and died." The first of these was unconditional surrender. "So that there can be no possible misunderstanding," Truman stated, "both Germany and Japan can be certain, beyond any shadow of a doubt, that America will continue the fight for freedom until no vestige of resistance remains!" To enthusiastic applause he declared: "Our demand has been and it *remains*—Unconditional Surrender!" (emphasis in original).[22]

But the issue was not as simple with regard to the Japanese as Truman made it out to be. He had inherited from Roosevelt an ongoing debate within the administration over how the formula should be applied to the emperor of Japan. The question took on ever greater urgency in the following months because it appeared that its resolution would have a decisive effect on when the war would end, thereby involving many thousands of lives on both sides. FDR's unwillingness to discuss definitions of unconditional surrender left Truman with few clues as to his predecessor's intentions.

Everyone agreed that Japan had long since lost the war by the spring of 1945. B-29 bombing raids were systematically destroying its cities; the naval blockade of its home islands was progressively becoming more effective; and by April American forces had recaptured the Philippine Islands and had invaded Okinawa, which lay only three hundred miles from Japan proper. The Soviet Union served notice in April that it would not renew its neutrality pact with Japan and began transferring troops to the Manchurian border. Finally, the long-awaited German surrender in early May meant that the United States and its allies could devote their entire resources against Japan in the future.

What was equally obvious, however, was that Japan still retained the ability to exact a fearsome toll should an invasion become necessary. The bloody struggle for Okinawa, which lasted until late June, provided a grim reminder that Japanese spirit remained high. They fought virtually until the last man at the cost of more than forty-seven thousand American casualties. Their army of two million men in the home islands could be expected to resist at least as fiercely in defense of Japanese soil. The first large-scale use of kamikazes (suicide aircraft) at Okinawa provided an even more nightmarish preview of things to come. Japan had thousands of trainers and obsolete fighters that could be converted into kamikazes with relatively little pilot training because of the short distances they would be required to fly while operating near Japanese shores.

Any alternative to invasion was desirable provided it did not compromise larger objectives. Those who might be called "retentionists" offered just such a prospect. They argued that all informed Japanese knew their situation was hopeless, and that moderates in the government were searching for a way out of the war. The unconditional surrender formula undermined the peace advocates because it guaranteed neither Hirohito's personal inviolability nor continuation of the imperial system. Because of the emperor's unique cultural/religious status within the national polity, no patriotic Japanese could advocate surrender without assurances that these minimal criteria would be met. Such assurances could be included in a public statement calling upon Japan to surrender, or given through third-party diplomatic channels.

Retentionists promised additional dividends. The only way to attain an orderly surrender was through an imperial rescript, without which Japanese troops everywhere might continue to fight regardless of what

orders the government in Tokyo issued. Later, perhaps as a constitutional monarch, the emperor would provide a stabilizing influence
on a society in transition. Retentionists minimized the threat of Japan
rearming for revanchist purposes, claiming that the militarists and their
allies would have been thoroughly discredited for having led the nation
to such a humiliating defeat. Besides, they pointed out, the United States
could not occupy Japan forever. Deposing the emperor instead of using
him as an instrument for change would cause an embittered Japanese
people to reinstall him or a successor as soon as they could. Under such
circumstances Japan once again would become a threat to peace in Asia.

"Abolitionists" warned against the seductive notion of an early peace.
As FDR had explained at Casablanca and repeatedly thereafter, the
goal of unconditional surrender was to enable the Allies to uproot and
destroy those institutions and philosophies in the Axis nations that had
brought on war in the first place. The monarchy was inextricably bound
up with Japanese militarism and the warrior tradition, abolitionists said,
regardless of the conduct of any particular incumbent. Continuation of
the imperial dynasty would provide a rallying point for the resuscitation
of militarism in years to come. Japanese "moderates," in this view, provided a frail reed upon which to base hopes for lasting peace. They "do
not differ materially in their national ambitions, their idea of Japanese
destiny, and their ruthlessness from the so-called militarists."[23] And
they had willingly cooperated with the latter when conquest appeared
to produce the desired results.

Understandable though it was to want to end the fighting as quickly
as possible, abolitionists believed that a premature armistice would
betray both the sacrifices already made and future generations if a
resurgent Japan chose the path of aggression again as Germany had done
after World War I. The only way to assure lasting peace was to fight it out
until unconditional surrender enabled the United States and its allies to
occupy Japan for as long as it took to achieve full democratization.

This debate, with variations introduced according to changing circumstances, continued virtually until the end of the war.[24] As the arguments necessarily were speculative, who could say which side was
correct? Would assurances about the emperor and the throne strengthen
Japanese moderates, as the retentionists predicted, or have the opposite
effect? Japanese spokesmen boasted that the hideous losses sustained
at Iwo Jima and Okinawa had weakened the American will to go on

fighting. Abandoning unconditional surrender would appear to validate this claim, bolstering the hard-liners' argument that holding out would produce even more favorable terms. At best the United States would offer a negotiated peace rather than undergo the bloodbath an invasion was sure to produce; at worst it surely would do so after suffering the crushing defeat on Japanese beaches militarists promised to administer.

There were domestic considerations as well. FDR had pledged that those responsible for the war at the very least would be removed from positions of responsibility, if not prosecuted as war criminals. Individuals familiar with Japan's political structure could debate (as they still do) Emperor Hirohito's culpability in bringing on the war. But most Americans, who had little idea of the intricacies of the Japanese system, tended to bracket him with Hitler and Mussolini as a great deal of wartime propaganda had encouraged them to do. There were few adults who had not seen newsreels or photographs of him astride his white horse reviewing Japanese troops, some of whom no doubt later killed or wounded American boys. To advocate the sanctity of one who to whatever degree bore responsibility for Pearl Harbor and atrocities such as the Bataan Death March was to invite charges of betraying FDR's legacy and the memory of those who had died in what was regarded as a war of treachery. Racist attitudes toward "Japs" also did not encourage forbearance with regard to the emperor.

Relations with the Soviet Union had implications for applying the unconditional surrender doctrine to Japan. Roosevelt had gone to Yalta believing that an invasion of the Japanese home islands probably would be necessary. Soviet participation in the war could save an untold number of American casualties. They could pin down Japanese forces in northern China and Manchuria, interdict shipping between Japan and the mainland, and provide air bases in Siberia for a bombing campaign against Japanese cities. Stalin as far back as October 1943 had promised Secretary of State Hull that the Soviet Union would join the conflict provided it received sufficient concessions to justify such an endeavor to the war-weary Soviet people. At the Teheran Conference a few weeks later, FDR had expressed his willingness to grant such concessions and he had them placed in writing at Yalta.[25]

The Yalta Far Eastern agreement provided for Soviet entry into the Pacific war two or three months after the end of hostilities in Europe.

In return the Soviets would receive from Japan the strategically located Kurile island chain and the southern half of Sakhalin Island. They would get from China a lease on Port Arthur for a naval base, a "preeminent" interest in the commercial port of nearby Dairen, and joint operation of the Chinese-Eastern and the South Manchurian railroads. Except for the Kuriles, all of these concessions had been seized by Japan from Imperial Russia in the war of 1904–1905. Stalin on his part expressed his "readiness" to conclude a pact of friendship and alliance with the American-backed Nationalist government of Chiang Kai-shek, an unstable coalition challenged by a vigorous Communist movement. FDR hoped such a pact would help Chiang consolidate control over all of China after Japan's defeat.[26]

During the period after Yalta, clashes with the Soviet Union over the governance and boundaries of Poland, the amount of reparations to be taken from Germany, and a host of other issues had strained the Grand Alliance. Even Roosevelt, who had dedicated himself to bettering Soviet-American relations throughout the war, became exasperated by Soviet behavior. Less than a week before his death, he approved a telegram to Winston Churchill stating that the military situation soon "will permit us to become 'tougher' [toward the Soviet Union] than has heretofore appeared advantageous to the war effort."[27] What appeared to American officials as systematic violations of the Yalta agreements involving Europe caused doubts about Stalin's intentions in the Far East. Such doubts naturally raised questions about the desirability of Soviet participation in the conflict, and about the role it would be in American interests for Japan to play in the postwar world.

Finally, there was the matter of atomic weapons. A month before leaving for Yalta, FDR had learned it was "reasonably certain" that one uranium "gun-type" atomic bomb with the explosive power of ten thousand tons of TNT "should be" available by August 1, 1945, and another by the end of the year. The scientists did not "believe" such bombs needed to be tested before use. At about the same time sufficient plutonium would be available to test an implosion device estimated to have the force of about five hundred tons of TNT. Subsequent weapons of this kind would increase in explosive power from one thousand to twenty-five hundred tons of TNT, "if some of our problems are solved."[28]

Roosevelt at Yalta could not count on such "best case" predictions, especially when they were hedged about with so many qualifications.

The scientists could not guarantee that the uranium bomb would be ready on time or that it would work. A test would have been desirable, whatever they might have believed, but would have been self-defeating. Production of enriched uranium for the gun-type bomb was so slow that a test would have used up all the available material, which is why they had turned to the plutonium bomb requiring implosion.[29] That this far more complicated device would be perfected on time was problematic. Previous "hopes" that an implosion bomb would be developed by late spring "have been dissipated by scientific difficulties which we have not as yet been able to solve." Who knew how many more "scientific difficulties" might be encountered in the future?

Although Roosevelt had to make agreements based on the requirements of conventional warfare, those who knew about the atomic program inevitably began to speculate on its possibilities. If the scientists could deliver on time, the United States might be able to "dictate our own terms" to Japan, as one individual put it, without a costly invasion.[30] Retentionists and abolitionists alike sought to incorporate this possibility into their arguments. Such a prospect also called into question previous assumptions about the importance of Soviet help in the war against Japan.

FDR's death thrust Harry S. Truman into this enormously complicated situation unexpectedly and without preparation. He had been Roosevelt's running mate for the usual reasons: he was expected to balance the ticket and he had not offended any powerful interest groups. He had seen the president on only a few ceremonial occasions since the 1944 election, and he had received no systematic briefings as to what was being done. Faced almost immediately with having to make numerous decisions as the war drew to an end in Europe, he was denied even the benefit of being able to concentrate on Asian affairs.

Truman had to function under another handicap. Roosevelt had conducted American foreign policy in a most haphazard fashion. In addition to his own often improvisational diplomacy with leaders such as Churchill and Stalin, he frequently had circumvented the State Department by relying instead on trusted personal aides. After the much-ignored Hull resigned for reasons of health in late 1944, FDR had replaced him with Edward R. Stettinius Jr., a man of modest intellectual gifts whose role was to carry out policies rather than to help design them. However well such an arrangement may have worked during

Roosevelt's lifetime, it deprived Truman of a strong, capable figure upon whom he could rely during the transition. He inherited instead a mixed bag of advisers, whose competing claims inhibited development of consistent, well-thought-out policies. This was especially true with regard to the war against Japan.

Taking Control

On the afternoon of April 12, 1945, while sitting for a portrait at his retreat in Warm Springs, Georgia, Franklin D. Roosevelt complained of a "terrific headache" and collapsed. Two hours later he was dead of a massive cerebral hemorrhage. Shortly after 7 P.M., in the Cabinet Room of the White House, Chief Justice of the Supreme Court Harlan Fisk Stone administered the presidential oath to Harry S. Truman before a small group of onlookers. Most were still in a state of shock from FDR's death, none more than Truman himself. Following the ceremony, he held a brief cabinet meeting during which he asked for cooperation in continuing Roosevelt's foreign and domestic policies. He added that he meant to be president in his own right, and intended to take full responsibilities for final decisions.[1]

One of Truman's most vexing problems during his first days in office was to determine just what FDR's foreign policies were that he had vowed to carry out. Roosevelt's tendency to improvise, to keep options open, and to work through a variety of individuals and agencies left his successor few clear guidelines to follow. The suddenness of his passing denied Truman the benefit of insights even a few extended conversations might have afforded. Truman had not been part of the administration's inner circles. With the war against Germany hastening to its end, the founding conference of the United Nations less than two weeks away, and relations with the Soviet Union growing steadily more poisonous, decisions had to be made in days or even hours that would have been difficult after extended study. But time was a luxury Truman did not have.

While awaiting the arrival of Chief Justice Stone for the swearing-in ceremony, Truman was approached by Secretary of State Stettinius on a matter he said could not wait. Differences with the Soviet Union over the government of Poland had reached such a stage that Churchill was threatening to go before the House of Commons to announce that negotiations had broken down.[2] Roosevelt, wishing to avoid such a drastic step, had authorized the drafting of a proposed joint communiqué to Stalin that he hoped might break the impasse. Stettinius wanted Truman to approve the message so it could be forwarded to Churchill before his announced deadline.

Roosevelt and Churchill had gone to Yalta in early February hoping that Stalin would consent to the formation of a representative provisional government for Poland. This interim regime would administer the nation until free elections could be held. Stalin had dashed their hopes by making the absurd claim that what was known as the "Lublin Committee," a handpicked, pro-Communist group installed by Red armies as they moved west, represented the will of the people and should be recognized as legitimate. After protracted discussions, Stalin agreed that an unspecified number of non-Communists from abroad and from within Poland might be invited to participate in a revised government. He insisted, however, that the Lublin group constitute its "kernel" or "nucleus." As Soviet occupying forces controlled the area, Roosevelt believed he had to accept such an arrangement as "the best I can do for Poland at this time."[3]

The tripartite commission formed in Moscow to preside over the reorganization almost immediately became stalemated when the Soviet member, Foreign Minister V. M. Molotov, insisted that the Lublin Committee have the authority to determine which Poles would be invited to join the coalition. To American Ambassador W. Averell Harriman's astonished protest that nothing in the Yalta agreement nor in any of the conversations held there even suggested arrogating such a right to the Lublin group, Molotov blandly replied that such was the *sense* of the accord. Unless this procedure were followed, he said, "we might make a mistake and find a fascist in our midst."[4]

As the deadlock continued throughout March, reports from within Poland indicated that the Lublin regime, backed by the Red Army and the NKVD, was systematically crushing political competition by large-scale arrests and deportations. American officials began to suspect that the stalemate had less to do with differing interpretations of the Yalta accord than with the Soviet desire to forcibly eliminate real or imagined challenges to the subservient Lublin regime.[5] Molotov's recently published reminiscences suggest that this interpretation was correct. When he expressed concern to Stalin that they might have conceded too much over Eastern Europe at Yalta, Molotov recalled, Stalin replied, "Don't worry, work it out. We can deal with it in our own way later. The point is the correlation of forces."[6]

Churchill early on had tried to persuade Roosevelt to join him in making a direct protest to Stalin over the Polish question. FDR refused because he hoped the Soviet leader would relent, and because he feared that strong language "might produce a reaction contrary to your intent." Several developments toward the end of March convinced Roosevelt that forbearance served no purpose. For some time the Soviets had been obstructing U.S. efforts to repatriate its prisoners of war from German camps in Poland overrun by Red armies. Now Molotov advised Harriman that repatriation would be expedited if Washington negotiated directly with the Lublin group. American officials interpreted this as a form of crude blackmail designed to compel de facto recognition of the puppet regime. At the same time Stalin began accusing the British and Americans of trying to arrange a separate peace with the German commander in Italy that would permit the Germans to transfer divisions to the Eastern front.[7]

On March 29 Roosevelt informed Churchill that "the time had come" to confront the Soviets over Poland. He included a copy of a cable he proposed sending to Stalin, informing him that the United States could not permit Lublin to exercise a veto over which Poles would be invited to participate in the reorganized government, nor would it recognize "a thinly disguised continuance" of that regime. The cable went out on April 1.[8] A few days later he replied to Stalin's charges regarding peace negotiations with the Germans, expressing his "bitter resentment" at the "vile misrepresentations" of Stalin's informants. Roosevelt also congratulated Churchill on the "strong" message *he* had sent to Stalin, adding that the military situation soon would enable them to become "tougher" with the Soviets.[9]

Stalin's reply to FDR about the Polish issue contained little that was new. In his response to Churchill, a copy of which he sent to Washington, he offered to "influence" the Lublin group to include in the reorganized government Stanislaw Mikolajczyk, an individual both the British and Americans regarded as the most widely respected Polish political leader.

This appeared to signal an opening, especially since Molotov only a few days earlier had declared the man unacceptable. Stalin also informed Roosevelt that he now regarded Anglo-American conduct in Italy as an example of "misunderstanding" between allies, rather than as an act of treachery. Churchill cabled FDR that this was "as near as they can get to an apology."[10]

Stalin's concessions seemed to indicate that standing up to the Soviets worked better than appealing to their sense of fair play. But Roosevelt feared that Churchill might go too far. The prime minister earlier had informed Stalin, "If our efforts to reach an agreement about Poland are to be doomed to failure I shall be bound to confess the fact to Parliament when they return from Easter recess." In an effort "to discourage him from making a hasty speech in Parliament on breakdown of Polish negotiations," Roosevelt on April 10 urged Churchill not to make any statements about Poland without prior consultation. To Churchill's request for his views, FDR replied on the eleventh that he would "minimize the general Soviet problem as much as possible," but that they "must be firm" and "our course thus far is correct."[11]

The proposed joint communiqué Stettinius discussed with Truman on the evening of Roosevelt's death, which was sent to Churchill the next day, offered a number of proposals for Stalin's consideration. The accompanying message, rewritten to suit the new circumstances, contained an appeal from Truman to "have another go at him [Stalin]." Public announcement that negotiations over Poland had broken down, the note continued, "will carry with it the hopes of the Polish people for a just solution to say nothing of the effect it will have on our political and military collaboration with the Soviet Union."[12]

Whether Truman's cable would have dissuaded Churchill from speaking out cannot be known. Stalin himself helped resolve the crisis. When Harriman informed him of Roosevelt's death, Stalin asked if there were anything he could do. Harriman suggested that he send Molotov to pay his respects to the fallen Roosevelt, then have him proceed to San Francisco for the founding conference of the UN. Stalin previously had declined to name his foreign minister to head the Soviet delegation on the ground that Molotov was too busy at home. Several Soviet statements had led Americans to believe that he was applying yet another form of pressure to compel formal recognition of Lublin before reorganization took place. Such a step, it was feared, would eliminate any incentive the Soviets might have for permitting the formation of at least a quasi-representative government.[13]

Stalin agreed to Harriman's request and also authorized Molotov to continue negotiations over Poland while he was in Washington. The Soviet leader undoubtedly wished to size up the relatively unknown Truman, but his willingness to discuss Poland at the foreign ministers' level implied a greater desire to reach agreement over what many American and British officials regarded as the test case for future cooperation among the Big Three. Churchill apparently found the prospects for a breakthrough sufficiently enticing to back off from his threat to go before the Commons. British Foreign Secretary Anthony Eden, already in Washington, thereupon informed Stettinius that "the PM won't speak. All he will say is that he is still hopeful."[14]

Truman's introduction to Soviet behavior must have seemed instructive. FDR's move to a stronger position during his last days apparently had led Stalin to withdraw his accusations of betrayal in Italy, to relent on the inclusion of a prominent non-Communist in the Polish government, and to permit renewed talks in Washington. Some officials, particularly Ambassador Harriman who had hurried back from Moscow after Roosevelt's death, urged the new president to keep up the pressure. The Russians despised weakness, according to this view, and would bully those who let them into making concession after concession without reciprocity or gratitude. Standing up to their more extreme demands provided the best way to establish a working relationship based on mutual respect. Such advice proved congenial to the new president, who admired decisiveness and who professed scorn for what he regarded as the unmanly language of diplomacy.[15]

Truman had another private conversation on the evening of Roosevelt's death, this one with Secretary of War Stimson. Promising to make a full presentation at a later date, Stimson briefly described an immense undertaking "looking to the development of a new explosive of almost unbelievable destructive power." This was, of course, the atomic bomb. Over the next few days James F. Byrnes, who recently had resigned as director of the Office of War Mobilization, and several other officials told Truman what they knew about the project.[16]

In his memoirs Truman claimed this was the first he had heard of the program. Elsewhere he had stated that Roosevelt told him about it during the election campaign the previous summer. Small matter. As with so many other issues, FDR had left only the roughest indication of his thinking about how to deal with this unprecedented new force, which bore enormous implications both for the war and for future world affairs. Truman would have to rely on the advice of those around him and, in the end, his own judgment.

The atomic program, code-named the Manhattan Project, had received high priority by late 1941 out of fear that Germany would acquire atomic bombs with which it might inflict unimaginable havoc on the allies. German scientists had discovered nuclear fission in 1938 and were thought to be well on the way to developing the technology to produce weapons based upon this process. During the summer of 1943 two of the most prominent physicists working on the Manhattan Project, Hans Bethe and Edward Teller, warned that there was "considerable probability" that Germany would have a large number of what they called "gadgets" ready to deliver on England, Russia, and the United States between November of that year and January 1944.[17]

Uncertainty about German progress had led to the recommendation by one study group that the first available atomic bombs be used against Japan. If Germany already had such weapons or was close to producing them, Hitler surely would retaliate. If German scientists had not yet achieved success a dud might provide them with the necessary technical information. Although Roosevelt had stated his willingness to use atomic bombs against Germany, it had become clear by the autumn of 1944 that the war in Europe would be over before they would become available. Consequently, a special air group was formed to begin training for raids on Japan using specially modified B-29 heavy bombers. By the time Truman took office Germany was collapsing, while Japan was demonstrating its resolve by inflicting heavy casualties on American invasion forces at Okinawa.[18]

One of Truman's first tasks was to assure the American people, and the rest of the world for that matter, of his commitment to the principles and goals of his predecessor. He did that in his April 16 address to a joint session of Congress, cited in the previous chapter, which was broadcast on the radio networks. He warned Germany and Japan that the United States would continue the war "until no vestige of resistance remains." Although much hard fighting lay ahead, he continued, this nation "will never become a party to any plan for partial victory" because to "settle for merely another temporary respite would surely jeopardize the security of all the world."[19]

The new president hardly could have said otherwise under the circumstances. It is unlikely he was even aware at this early date of the considerable sentiment within official circles for informing the Japanese that they might retain the emperor in order to make capitulation less repugnant to them. Nonetheless he had gone on record as endorsing the idea that unconditional surrender was necessary to establish a lasting peace, and had pledged himself to attaining that goal. This and other public statements made it difficult for him later on to advocate peace terms that would appear to repudiate Roosevelt's legacy and his own solemn promises.

During the next week Truman struggled to get a grip on the many issues confronting him in an atmosphere of crisis caused by two approaching deadlines: Molotov's scheduled arrival in Washington on April 22 and the opening of the UN conference in San Francisco a few days later. They were connected because of Stalin's demand that the as yet unaltered Lublin regime in Poland be invited to send a delegation to San Francisco. Truman faced a painful dilemma. Yielding to the Soviets would invite charges of "selling out" Poland and jeopardize Senate passage of the UN treaty. Failure to reach agreement with Molotov might lead Stalin to boycott the organization with equally disastrous results. He might also reconsider his promise to enter the war against Japan.

Molotov's negotiations with Stettinius and Eden began on an inauspicious note. On the eve of his arrival on the twenty-second, word came that the Soviets had signed a mutual assistance pact with Lublin despite Anglo-American protests. Molotov himself proved intransigent. Refusal to accept Soviet terms, he warned, would provoke an open fight over seating a delegation from Lublin at the San Francisco conference. If the Soviets lost, he made clear, they might withdraw from the UN. Privately, Eden urged Stettinius to "mobilize the President to talk like a Dutch Uncle" to Molotov if the foreign ministers could not agree. When no progress was made the next morning, Stettinius persuaded Truman to meet with Molotov that evening to explain to him "in blunt terms the effect of his attitude on future cooperation between the great powers."[20]

Before seeing Molotov, Truman called a meeting of his secretaries of State, War, and Navy, the army and navy chiefs of staff, Ambassador

Harriman, and others. After Stettinius outlined the points of contention over Poland, Truman told the group that carrying out agreements with the Soviets so far had been a "one way street," and he did not intend to let this continue. He said he would go on with the plans for the UN conference and if the Soviets chose to withdraw over the Polish question, "they could go to hell." He then asked those present to state their views.

Stimson, who spoke first, urged caution. Worried for some time that the dispute over Poland might cause a rupture with the Soviets, but caught unawares by the impromptu meeting, he later complained in his diary, "All this was fired at me like a shot from a Gatling gun." In any event, he regarded it as nowhere near important enough to risk a break with the Soviets, and pointed out how important Poland was to them. Only Army Chief of Staff Marshall supported him. Marshall stressed the need to have the Soviets join the Pacific war as soon as possible, instead of waiting until "we had done all the dirty work."

Major General John R. Deane, who commanded the United States military mission to the U.S.S.R., disagreed. He said the Soviets would enter as soon as they were able because delay would cause "a letdown" for their exhausted people. Deane added that his experiences in Moscow had convinced him that "we should be firm when we were right." Others concurred, whether out of conviction or deference to the president's opening remarks.[21]

Truman could not have failed to notice that those who had negotiated with the Soviets personally were unanimous in recommending firmness. Stimson and Marshall lacked such background. Deane's estimate of Soviet intentions with regard to Japan, furthermore, appeared to address Marshall's worry about timing. That Anthony Eden, presumably speaking for Churchill, had suggested talking to Molotov "like a Dutch Uncle" added to the consensus among the old hands that "standing up to" the Soviets offered the best hope of breaking the impasse. Truman asked Stettinius and Harriman, both advocates of this policy, to stay on after the meeting to help prepare notes on the points to be discussed with Molotov.

Molotov, along with Soviet Ambassador Andrei Gromyko and an interpreter, was ushered into the president's office at 5:30 that evening. With Truman were Leahy, Stettinius, Harriman, and the American interpreter, Charles E. Bohlen. After the formalities, Truman "went straight to the point," as he later put it. He said he and Churchill had gone as far as they could to affect a reasonable settlement of the Polish issue, but that they could not recognize a government that was not "representative of all democratic elements." Although the United States was going ahead with the UN conference regardless of disagreements, failure to resolve the Polish question would cast "serious doubts" on the future of Big Three unity. Then, obviously referring to a postwar loan for the U.S.S.R., he warned that "economic measures in the foreign field" would stand little chance in Congress without public support. He concluded by expressing his hope that Molotov would be authorized to continue discussions at San Francisco, and handed him a message for Stalin containing the points he had just made orally.

Molotov then asked to make a few observations. He said that thus far the three governments had resolved differences as equals. There had been "no case where one or two of the three had attempted to impose their will on another," which is clearly what he was accusing the United States and Great Britain of trying to do over Poland. When Truman replied that all they were asking was that the Soviets abide by the Yalta accord, Molotov insisted that his government stood by it "as a matter of honor." The talk grew ugly as the president repeated several times his charge that the Soviets had failed to comply with the Yalta decision, which Molotov steadfastly denied. Finally, according to Bohlen's notes, Truman ended the meeting abruptly: "That will be all, Mr. Molotov, I would appreciate it if you would transmit my view to Marshal Stalin."[22]

Truman's memoirs have Molotov at the end complaining, "I have never been talked to like that in my life," and himself replying, "Carry out your agreements and you won't get talked to like that." This version, written at a time when the Roosevelt and Truman administrations were being accused of being "soft on Communism," has proven irresistible to historians even though it is of dubious authenticity. Bohlen himself denied any such exchange took place. Yet there is no question that Truman lost his temper and used "language that was not at all diplomatic," as Leahy put it in his diary.[23]

Truman's first attempt at personal diplomacy was an embarrassment. The paper he had spoken from during the first part of the meeting enunciated the firm positions Harriman, Stettinius, and Eden had recommended he take. Harriman, who had specifically warned against bluster, was appalled that Truman "went at it so hard" because it gave Molotov "an excuse to tell Stalin that the Roosevelt policy was being abandoned." Harriman later stated that after the meeting he cautioned Truman against pushing the Soviets too far.[24]

Truman himself had second thoughts. A few days later he told former ambassador to the Soviet Union Joseph E. Davies that he had given Molotov "the one-two to the jaw." Then he asked, "Did I do right?" He did not argue when Davies, a staunch admirer of the Soviet Union who had met with Molotov privately a few hours before the latter's row with Truman, replied that tough talk would serve only to confirm Soviet suspicion about their allies' intentions.[25] Most important, the confrontation failed to produce results. A divisive struggle over seating the Lublin delegation took place at San Francisco and, although the Soviets did not walk out when they lost, the Polish issue continued to fester for weeks.

Meanwhile, Stimson met with Truman on April 25 to brief him in detail about the atomic program. Stimson brought with him a summary prepared by Major General Leslie R. Groves, Commanding General of the Manhattan Engineer District, and two of Stimson's assistants, George L. Harrison and Harvey Bundy. The secretary and Bundy also had drawn up another memorandum giving "an analytical picture of what the prospects of S–1 [code word for the atomic bomb] are and the problems it presents to this country." Groves joined the meeting after it began, having taken a different route to avoid arousing the suspicions of White House reporters.

In a session lasting about three quarters of an hour, Stimson first discussed his memorandum, which began, "Within four months we shall in all probability have completed the most terrible weapon ever known in human history, one bomb of which could destroy a whole city." The thrust of the document was that because the process of constructing atomic bombs could not be kept secret indefinitely, the United States bore an enormous responsibility to devise effective means of international control over this terrible new weapon. To prepare for this task, Stimson proposed that a committee be formed to recommend policy to the president and the Congress "when secrecy is no longer in full effect." Groves then joined the meeting to go over his more technical report.

Following the briefing on Groves's paper, the three men discussed political issues with particular emphasis on Russia. No one took notes, but Stimson's memorandum and his diary entries during this period indicate the advice he probably gave. Although in the future even small nations might be able to produce atomic bombs, his memo pointed out, the only one likely to do so "within the next few years" was the Soviet Union. Agreement with the Soviets, therefore, was indispensable to constructing "a pattern in which the peace of the world and our civilization can be saved."[26] Considering the stakes, allowing such a comparatively minor issue as the Polish question to cause a rupture between the United States and the U.S.S.R. would constitute the greatest folly.

Truman's published account of the session emphasized Stimson's concern with the effect of the bomb on the future of "civilization" as well as on the present war. In contrast, Truman alluded to an earlier talk with future secretary of state Byrnes, during which Byrnes had said that because the bomb was capable of "wiping out entire cities" it "might well put us in the position to dictate our own terms at the end of the war." Some writers, taking these words out of context, have tried to make it appear that Byrnes was referring to dictating terms to the Soviet Union. Nothing in Truman's prose warrants such an interpretation. His next sentence, "Stimson, on the other hand, seemed at least as much concerned with the role of the atomic bomb in the shaping of history as in its capacity to shorten this war," makes it clear that Byrnes was talking about Japan.[27]

The meeting was significant for what was not discussed as well as for what was. None of the written accounts left by the three participants even suggests that there was any discussion about whether or how the bomb should be used against Japan, nor did Stimson include such matters among those to be taken up by the committee he proposed. As both Byrnes and Stimson had referred to the bomb within the context of destroying cities, Truman had reason to assume that FDR intended to use the new weapon in this manner if it would shorten the war. The latter's authorization for the training of a special bombing unit for operations against Japan as well as Germany signified such intent.[28]

The degree to which the assumption of use permeated the thinking of officials responsible for the program can be seen in several ways. Two days after Truman's briefing a previously named group designated the Target Committee held its first meeting in the Pentagon. Composed of scientists from the Manhattan Project and air force personnel, the committee was chaired by Groves's deputy, Brigadier General Thomas F. Farrell. After a discussion of probable weather during the period when the first bombs were likely to become available, the committee took up

Groves's charge that "the targets chosen should be places the bombing of which would most adversely affect the will of the people to continue the war." "Beyond that," Groves had instructed, "the targets" (he delicately refrained from using the word "cities") should be those of military importance that had suffered the least damage by conventional air raids. At no time during its existence did the committee consider alternative sites for demonstration purposes such as uninhabited Pacific islands or areas in Japan proper.[29]

Groves's instructions surely had the approval of his superiors, Stimson and Marshall, for they remained in effect throughout subsequent deliberations. Using the bomb in a way that "would adversely affect the will of the people" meant that it was most highly valued for its psychological effect. Later orders to spare designated cities from conventional bombing, after all, guaranteed that whatever contributions they made to the war effort would continue unabated until the last moment.[30] It was not the loss of an industrial center or military installation that was expected to compel the Japanese to surrender, but the sheer enormity of what had been done to them and would continue to be done until they capitulated.

The wording of a memorandum Harrison and Bundy prepared for Stimson on May 1 also is revealing. Referring to the secretary's meeting with Truman, they urged that the proposed committee be formed quickly because of the "possibly short time available before actual military use." Among other things, Harrison and Bundy pointed out, the committee would have to prepare statements by the president and the War Department to be given out "as soon as the first bomb is used." Outlining other steps that should be taken "as soon as possible after use," the memorandum simply presumed the weapon would be employed against Japanese cities as soon as it became available. That its authors believed they were in any way deviating from their chief's line of thinking is unlikely.[31]

Stimson followed his subordinates' advice to move quickly. The next day he met with Truman to secure approval of those he proposed inviting to serve on the committee. He also suggested that the president name a personal representative. Truman replied that he thought there was no need for this, but agreed at Stimson's urging. On the third, Stimson telephoned to suggest Byrnes for the position. Truman called back later in the day to say that Byrnes would take it. Stimson sent out invitations to Assistant Secretary of State William L. Clayton; Undersecretary of the Navy Ralph A. Bard; Vannevar Bush, director of the Office of Scientific Research and Development (OSRD); Carl T. Compton, Chief, Office of Field Service, OSRD; and Byrnes. All accepted. Stimson would serve as chairman and Harrison as his alternate.[32]

Byrnes's inclusion on the committee as the president's representative was an obvious choice. It was known that he would replace Stettinius as secretary of state in the near future, and he had Truman's ear since the latter had sent a plane to fetch him to Washington on the evening of Roosevelt's death. Technically out of government since his resignation as director of the Office of War Mobilization, Byrnes made frequent trips to the capital to consult with Truman and other officials in their offices or in his suite at the Shoreham Hotel. Harrison and Bundy were "tickled to death" that Byrnes had agreed to serve on the committee because his status helped ensure that its recommendations would receive Truman's closest attention.[33]

Although scholars have noted that Stimson coined the title "Interim Committee" to forestall later charges that the administration had usurped congressional powers, they have paid insufficient attention to how much this concern influenced his beliefs about the committee's proper functions. He spelled these out in the first, informal meeting on May 9. The group was to "study and report on the matter of temporary war-time controls and publicity, and to make *recommendations on post-war research, development, and control, and on legislation necessary for these purposes*" (emphasis added). He made clear later that he wanted emphasis placed on legislation for domestic controls "with the problem of international relations and controls to be dealt with by the Permanent Post-War Commission that would be established by law."[34]

The distinction between what he regarded as the legitimate exercise of the president's wartime powers and the need to secure congressional approval for more permanent arrangements when the fighting ended was crucial. For the latter the administration could only draw up proposals to submit "when secrecy was no longer in full effect," as he put it in his original memorandum to Truman. An active participant in the struggle over the League of Nations in 1919–1920, Stimson was well aware that the Senate—restive over its diminished role during the war—would insist upon full exercise of its prerogatives in peacetime. To present that body with agreements that could not be defended as having been necessary for the war effort, particularly on such a momentous question as atomic energy, would invite repudiation with possibly disastrous repercussions for future negotiations with the Soviets or anyone else. As will be seen, well-meaning scientists and others who during this period were urging government officials to take immediate, dramatic action along these lines seemed utterly oblivious to the way the United States government worked.

On May 8, the day before the Interim Committee first met, Truman held a press conference to announce the end of the war in Europe. Following his remarks about Germany, he read another statement calling upon the Japanese to surrender. Alluding to the destruction already visited upon them, he warned that "Our blows will not cease until the Japanese military and naval forces lay down their arms in unconditional surrender." He outlined what this would mean to the Japanese people: an end to their suffering, the ouster of military leaders responsible for their plight, and the return home of soldiers and sailors to families and jobs. "Unconditional Surrender does not mean," he concluded, "the extermination or enslavement of the Japanese people."[35]

Truman referred twice to the unconditional surrender of Japanese military forces rather than of the government. Those who have claimed that this represented a softening of terms to make capitulation more palatable to Japanese leaders almost certainly are wrong. Such phrasing had been commonplace in position papers put together by various committees, where it was used interchangeably with "unconditional surrender" just as Truman had done. The wording probably derived from the fact that Japanese troops were widely dispersed throughout Asia, and was intended to serve as a warning that the United States would not slacken its efforts until *all* had surrendered.

Truman had told Acting Secretary of State Joseph C. Grew (Stettinius was at the UN conference in San Francisco) the day before that he intended to "touch on the subject of Japan" in his V-E address without hinting that any change of policy was in the offing. When Grew asked permission to issue his own statement to combat rumors that Japan was seeking peace, Truman approved without even asking what the acting secretary intended to say. Such behavior is incomprehensible on Truman's part if he intended to suggest a new departure that Grew might inadvertently contradict. In any event, neither Truman nor any of the high-level officials involved in the debate over surrender terms either then or later suggested that the president's May 8 announcement constituted a revision of the unconditional surrender doctrine.[36]

Truman's statement originally had been written several weeks earlier for Roosevelt's use by Navy Captain Ellis M. Zacharias of the Office of War Information. Zacharias was an intelligence officer and longtime student of Japan. A few hours after the press conference, he made the first of a series of radio broadcasts designed to help persuade the Japanese to surrender. Zacharias repeated the presidential statement and sought to assure the Japanese that unconditional surrender was purely a military act signifying the end of resistance. He emphatically denied any intent to destroy their nation or its culture. "Your future lies in your own hands," he concluded. "You can choose between a wasteful, unclean death for many of your forces, or a peace with honor."[37]

The Japanese responded with defiance. In a statement adopted at a special cabinet session and approved by the emperor, the government declared its commitment to the "complete destruction of the unjust ambition of the United States and Great Britain, which are attempting to trample down Greater East Asia."[38] The state-controlled press and radio warned the Japanese people that defeat would mean the end of their society regardless of what the treacherous enemy might say to deceive them. All this was for public consumption, of course, but no one in the Japanese government at that time seems to have perceived Truman's address as implying a change in policy. The MAGIC intercepts (decryptions of Japanese diplomatic codes) contain no messages from Tokyo to its diplomats abroad requesting that they seek clarification from their Western contacts.

Relations with the Soviet Union took a turn for the worse only a few days after Germany's surrender. On May 11 Truman approved a proposal to scale back Lend-Lease shipments for the Soviet Union to those supplies and materials intended for use against Japan. The curtailment was mandated by legislation, about which the Soviets had been made fully aware, but its unduly strict implementation by subordinate officials placed the administration in an awkward spot. Instructions were issued to unload ships destined for the Soviet Union and to reroute those already at sea. These orders were rescinded within hours, but the damage had been done. Everyone understood that the Soviets would interpret what had happened as a crude attempt to apply economic coercion.[39]

Truman realized something had to be done to prevent relations with the Soviets from deteriorating further. Two days after the Lend-Lease fiasco, he dined alone with Davies who had been trying to patch things up with the Soviets since the president's confrontation with Molotov. In addition to talking with Truman and other American officials, Davies on May 2 had sent a "My Dear Friend" message to Molotov congratulating him on the "dignity, bigness of mind, and brilliant ability" he had shown both in Washington and in San Francisco, and assuring him that Truman wanted to get along with the Soviets.[40]

During their conversation, Truman authorized Davies to bypass regular diplomatic channels to invite Stalin to a Big Three conference in July. As a stopgap, he also asked Davies to go to Moscow as soon as possible in an effort to reverse the dangerous trend of Soviet-American relations. Davies said he could not make such an arduous trip because of poor health, but in turn suggested that the president himself meet with Stalin before the summit began. Truman agreed. The next day Davies sent another personal message to Molotov, telling him that Truman had suggested a Big Three meeting and asking if the president and Stalin could get together "for a few days before that."[41]

Truman moved quickly to find another personal emissary to Stalin after Davies begged off. Ambassador Harriman suggested Harry Hopkins, who had been Roosevelt's closest adviser, had sat at his side at Yalta, and was known as a staunch ally of the Soviets. Truman apparently had some doubts about FDR's former aide, because he first sounded out several people who had worked with him "as to their viewpoint on Mr. Hopkins' integrity." This included a visit to the Bethesda Naval Medical Center to consult with the ailing former secretary of state, Hull. Satisfied that Hopkins was "perfectly loyal and his integrity was beyond question," Truman asked him to undertake the mission. When Hopkins agreed, despite his own ill health, the president cabled Stalin on May 19 asking that the envoy be received as soon as he could get to Moscow.[42]

As with his approach to Davies, Truman did not confer with advisers such as Byrnes and Leahy before asking Hopkins to see Stalin. When Byrnes learned about the mission, he visited the White House "to tell me I should not send Harry Hopkins to Russia." Truman was unmoved. "I told Jimmie I thought I would send him." A few days later, Leahy complained to his diary that the decision was made "without consulting me."[43]

In addition to Hopkins's identification with Rooseveltian diplomacy, Truman had another reason to hope the mission would be productive. The day after FDR's death, Stettinius had told the new president that Hopkins was "the one person who really thoroughly understood" Roosevelt's relations with Stalin and Churchill. The next morning Truman had met with Hopkins, who described Stalin as a "rough, tough Russian," but one who could be "talked to frankly." Byrnes, who also had been at Yalta, agreed. He likened Stalin to an American political boss of a type Truman was familiar with: a shrewd horse trader, but one whose word could be trusted.[44]

How could these assessments of Stalin be reconciled with his behavior since Yalta? Harriman and Bohlen, among others, provided an answer. They claimed that Stalin represented those in Moscow who genuinely sought cooperation, while Molotov headed a faction of hard-liners bent upon undermining the relationship. Stalin had grown "deeply and unjustifiably suspicious" of American motives, Harriman warned Truman, because his foreign minister had been deceiving him.[45] The president found this interpretation persuasive: a few days later he told a Treasury Department official that Stalin had not known "half the things that were going on" because the "Molotov clique" had misled him. Negotiating directly with Stalin, therefore, offered the best way to nullify Molotov's baneful influence.[46]

Hopkins's most pressing assignment was to secure agreement with Stalin over the still deadlocked Polish question. Truman's instructions are illuminating. He told Hopkins to impress upon Stalin that what happened in Eastern Europe "made no difference to U.S. interests" except insofar as "World Peace is concerned." Poland should have elections as free as American political bosses would allow "in their respective bailiwicks." Finally, Hopkins should seek some gesture from Stalin "*whether he means it or not* to keep it before our public that he intends to keep his word," which is what any "smart political boss" would do (emphasis added).[47] Truman was willing to concede the Lublin group's domination over Poland, provided appearances were kept that would protect the administration from charges of betrayal.

Truman also told Hopkins to seek "as early a date as possible on Russia's entry into the war against Japan" and to sound out Stalin's intentions toward China.[48] These matters were related. The Yalta Far Eastern accord provided that the Soviets would join the conflict "two or three months" after V-E Day. Their help against Japan would save American lives should an invasion prove necessary, and there still was no guarantee that atomic bombs would be available as an alternative or that they would be sufficient. Part of Stalin's reimbursement, however, had been recognition of Russia's "pre-eminent interests" in the key Manchurian port of Dairen and connecting railroads. Soviet behavior in Eastern Europe had caused Grew, Harriman, and others to question whether they would interpret "pre-eminent interests" in such a way as to compromise Chinese sovereignty over Manchuria. Truman wanted Stalin's assurance that they would not.[49]

Finally, Hopkins was to invite Stalin to a Big Three conference in mid-July at a place of the latter's choosing. This would provide opportunity to negotiate issues without having to go through Molotov. Truman lacked FDR's confidence in his own personal charm, of which he had little, but prided himself on his capacity for "plain talk." And that, according to Hopkins and Byrnes, was what would be most effective with Stalin. Truman hoped such a meeting would "overcome the misunderstandings and difficulties which have risen since Germany folded up."[50]

Churchill remained to be dealt with. For some time he had been urging Truman to call a Big Three conference, and further desired to meet with the president before then. Truman by this time had grown irritated with the prime minister over his persistent requests to take a tougher stance toward the Soviet Union. He told Davies on May 21 that "I was having as much difficulty with Prime Minister Churchill as I was with Stalin," and he also wished to avoid the appearance of "ganging up" on Russia. When Davies said he thought he could make Churchill "see the light," Truman asked him to go to London if his health permitted. Davies accepted, thereby assuming the unenviable task of conveying word that the president intended to meet with Stalin rather than with Churchill before the summit.[51]

Truman's reliance on this fervent advocate of Soviet-American harmony refutes the notion that he was a captive of hard-liners such as Leahy. The president apparently consulted no one about asking Davies to serve as his personal representative to Moscow. He certainly did not do so before authorizing the former ambassador to bypass the State Department in requesting a Truman-Stalin meeting. He told him about the atomic bomb, gave him full access to top-level diplomatic correspondence in the White House Map Room, and asked him to undertake a most sensitive mission to Churchill only a few days after the Soviets announced that Davies had been awarded the Order of Lenin. "Ain't that sompin,' " Truman noted in his diary, and the next day gave Davies a handwritten note for Churchill stating, "You may talk freely and frankly to him, as you would to me."[52]

The president's attitude toward negotiating with the Soviets had changed significantly since his unfortunate confrontation with Molotov. Persuaded by those who emphasized Stalin's moderation and by the view that Molotov was responsible for much of the friction that had developed, he concluded that face-to-face discussions with the Soviet leader offered the best way to reach accommodation. His self-assurance had grown in the process. He had not hesitated to go outside his official circle of advisers in arranging such meetings for himself and for Hopkins, and his willingness to confer alone with Stalin bespoke growing confidence in his own abilities.

CHAPTER 3

Consideration of the Bomb and Preparations for the Summit

Truman's decision to send Harry Hopkins to Moscow marked a renewed effort to establish a working relationship with the Soviet Union. Hopkins had first met Stalin in July 1941, when many thought the Soviet Union must collapse under the German onslaught. Dispatched by Roosevelt to assess Soviet prospects and needs, Hopkins had been impressed by Stalin's calm determination and had requested all aid possible. He retained his admiration for the Soviet leader, and talk of inevitable Russian expansion in Europe and the Far East "makes Harry wince," as one official put it after visiting him on the eve of his departure.[1] Truman would be encouraged by his envoy's achievements in Moscow, which in turn influenced the president's judgments about how to proceed in the war against Japan.

Hopkins, accompanied by Ambassador Harriman, met with Stalin and Molotov six times between May 26 and June 6. Although initially there was some confusion over Hopkins's invitation to a Big Three conference and Davies's earlier request for a Truman-Stalin meeting, about which Hopkins was uninformed, the marshal agreed to attend a summit beginning on July 15 in the vicinity of Berlin. He was less cordial in vehemently denouncing the Lend-Lease curtailment, which he branded as "unfortunate and even brutal." Eventually he relented, however, and pronounced himself satisfied with Hopkins's explanation that the matter had been a "technical misunderstanding" rather than an effort to apply economic pressure.[2]

Discussions about Poland took place during five of the six sessions. Hopkins denied that the United States had any ulterior motives there, but tried to convince Stalin how important the issue was as a "test case" for future cooperation among the Big Three. Stalin professed to accept his assurances and blamed the British for trying to create an anti-Soviet buffer state. By May 31 they had agreed on a list of those Poles who would be invited to work with the Lublin group on reorganization. That Stalin could determine who would be acceptable exposed the fiction of Lublin's autonomy, but he kept up the pretense by warning Hopkins that the regime would allow other Poles no more than four of the eighteen or twenty positions in the new government.[3]

When conversation turned to the Pacific war, Stalin said Soviet forces would be ready to invade Manchuria by August 8, three months after V-E Day. He added that operations would not begin until agreement was reached with China affirming Soviet rights as spelled out in the Yalta accords in order to justify the move "in the eyes of the Soviet people." He endorsed the unconditional surrender policy as necessary to destroy Japan's military potential, and said that overtures for a negotiated peace should be rejected as the Japanese wanted to "retain intact their military cards and, as Germany had done, prepare for future aggression." He also favored abolishing the emperorship because the ineffectual Hirohito might be succeeded by "an energetic and vigorous figure who could cause trouble." Harriman assured Stalin that "there was no intention on our part" to deviate from Roosevelt's commitment to unconditional surrender.

Stalin's comments about China were all the Americans could have asked. He said that the United States, as the only nation possessing the necessary financial resources, would have to play the leading role in rehabilitating China. He supported unification under Chiang Kai-shek—"the best of the lot"—and disavowed territorial interests in Manchuria or elsewhere. He also promised to maintain an Open Door policy with regard to trade in the port city of Dairen. Small wonder that Hopkins closed his report to Washington with the comment, "We were very encouraged by the conference on the Far East."[4]

An unforeseen emergency arose during the final meeting on June 6. Controversy had erupted in San Francisco over the scope of the veto power permanent members of the UN Security Council could exercise. The Soviet representative, Andrei Gromyko, had insisted on such a broad construction that Stettinius was certain it would be rejected by the United States Senate and the smaller nations. Alarmed that the conference would break up if the issue were not resolved quickly, he secured Truman's permission to have Hopkins and Harriman broach the matter personally with Stalin.[5]

Beginning his message with the by now familiar refrain that "Marshal Stalin did not know himself of some of the decisions that were being taken," Stettinius urged Hopkins to impress upon him that the United States "could not possibly join" the UN on the basis of Gromyko's "wholly new and impossible interpretation." When Hopkins raised the issue, Molotov not unexpectedly defended Gromyko's position. There followed a conversation in Russian between Stalin and Molotov, according to Bohlen's notes, which revealed that Stalin "had not understood the issues involved and had not had them explained to him." Stalin ended the exchange by pronouncing the matter trivial, then told Hopkins that the Soviets would accept the American view. The crisis was over.[6]

The Hopkins mission confirmed the belief that the best way to deal with the Soviets was to negotiate directly with Stalin. He had lived up to Hopkins's earlier description of him as a "rough, tough Russian" in his blunt denunciation of Lend-Lease curtailment and his refusal to allow non-Lublinites more than a few positions in the reorganized Polish government. His approval of some American-sponsored Poles, on the other hand, provided the fig leaf Truman had sought. That was what any smart political boss would do. Finally, the way he so readily settled the UN controversy corroborated the notion that the "Molotov clique" had been sabotaging relations by deliberately misleading him.

Truman responded enthusiastically to the Hopkins-Stalin agreement over Poland. "He told us he was a little excited this morning," an aide noted, because Hopkins "had messaged him that the Polish dispute, which has been causing much worry over the Russian attitude, had been settled."[7] Truman immediately forwarded to Churchill the list of Poles Stalin and Hopkins had agreed on, saying it had his "wholehearted approval" and assuring the dubious Briton that "this is the best solution we can hope for under the circumstances."[8]

He was similarly pleased about the Far East. To meet Stalin's condition that a Sino-Soviet treaty must be concluded before the Soviets would go to war with Japan, Truman had Hopkins inform him that the United States would provide air transportation for Chinese Foreign Minister T. V. Soong—then at the San Francisco Conference—to reach Moscow by July 1. The president told Davies at dinner on June 4 that he wanted the treaty completed before the Big Three meeting. Two days later he informed Stimson that Stalin had guaranteed that Manchuria would remain "fully Chinese," except for Port Arthur and "the settlement of Dairen which we had hold of [Stalin's assurance of an Open Door]." When Stimson, who had not been consulted about the Hopkins mission nor kept informed of its progress, cautioned that joint control of the railways would result in Soviet domination, Truman replied that he "realized that but the promise was perfectly clear and distinct." The next day he confided to his diary, "We may get a peace yet . . . I'm not afraid of Russia. They've always been our friends and I can't see any reason why they shouldn't always be."[9]

Churchill dashed Truman's hope for further improving relations with the Soviets by a personal meeting with Stalin. Davies had met with the prime minister on the evening of May 26, the day talks in Moscow began. Churchill proceeded to "blow off" when Davies informed him that Truman intended to confer alone with Stalin before the Big Three conference. The prime minister denounced what he regarded as betrayal in such strong terms that Davies threatened to walk out.[10] Churchill eventually calmed down, but notified the president that "I should not be prepared to attend a meeting which was a continuation of a conference between you and Marshal Stalin."[11] Truman abandoned the idea.

On May 27, a Sunday, Stimson told Truman that he intended to devote himself exclusively to atomic affairs during the next few days in preparation for two sessions of the Interim Committee.[12] Earlier deliberations had been devoted largely to drafting public statements to be issued by the president and by Stimson after the bomb had been used. The committee had agreed to appoint an advisory group designated the Scientific Panel. It consisted of Arthur H. Compton, Ernest O. Lawrence, and J. Robert Oppenheimer, the directors of atomic projects at Chicago, Berkeley, and Los Alamos respectively; and Enrico Fermi, who had supervised the first nuclear chain reaction in 1942.[13] A panel of industrialists also was named. Stimson hoped that consultations with these groups would provide the specialized information necessary to formulate sound recommendations to the president.

The committee met with the Scientific Panel at the Pentagon the morning of May 31. Generals Marshall and Groves attended by invitation. After welcoming the scientists, Stimson outlined to them the Interim Committee's responsibilities for developing proposals on atomic matters such as wartime controls and postwar legislation. He invited them to express their views "on any phase of the subject," but emphasized that he and General Marshall bore responsibility for counseling the president on military use. He assured them, however, that he and Marshall were well aware that the bomb was not just another instrument of warfare but a force that "must be controlled if possible to make it an assurance of future peace rather than a menace to civilization."

The first subject addressed was the future potential of nuclear weaponry. Prospects were awesome. The plutonium device scheduled to be tested, as well as those bombs that would be constructed for use against Japan, would have an estimated explosive force of two thousand to twenty thousand tons of TNT. "Second stage" bombs, expected to be available within two years, would provide the equivalent of fifty thousand to one hundred thousand tons of TNT. "Third stage" hydrogen weapons, having the power of ten million to one hundred million tons of TNT, would take approximately three more years after that. Once the technological difficulties were solved, moreover, the materials for each stage would be cheaper and obtainable in larger quantities than the stage before.

The domestic program and international controls were taken up next. After a discussion led by Lawrence, Arthur Compton, and Carl Compton, Stimson summarized the group's consensus over domestic procedures as follows: "Keep our industrial plant intact; build up sizable stock piles of material for military use and for industrial and technical use; and open the door for industrial development." Debate over international controls was inconclusive. Those who spoke agreed that atomic "secrets" could not be kept, but some were dubious that a control body would be able to provide effective means of inspection, which they deemed crucial. At this point Stimson left the meeting to attend a ceremony at the White House.

Russia, the most immediate concern, was taken up next. Oppenheimer proposed raising atomic matters "in the most general terms" with the Soviets "without giving them any details of our productive effort," and expressing interest in future cooperation with them. Marshall pointed out that many allegations about the seemingly uncooperative attitude of the Soviets were unfounded, and said he had no fear that they would divulge information given them about the atomic bomb to the Japanese. He suggested inviting two prominent Russian scientists to witness the forthcoming test.

Byrnes dissented. At a previous meeting he had voiced dismay over how little the United States had benefited from its association with Great Britain in the atomic project. Now he warned that the Soviets would use the British precedent to ask full partnership in the enterprise. He proposed instead that the United States "push ahead" as fast as possible to retain the lead "and at the same time make every effort to better our political relations with Russia." His opinion, according to the minutes, "was generally agreed to by all present." After more talk about the prospects of international control, the meeting adjourned for the morning.[14]

During informal conversation at lunch, by which time Stimson had returned, someone asked about the effectiveness of a demonstration before using the bomb against Japanese cities. Oppenheimer, who sat on the Target Committee which already had compiled a list of cities as prospective targets, replied that he could think of no display that would be sufficiently impressive to induce the Japanese to surrender. Other considerations were that it might prove to be a dud, that the Japanese might bring prisoners of war to the demonstration area, and that they would make every effort to destroy the carrier in flight.[15]

The afternoon session began with further talk over use of the bomb. Someone made the point that conventional raids already were capable of inflicting comparable damage. Oppenheimer replied that the spectacular visual effects of an atomic explosion would provide incontrovertible evidence that an entirely new force was responsible. Following a lengthy discussion of targets and effects, Stimson reviewed the group's conclusions: the bomb should be used without warning; it should not be dropped on a "civilian area," but "we should seek to make a profound psychological impression on as many of the inhabitants as possible." He agreed with the suggestion of James Bryant Conant, chairman of the National Defense Research Committee, that the most desirable target would be "a vital war plant employing a large number of workers and closely surrounded by workers' houses." Several other topics were discussed and the scientific panel was asked to draft a memorandum on creating an international organization for control of atomic energy.[16]

The next morning, June 1, the committee with Marshall and Groves again in attendance met with four executives of companies involved in various phases of the Manhattan Project. Stimson began by telling the industrialists, as he had the scientists, that although he and General

Marshall carried the burden of advising the president on use of atomic bombs in the present war, both realized the larger implications involved. Alluding to the need for international control, Stimson said that one of the most important considerations "was the question of how long it would take other nations to catch up with the United States," and asked for their estimates.

Everyone understood that "other nations" meant the Soviet Union. Several of the businessmen offered alternate timetables depending on whether the Soviets had access to German scientists and technicians, or on how much information they might acquire through espionage. Each individual's calculations were confined to the particular process his own company was engaged in, but a composite picture emerged. The Soviets could be expected to be able to build their own bombs within five to ten years. This lay between an earlier calculation of three to four years by Bush and Conant, and General Groves's prediction of a twenty-year lag.

Following lunch there was brief deliberation over international control with the industrialists, who then left along with Stimson. At 2:15 the committee reassembled in Harrison's office. After further talk about postwar organization and congressional appropriations, Byrnes returned to the question of using the bomb. He recommended that the committee inform Stimson of its present view that "the bomb should be used against Japan as soon as possible; that it be used on a war plant surrounded by workers' homes; and that it be used without prior warning." He went on to say it was the committee's understanding that the "small bomb" (plutonium-implosion type) would be used in the test and the "large bomb" (uranium-gun type) would be used "in the first strike over Japan."[17]

Most accounts exaggerate the importance of the May 31 and June 1 meetings, especially with regard to using the bomb. The Interim Committee had been constituted to draft public statements and to draw up proposals on domestic development and international control of nuclear research, *not* to make recommendations on use. Stimson had made clear to members of the committee and of both panels that although they were free to air their views on any aspect of the subject, determination of whether and how to employ the bomb against Japan was a military matter about which he and Marshall shared accountability for advising the president. For some assistant secretary or scientist (the subject was not discussed when the businessmen were present) to have claimed greater knowledge of the military situation at that time, let alone when the bomb became available, would have been presumptuous to say the least. None did.

Nor did the committee have any real influence over how the bomb should be used. The issue was not on the agenda and was raised during the meeting with the Scientific Panel only as a continuation of the impromptu conversation begun at lunch. No one challenged the goal of inflicting the greatest possible shock on the Japanese, and the criteria discussed were identical to those that General Groves already had conveyed to the Target Committee weeks earlier. Indeed, Stimson had Groves provide him with a list of cities proposed by that group in time for the meeting.

The net result of the two sessions was largely to endorse what already had become the operative assumptions about use. Arthur H. Compton later recalled that throughout the discussions "it seemed a foregone conclusion that the bomb would be used." When various kinds of demonstrations were mentioned, he wrote, "One after the other it seemed necessary that they should be discarded."[18] Byrnes's proposal on June 1 that the committee convey its views to Stimson—views already agreed to the day before in discussions Stimson himself led—can best be seen as an insurance policy. Aware that some scientists were lobbying against military use of the bomb, Byrnes made sure the record indicated that a group including four of the world's most eminent physicists (three were Nobel laureates) had been unable to recommend any viable alternative to dropping it on Japanese cities.

Just as Stimson in his capacity dominated deliberations over use, Byrnes in his prevailed on the matter of disclosure to the Soviets. As Truman's personal representative on the committee, he presumably was familiar with the president's thoughts on the subject. As the next secretary of state, he would inherit major responsibilities for dealing with the Russians. Byrnes undoubtedly had in mind the forthcoming meeting with Stalin, but the notes do not reveal whether he mentioned it in making his argument against disclosure. In any event, although Bush, Conant, Oppenheimer, and others favored informing the Soviets, no one challenged Byrnes at this time.

Perhaps the most significant result of the sessions were the estimates as to when Russia would be able to produce its own bombs. Unlike those who urged that overtures to the Soviets be made immediately to gain their trust, Stimson wanted to make sure that effective controls were in place before sharing the results of American research. From this point of view, the prediction that it would take the Soviets five to ten years to acquire nuclear capability meant that while creation of an inspection system was necessary, it need not be done hastily or without congressional approval. He therefore instructed the committee to concentrate on drafting legislation for domestic regulation, "with the problems of international relations and controls to be dealt with by the Permanent Post-War Commission that would be established by law."[19]

Stimson discussed the committee's findings with the president on June 6. Truman said that Byrnes already had briefed him and had seemed "highly pleased" with the results. Stimson's first point was the recommendation that there be no revelation of "our work on S-1 until the first bomb had been successfully laid on Japan." He warned that "the greatest complication" was what might happen at the Big Three meeting. Truman replied that he had scheduled it for July 15 to allow time for the test. The secretary pointed out that there still might be delay, and if there were and the Russians "should bring up the subject" and asked to be admitted to partnership, the best response was the "simple statement that as yet we were not quite ready to do it."

With regard to future controls, Stimson reported that the "only suggestion" the committee could come up with was that each nation should promise to make public all work it was doing on atomic energy and that an international organization be formed with "full power of inspection." He said he realized the proposal was imperfect and that Russia might not cooperate, but in that event "we were far enough ahead of the game to be able to accumulate enough material to serve as insurance against being caught helpless." He advised that no dissemination of information be made until a control system was functioning. The two men then discussed "further quid pro quos which should be established in consideration for our taking them [the Soviets] into partnership," mentioning Poland, Romania, Yugoslavia, and Manchuria.[20]

Stimson's meeting with Truman is revealing. The secretary's advice that there be no disclosure to the Soviets until after the bomb had been "successfully laid on Japan" provides yet another example of the assumption that it would be used when ready if the Japanese had not yet capitulated. So does Byrnes's account of his talk with the president five days earlier. Advised that the Interim Committee would recommend using the bomb without warning, according to Byrnes, the president said "regrettable as it might be, so far as he could see, the only reasonable conclusion was to use the bomb."[21]

Stimson's report also shows that it was taken for granted that the Soviets knew about the Manhattan Project, although presumably not how close it was to fruition. The secretary's concern about how to respond if the Russians "should bring up the subject" makes no sense otherwise, for the Soviets could not be expected to mention a subject they knew nothing about. He and Groves had told Roosevelt six months earlier that the Soviets were spying on the program. The file Groves kept on such activities, furthermore, contained numerous accounts of Soviet officials expressing interest in obtaining high-grade uranium ore and information on nuclear research. One report stated that a member of the Radiation Laboratory in Berkeley had given information about the program to an American Communist named Steve Nelson, who in turn had conveyed it to a Soviet official in San Francisco. The general understandably concluded, "The Russian government is working on uranium fission."[22]

Such fears were confirmed by a memorandum British Chancellor of the Exchequer Sir John Anderson had sent to Groves in March 1945. Anderson, Stimson's counterpart in the British atomic program, had met with the prominent French scientist, Frederic Joliot-Curie, on February 23. France had worked with Great Britain on atomic affairs before Hitler's victory in 1940, and several French scientists who fled had been or were employed on the Manhattan Project. Now the French insisted on being taken in as associates, threatening to turn to the Russians if denied. Joliot-Curie told Anderson that approaches already had been made and that the Soviets had expressed interest in collaboration. They had refused, however, to divulge any information about their own work.[23]

Finally, Stimson's discussion with Truman about obtaining quid pro quos from the Soviets in return for admitting them to partnership must be understood in context. The decision not to mention the bomb at the Big Three meeting obviously precluded using it as a bargaining counter there, even though all the issues cited were sure to be taken up. With the memories of what had happened after Yalta still fresh, Stimson and Truman hoped that the prospects of being taken in as partners would influence the Soviets to carry out in good faith agreements made before and during the upcoming summit conference.

A thesis that unaccountably has been treated with respect by historians who should know better is that during these weeks Truman and his advisers were acting out an elaborate hoax. What appeared to be conciliatory gestures, such as the Hopkins mission, were designed to fool the Soviets into thinking that the United States genuinely sought accommodation. Hopkins was an unwitting dupe, according to this scenario, whose real mission was to baby Stalin along in order to *put off* resolution of issues such as Poland. All the while Truman was secretly preparing for a "delayed showdown" at the Big Three conference during which he intended to rely upon the atomic bomb to bully Stalin into accepting American dictates.

This plot, the story continues, was revised in light of Stimson's June 6 meeting with Truman. Previously the secretary had deemed it sufficient that Truman himself knew from the test whether he had this new force at his disposal. Now, as a result of discussions with the Interim Committee, Stimson advised waiting until the bomb had been "successfully laid on Japan" to guarantee that Stalin would be sufficiently awed. What he referred to as "the greatest complication" was the possibility that the weapon would not be ready for use against Japan by the time the summit began in mid-July. "Stimson's fear that the bomb might not be publicly demonstrated before the negotiations," Gar Alperovitz has it, "proved to be only too correct."[24]

All this is fiction. There is no evidence that a "delayed showdown" was planned—it certainly was not discussed by the Interim Committee—or that the Hopkins mission was intended as a smoke screen. And, as shown previously, Stimson's remark about "the greatest complication" referred to a Soviet request for partnership. The claim that he was talking about use of the bomb against Japan prior to the summit conference is based on a distortion of what he wrote in his diary and is refuted by the facts.

The uranium bomb, *Little Boy*, was scheduled to be ready for use by August 1. Because of its simplicity and through a trial that became known as the "Dragon Experiment"—dropping a slug of uranium compound through a hole in a nearly critical mass of the same material "so that for a split second there was the condition for an atomic explosion"—scientists were confident it would work.[25] What was to be tested was not a bomb but an implosion-type plutonium device suspended in a tower. Assuming success, far more was involved than merely stuffing another one inside a casing and screwing down the lid. The plutonium bomb, *Fat Man,* was an extremely complicated mechanism, some components of which would not be ready until late July, and more time would be required to get it to the Pacific. Regardless of how early the device was tested, therefore, Stimson *knew* when he talked to Truman that there was absolutely no chance *Fat Man* would be operational before *Little Boy* in early August, much less by the time the summit met. As Byrnes had pointed out at the Interim Committee meeting, the gun-type bomb would be used "in the first strike over Japan."[26]

Truman did not want a showdown of any kind, as his attitude toward Poland makes clear. Having failed to budge the Soviets through tough talk, his instructions to Hopkins and his lack of concern over the tiny number of seats Stalin was willing to allow non-Lublinites indicate that he was by then willing to settle for appearances. Byrnes was equally forbearing. He likened the settlement to any political compromise where the party "in a commanding position" accepts "other elements" for the sake of cooperation. After discussing Poland with Hopkins and Davies on June 13, Truman expressed satisfaction that "we are in better position for a peaceful conference than we were before."[27]

The president likewise wanted to settle the Manchurian issue before the Big Three conference. Three days after his talk with Stimson about the bomb, during which he had mentioned Hopkins's "accomplishment" with regard to Manchuria, he and Acting Secretary of State Grew met with Chinese Foreign Minister Soong, who had flown in from the San Francisco Conference. Truman told Soong how pleased he was by Stalin's stated intentions, then handed the minister a message that the American ambassador in Chungking was to deliver to Chiang Kai-shek on June 15. The message listed seven points constituting the "understanding" Hopkins had reached with Stalin and repeated verbatim the Yalta Far Eastern accord, which until then had been kept from the Chinese to avoid a leak. Soong also was shown Truman's instructions to the ambassador: "Inform Chiang Kai-shek that President Roosevelt at Yalta agreed to support these Soviet claims upon the arrival of Russia in the war against Japan. I am also in agreement." Copies of these instructions were sent to Churchill and to Stalin.[28] Soong was alarmed by some of the arrangements FDR had agreed to at Yalta. A Soviet lease on Port Arthur was a painful reminder of the days when stronger nations carved up China by extracting "leases" from its impotent government. Equally ominous, what was meant by Soviet "preeminent interests" over Dairen and the vital connecting railways? On these and other matters Soong tried in vain to get some sense of what the Americans regarded as reasonable interpretations of Russian claims. China would be helpless in dealing with the Soviets alone, he pointed out, yet all he was told was that the United States adhered to the Yalta accord and that he would have to work out the details with Stalin. Chiang's subsequent request that the United States and Great Britain participate in the negotiations, and that Port Arthur be designated a joint naval base of the four powers, also was turned down.[29]

Truman refused to back the Chinese because their priorities were not his. However much they resented a Soviet lease on Port Arthur, FDR had agreed to it and to Russia's "preeminent interests" in Dairen and the railways. Truman endorsed these provisions of the Yalta accord as he stated in his message to Chiang. Besides, such matters simply did not concern him much provided the Soviets kept their pledges on matters of greater importance to the United States. Recall his reply to Stimson when the latter warned that joint control of the rail lines would result in Soviet domination: "He said he realized that but the promise [that Manchuria would remain "fully Chinese" and that an Open Door would be maintained in Dairen] was perfectly clear and distinct." Stalin could not be expected to carry out his end of the bargain without compensation the Chinese would have to pay.

Truman wanted to facilitate Russian entry into the war against Japan. He also sought Stalin's support for the unification of China under Chiang and an Open Door in Manchuria, even though the latter was primarily symbolic. Trade with Manchuria never had been large, but the Open Door had been a historic American policy and he had no wish to be accused of abandoning it. Attainment of these objectives, Stalin had assured Hopkins, hinged upon the successful conclusion of Sino-Soviet negotiations. Truman made clear to Soong that the United States expected Chinese concessions, and he had Davies meet privately with the foreign minister to urge that a treaty be concluded before the summit began.[30]

The last major issue Truman hoped to resolve before the Big Three meeting involved reparations from Germany. At Yalta the Soviets had requested that a total of $20 billion in capital equipment and goods be extracted from Germany, with half going to Russia. Neither Roosevelt nor Churchill had questioned the Soviet share, but both opposed naming a figure before on-site inspections revealed what Germany could afford to pay without reducing its population below a minimal standard of living. Out of deference to the Soviet appeal that they needed an approximate figure for their own postwar planning, FDR reluctantly agreed that a tripartite reparations commission could use in its "initial studies" a sum of $20 billion as a "basis for discussion." He did so under the assumption that the figure was a target to be sought after a physical inventory had been made to determine Germany's capacity to pay.[31]

Truman was adamant about only two aspects of reparations. He did not want the United States placed in the position of having to subsidize the German economy because of excessive extractions, and he would not be party to any agreement involving German slave labor. On May 19, the same day he asked Hopkins to go to Russia, he talked with Edwin W. Pauley, whom he had recently appointed head of the American delegation to the Reparations Commission. Pauley was preparing to embark on an inspection tour of Germany before proceeding to Moscow where the commission would meet. Truman believed that the issue of forced labor rather than the amount of reparations would be the "main stumbling block" to an agreement. He told Pauley "to use his best judgement" but "under no circumstances to commit us to anything resembling slave labor."[32]

By the middle of June, then, prospects for a "peaceful conference" appeared good. Truman had scheduled it to coincide with the atomic test, but not in order to intimidate the Russians. He had decided to issue an American-British-Chinese ultimatum to Japan during the conference rather than an earlier, unilateral one as some of his advisers had been urging.[33] The three powers, after all, had jointly issued the Cairo Declaration in 1943 committing them to unconditional surrender and to divesting Japan of its overseas possessions. Knowledge of a successful test at the outset of the conference would influence the ultimatum's content and permit its issuance in time for the Japanese to reply before the first bomb was ready for use. It would also help determine future strategy.

The goal of forcing the Japanese to surrender through psychological shock had been predicated on the assumption that at least two atomic bombs be available, more if necessary. Everyone assumed that the

Japanese military would try to conceal or minimize the first explosion, which was one of the reasons for rejecting a demonstration. The idea was to convince them that the United States had such weapons in production and could drop one after another indefinitely. Successful detonation of the plutonium device would meet this requirement even if any particular *Fat Man* malfunctioned. Should the device prove unworkable, only *Little Boy* remained. There was just one and even it could not be guaranteed, if for no other reason than that the aircraft delivering it might crash or be shot down.

Results of the nuclear trial had implications for negotiations with the Soviets at the conference, of course. Roosevelt had agreed to Stalin's terms for joining the war to reduce American casualties if an invasion proved necessary. Truman wanted Soviet participation in any event—it might help convince the Japanese that their situation was hopeless—but the test's outcome would influence how far he would be prepared to go if Stalin should try to raise the ante.

Meanwhile, with the availability of atomic bombs uncertain, and with no guarantee that the bombs could compel surrender even if they were available, Truman had to determine whether to approve plans for invasion or to rely on conventional bombing and naval blockade as some of his advisers urged. Okinawa afforded a preview of coming attractions. Since April 1 the Japanese had fought with a ferocity that mocked any notion that their will to resist was diminishing. They could be expected to defend their sacred homeland with even greater fervor, and kamikazes flying at short range would be even more devastating.

On June 14 the president had Admiral Leahy notify the Joint Chiefs of Staff that a meeting would be held on the eighteenth so that Truman could be "thoroughly informed as to our intentions and prospects in preparation for his discussions with Churchill and Stalin." The chiefs were asked to provide estimates of the time required and casualties expected in defeating Japan by invasion, for which they already had issued a preliminary directive on May 25, compared with relying on air bombardment and blockade. "He desires to be informed," the memorandum concluded, "as to exactly what we want the Russians to do." On the evening before he met with the chiefs, Truman wrote in his diary: "I have to decide Japanese strategy—shall we invade Japan proper or shall we bomb and blockade? That is my hardest decision to date. But I'll make it when I have all the facts."[34]

Truman summoned the chiefs against the backdrop of reports from Japan that a decision had been made at the highest levels to fight the war to a finish. On June 8 an imperial conference adopted "The Fundamental Policy to Be Followed Henceforth in the Conduct of the War," the heart of which read: "With a faith born of eternal loyalty as our inspiration, we shall . . . prosecute the war to the bitter end in order to uphold the national polity, protect the imperial land, and accomplish the objectives for which we went to war."[35] The president had no reason to believe that the proclamation meant anything other than what it said.

Advice and Dissent

On the morning of June 18, 1945, the day of Truman's scheduled conference with the Joint Chiefs of Staff, he talked with Acting Secretary of State
Grew about making a public statement calling upon Japan to surrender.
A few days before, Grew had submitted for the president's attention
a draft of such a statement proposing to assure the Japanese that, once
certain criteria had been met, they would be permitted to determine their
own form of government and to pursue peaceful economic relations
with other nations. Grew thought the best psychological moment to
issue the declaration would be immediately after the fall of Okinawa,
expected any day.

Truman told Grew that he had "carefully considered" the draft, but
that while "he liked the idea he had decided to hold this up until it could
be discussed at the Big Three meeting."[1] Possibly he thought a unilateral
announcement would violate the spirit of the Cairo Declaration of 1943,
in which the United States, Great Britain, and China had pledged to
continue the war until Japan surrendered unconditionally. Truman's
decision ended debate over *when* an appeal should be released, but appeared to indicate that one would be forthcoming. Various individuals
and committees intensified their efforts to come up with a formula that
would influence the Japanese without alienating the American people.

Truman met with the chiefs at 3:30 that afternoon: Generals Marshall
and Ira C. Eaker (sitting in for Army Air Forces chief Henry H. Arnold
who was on an inspection tour in the Pacific), and Admirals Leahy and
Ernest J. King, navy chief of staff. Secretary of the Navy James Forrestal,
Stimson, and Assistant Secretary of War John J. McCloy also attended.
Stimson earlier had developed a migraine and asked McCloy to sit in

for him, but at the last minute decided the meeting was too important to miss. Truman began by alluding to Leahy's memorandum stating the purposes of the meeting, then asked Marshall for his views.

Marshall read a digest of the memorandum his staff had prepared for the session. The gist of it was that the chiefs, supported by General Douglas MacArthur and Admiral Chester W. Nimitz, believed that an invasion of Kyushu, southernmost of the Japanese home islands, "appears to be the least costly worth-while operation following Okinawa." A lodgment in Kyushu, he said, was essential both "to tightening our strangle hold of blockade and bombardment on Japan, and to forcing capitulation by invasion of the Tokyo Plain [on the main island of Honshu]." The chiefs recommended a target date of November 1 because by that time bombing "will have smashed practically every industrial target worth hitting," the Japanese navy "if any still exists, will be powerless," and sea and air power "will have cut Jap reinforcement capabilities from the mainland to negligible proportions." A later date would give the Japanese more time to prepare defenses and bad weather might delay the invasion, "and hence the end of the war," for up to six months.

Marshall also justified the Kyushu operation on the grounds that if the Japanese "are ever willing to capitulate short of complete military defeat," it would be from a combination of air bombardment and naval blockade, an invasion "indicating the firmness of our resolution," and "the entry or threat of entry of Russia into the war." With regard to casualties, he said that campaigns in the Pacific had been so diverse "it is considered wrong" to give estimates. All he would say was that casualties during the first thirty days of the Kyushu invasion should not exceed those suffered in taking Luzon in the Philippines—thirty-one thousand men killed, wounded, or missing in action. He concluded on this point by saying, "It is a grim fact that there is not an easy, bloodless way to victory in war." After reading a message from MacArthur supporting the operation, Marshall said his own personal opinion was that it was "the only course to pursue." Air power alone had been unable to defeat Germany, and it would not be "sufficient to put the Japanese out of the war."

Admiral King said he fully endorsed Marshall's remarks, and that the more he studied the matter the more he was impressed by the strategic location of Kyushu, which he considered "the key to the success of any siege operations." In his opinion "we should do Kyushu now, after which there would be time to judge the effect of possible operations by the Russians and the Chinese." He stated that they should also begin preparations for invading the Tokyo plain because "if they do not go forward now, they cannot be arranged for later." Once started, however, they "can always be stopped if desired."

When the president asked for Leahy's comments, the admiral questioned Marshall's casualty estimate. He said that the troops at Okinawa had suffered 35 percent casualties, and because "of the similarity of fighting" that percentage should be applied to the number of troops participating in the Kyushu operation. King replied that there would be more room to maneuver on Kyushu, and said he thought the most realistic figure lay somewhere between the losses incurred on Luzon and on Okinawa. After a brief discussion about Japan's ability to reinforce Kyushu, Leahy again stressed the difficulties in taking "another island." This led Truman to complain that the proposed operation was "practically creating another Okinawa closer to Japan, to which the Chiefs of Staff agreed."[2]

Truman's dismay was largely due to Leahy. Leahy had been trying to persuade him that Japan could be defeated by air and naval power without any more landings.[3] This accounts for Truman's diary entry the day before stating that the decision he had to make was "shall we invade Japan proper *or* shall we bomb and blockade?" (emphasis added). It also accounts for the admiral's repeated insistence that the Kyushu operation would be bloodier than either Marshall or King predicted.

But Leahy had no constituency. He had retired as chief of naval operations in 1939. After a brief tenure as governor of Puerto Rico, in 1940 he was named ambassador to the Vichy government of France where he served until the summer of 1942. He then became FDR's personal chief of staff and, upon Marshall's recommendation, also was appointed to the newly formed Joint Chiefs of Staff. Marshall wanted the Army Air Forces represented on the JCS and knew the navy would not accept being outnumbered. He also intended that Leahy in his dual capacity would provide liaison with the president. Leahy chaired JCS meetings, usually said very little, and tried to act as honest broker despite his tie to the navy. "His chief function," as the historian of the JCS has written, "was to keep the JCS and the President informed of each other's positions."[4] King, as chief of naval operations and navy chief of staff, spoke for that branch, and he supported Marshall.

Eaker made it unanimous among those who represented the services. He "agreed completely" with Marshall, and said he had just received a cable from Arnold in which the latter also "expressed complete agreement." Eaker said that existing plans called for the use of forty groups of heavy bombers against Japan, and that these "could not be deployed without the use of airfields on Kyushu." Those who advocated the use of unsupported air power, he continued, overlooked the "very impressive fact" that air casualties, then running at 30 percent per month, "never fail to drop as soon as the ground forces come in." He concluded by emphasizing that "delay favored only the enemy and he urged that there be no delay."

Secretaries Stimson and Forrestal agreed with the chiefs. Stimson believed "there was no other choice," but added that there was a "large submerged class in Japan who do not favor the present war and whose full opinion and influence had never yet been felt." He said that this class would defend Japan against invasion, but in the meantime he hoped something would be done to "arouse them and to develop any possible influence they might have." He meant, of course, assuring the Japanese that unconditional surrender did not mean destruction of their nation. Truman, having talked about the matter with Grew that morning, replied that "this possibility was being worked on all the time."

The president then said that one of his objectives at the Big Three conference would be "to get from Russia all the assistance in the war that was possible." He therefore wanted to know "all the decisions that he would have to make in advance" so as to occupy "the strongest possible position in the discussions." Leahy responded that he disagreed with those who claimed that anything short of unconditional surrender meant "that we will have lost the war." He said he had no fear of "menace from Japan in the foreseeable future" if terms were modified, but he did fear that insistence on the doctrine would "increase our casualty lists." Truman answered that he had "left the door open for Congress" to take the lead but that "he did not feel that he could take any action at this time to change public opinion on the matter."[5]

What Truman meant by his reference to leaving the door open to Congress is unclear, although some members at the time were calling for a negotiated peace. As for himself, as recently as June 1 he had reaffirmed his commitment to unconditional surrender in a special message to Congress. Citing the Japanese attack on Pearl Harbor, the Bataan death march, and the "barbarous massacres in Manila," he said that while their dreams of conquest had been destroyed, they have not "given up hope." That hope was that war weariness "will force us to settle for some compromise peace short of unconditional surrender." "They should know better," he scoffed, and pledged that the United States would "see the fight through to a complete and victorious finish."[6] To openly abandon the formula only weeks later would have placed him in the position of doing precisely what he had promised the American people he would not do.

Truman said he considered "the Kyushu plan all right from the military standpoint" and directed the chiefs to "go ahead with it." After discussion of the situation in China and the possibility of having a supreme commander in the Pacific, the president summed up. He had called the meeting to learn "how far we could afford to go in the Japanese campaign." "He had hoped that there was a possibility of preventing an Okinawa from one end of Japan to the other," but "he was clear on the situation now" and was "quite sure" the chiefs should proceed with the invasion plans.

King made a final point about negotiations with the Russians. Regardless of the desirability of having them enter the war against Japan, he said, "they were not indispensable and he did not think we should go so far as to beg them to come in." While the cost of defeating Japan would be greater without Soviet help, there was no question in his mind that "we could handle it alone." Realization of that fact, he concluded, "should greatly strengthen the President's hand in the forthcoming conference."[7]

The next statement in the rough draft of the minutes, omitted in the final version, reads: "The President and the Chiefs of Staff then discussed certain other matters."[8] These matters involved use of the atomic bomb. As the session was breaking up, Truman said that no one was going to leave without giving his opinion and he asked McCloy what he thought. According to McCloy's later accounts, he replied that he believed the atomic bomb would make invasion of Japan unnecessary. He thought a warning should be issued to the emperor stating that the United States possessed atomic weapons and would use them unless Japan surrendered. The discussion that followed was inconclusive because of the stubborn fact that no one could be certain the bombs would work.[9]

In his memoirs Truman claimed that dropping atomic bombs on Japan avoided an invasion that would have cost 500,000 American lives.

Stimson, Byrnes, and others in their recollections mentioned the same or even higher figures, which then began appearing in scholarly and popular accounts on the subject.[10] Some critics have attacked such estimates as gross exaggerations. As evidence they most often point to a document prepared by the Joint War Plans Committee (JWPC) for the chiefs' meeting with Truman. The committee estimated that the proposed landings in southern Kyushu, followed by invasion of the Tokyo plain, would cost 40,000 dead, 150,000 wounded, and 3,500 missing in action for a total of 193,500 casualties.[11]

That those who participated in a controversial decision would inflate the consequences of the path not chosen is unremarkable, if not particularly admirable. Some of their critics profess to see a more sinister motive at work. The lower casualty estimate, they argue, calls into question the very idea that atomic bombs were dropped to avoid the losses invasion would incur. By discrediting that justification as a cover-up, they seek to give credence to their own allegations that the bombs really were used to impress the Soviet Union rather than to defeat Japan.[12]

Perhaps only an intellectual could assert that 193,500 anticipated casualties were too insignificant to have caused Truman to use atomic bombs.[13] Actually, this figure referred only to ground combat. It did not include naval losses (estimated at 9,700 for Kyushu alone) or the unpredictable number of casualties kamikazes would inflict on crowded troop transports—which would be their primary targets. That is not all. These writers have conveniently ignored the disclaimers sprinkled throughout the JWPC report: that casualties "are not subject to accurate estimate" and that the projection "is admittedly only an educated guess." Most important, they neglect to mention that the figures that do appear never were shown to Truman. And, as will be shown in chapter 7, these numbers in any event had become irrelevant by the time the first atomic bomb was dropped.

When the JWPC report reached the next higher level, the Joint Staff Planners, few changes were made except for the casualty estimates. These were omitted with the comment that they "are not subject to accurate estimate." The amended document was next passed along to Assistant Chief of Staff General John E. Hull. In a memorandum to Marshall entitled "Amplifying Comments on Planners' Paper for Presentation to the President," Hull wrote that "it is considered wrong to give any estimate in numbers" for the proposed operations. He merely listed the casualties involved in several previous campaigns and stated, "There is reason to believe that the first 30 days in Kyushu should not exceed the price we paid for Luzon." It was Hull's memorandum that Marshall read at the meeting with Truman.[14] Hull later told an interviewer that casualty estimates had run "from a few hundred thousand to a million men to do the thing."[15]

The five hundred thousand figure Truman used in his memoirs did not come out of thin air. In August 1944 a JCS study of the losses suffered on Saipan predicted that invading Japan would "cost a half a million American lives and many more that number in wounded."[16] That estimate never was officially revised and may have been passed along to the president by Leahy, who stressed how costly an invasion would be, or by someone else. In late May 1945, at Truman's request, former president Herbert Hoover submitted a memorandum on ending the war in Japan. In it he stated that a negotiated peace with Japan "will save 500,000 to 1,000,000 lives." Truman gave the memorandum to Stimson for review by War Department staff. The resultant analysis stated that Hoover's estimate was too high, but Stimson in his covering letter to the president emphasized that a war to the finish would cost "a large number of lives."[17]

Whether such dramatic numbers stuck in Truman's memory because of the chiefs' unwillingness to provide *any* estimates of total casualties at the June 18 meeting or later can only be guessed. Differences among them over anticipated losses on Kyushu during the first thirty days added to the confusion. Would they equal the thirty-one thousand suffered on Luzon (Marshall), or the much larger rate as on Okinawa (Leahy), or somewhere in between (King)? MacArthur's headquarters had submitted an estimate of fifty thousand (although the general himself said this was high), and Nimitz placed the number at forty-nine thousand.[18] Whatever his culpability for citing inflated figures later, there can be no doubt that Truman at the time feared a bloodbath and wanted to prevent "an Okinawa from one end of Japan to the other."

Three days after Truman's meeting with the JCS, the Interim Committee convened to discuss among other things a petition it had received from a component of the Manhattan Project designated the Metallurgical Laboratory, based at the University of Chicago. The Met Lab, as it was called, had been crucial during the developmental stages of the program, but its role had been reduced to the point where the Interim Committee had discussed phasing it out altogether.[19] Some at the Met Lab had been alienated ever since the project had been placed under General Groves's heavy-handed control, thereby reducing them to the status of employees rather than associates to be consulted. Now, with the group's future uncertain and atomic bombs nearing readiness, they were appalled that momentous decisions would be made by politicians and military men advised only by a few scientists whom they regarded as having been coopted. When Arthur Compton, director of the Metallurgical Project (of which the Met Lab was a part) and a member of the Interim Committee's Scientific Panel, invited the dissidents to submit their views, they eagerly complied.

On June 12 Compton forwarded for the Interim Committee's attention what became known as the Franck report, named for Nobel Laureate James Franck who chaired the Met Lab's hastily formed Committee on Political and Social Problems. Fearful that the report might bog down in channels, by intent or otherwise, several members of the Met Lab committee persuaded Franck to deliver it personally to Compton in Washington. Compton tried to arrange a meeting between Franck and Stimson; when informed that Stimson was out of town, he personally handed the report, with a covering letter, to the Interim Committee secretary, R. Gordon Arneson.[20]

The Franck report drew a horrifying picture of a future world in which an aggressor nation, using far more powerful nuclear weapons than those now being developed, could literally destroy another society. The United States would be especially vulnerable because its population and industry were so concentrated. Such an eventuality could not be avoided either by keeping secret the procedures for building atomic bombs or by trying to monopolize the sources of uranium ore. Other nations sooner or later would acquire the ability to construct nuclear weapons, and uranium deposits were too widespread for any one nation or coalition to corner them all. With regard to the Russians, their experience in nuclear research "is entirely sufficient to enable them to retrace our steps within a few years," and the likelihood that they had no uranium reserves "in a country which covers $1/5$ of the land area of the earth (and whose sphere of influence takes in additional territory) is too small to serve as a basis for security."

The only way to avoid nuclear catastrophe, the report stated, was through international control based on "mutual trust and willingness on all sides to give up a certain part of their sovereign rights." Assuming international agreement to prevent nuclear war was the "paramount objective," using atomic bombs against Japan "may easily destroy all our chances of success." How could the rest of the world trust a nation capable of using such weapons when it proclaimed its desire to abolish them? The number of American lives that might be saved, therefore, "may be outweighed by the ensuing loss of confidence and by a wave of horror and repulsion sweeping over the rest of the world." Besides, the devastation already visited upon Japanese cities and the "comparatively low efficiency and small size" of the first bombs made it "doubtful" that they would be "sufficient to break the will or ability of Japan to resist."

The Chicago scientists proposed instead a nuclear demonstration in the desert or on an uninhabited island, to which representatives of the United Nations would be invited. This would enable the United States to say to the world, "You see what sort of a weapon we had but did not use," thereby enhancing its moral prestige in the campaign for international control. Following the demonstration, nuclear weapons "might perhaps be used against Japan if the sanction of the United Nations (and of public opinion at home) were obtained, perhaps after a preliminary ultimatum to Japan to surrender." "This may sound fantastic," the authors admitted, but the enormous destructive power of nuclear weapons required "new and imaginative methods."

Compton said in his accompanying letter that the Met Lab document would be discussed during the next few days by the Scientific Panel, which would then report to the Interim Committee in time for its next meeting. He also pointed out that the document omitted two important considerations:

(1) that failure to make a military demonstration of the new bombs may make the war longer and more expensive of human lives, and

(2) that without a military demonstration it may be impossible to impress the world with the need for national sacrifices in order to gain lasting security.[21]

The Scientific Panel drew up its response to the Franck report on June 16. There were three points made. First, that the United States should inform all its major allies that atomic bombs might soon be available and that their suggestions about using this development to improve international relations would be welcomed. Second, that opinion among scientists ran from those who advocated a "purely technical demonstration" so as not to prejudice chances for establishing control to those who emphasized "the saving of American lives by immediate military use" and who believed that such use would "improve the international prospects." Panel members favored the latter views: "we can propose no technical demonstration likely to bring an end to the war; we see no acceptable alternative to direct military use." The third point was that "we, as scientific men" had "no claim to special competence" in solving the military, social, and political problems created by atomic power.[22]

The Interim Committee met at 9:30 A.M. on June 21, with George Harrison chairing in place of the elderly Stimson who was resting at his Long Island estate. The morning session was taken up with discussion of the various official statements that were to be issued after the first bomb was dropped. After lunch, the group considered three papers from the Scientific Panel, including the one written in reply to the Franck report. Harrison explained that the Met Lab document had been forwarded to the Scientific Panel for its response, and that its members "saw no acceptable alternative to direct military use." The committee thereupon reaffirmed the position it had taken at the meetings of May 31 and June 1: that the weapon be used without warning at the earliest opportunity, on a "military installation or war plant surrounded by or adjacent to homes or other buildings most susceptible to damage."[23]

Although the committee almost certainly would have rejected the Franck report in any case, knowledge that the man most responsible for it was Leo Szilard helped ensure that it would be regarded with skepticism. Szilard was a brilliant physicist who had become obsessed with the idea of producing a nuclear chain reaction during the early 1930s. He had been one of those responsible for Albert Einstein's letter to Roosevelt that had launched the American atomic program in 1939, had designed with Enrico Fermi the apparatus that created the first self-sustained chain reaction in December 1942, and had contributed innumerable ideas since.[24] He also was arrogant, intemperate in argument, and absolutely certain about whatever position he took even if he recently had changed it. He had clashed repeatedly with committee members Bush and Conant, who knew he distrusted them as housebroken bureaucrats, and he had personally alienated Byrnes and Groves, who was at the meeting by invitation.

Szilard had dedicated himself to the task of building atomic bombs out of fear that Nazi Germany would acquire them first. He had frequently criticized what he regarded as the army's bungling management of the program—its emphasis upon compartmentalization for security purposes, for instance—because he believed it retarded progress. More recently, especially after it had become clear that Germany posed no threat, he had grown increasingly concerned about the implications of nuclear weapons for the future of humanity. Unlike those of his colleagues who preferred to stick to their lasts, Szilard believed that scientists like himself should have a major role in shaping policy because they alone had both the knowledge and the imagination to deal intelligently with this unprecedented new force.

Groves and Szilard had become enemies almost from the day they met. To Szilard, Groves was an authoritarian clod to be resisted at every turn. Groves regarded Szilard as at worst a spy, at best a loose cannon that had to be tied down or, better yet, thrown overboard. As early as October 1942, Graves had tried to have Szilard—a Hungarian-born Jew who had fled Hitler's Germany—interned as an enemy alien. Since then the general had conducted a vendetta: he had Szilard placed under FBI surveillance and his mail opened, and had him discharged from the Met Lab for several months in 1943 over a patent dispute.[25] Most recently, at the Interim Committee's meeting on May 31, Groves undoubtedly had Szilard in mind when he proposed dismissing "certain scientists of doubtful discretion and uncertain loyalty."[26] At that time Groves was particularly infuriated by Szilard's efforts to secure a meeting with the president, which in turn led to Byrnes's encounter with the mercurial scientist.

For years Szilard had advocated international control as the only effective way to neutralize the atomic threat. The problem was how to achieve it. In early 1944 he had written Vannevar Bush that atomic bombs *must* be used in combat so that "the fact of their destructive power" would sufficiently shock the public into making the sacrifices necessary for peace. He even advocated preemptive war, if necessary, to secure control of the world's uranium deposits.[27] Such ideas he later would condemn as ignorant and dangerous.

On March 12, 1945, Szilard completed a memorandum intended for President Roosevelt's eyes. Warning of a future without arms control, during which atomic bombs might be smuggled into cities or delivered by long-range rockets, he argued that the United States had to reach agreement with the Soviets. The best time to approach them, he wrote, would be "immediately after we demonstrated the potency of atomic bombs" by using them against Japan or by staging a demonstration at an appropriate time. Meanwhile, research on second-stage weapons should proceed at full speed as yet another inducement for the Soviets to cooperate. Such progress also would place the United States in a better position should attempts to establish arms control prove unsuccessful.[28]

Having no access to the White House himself, Szilard turned once again to Einstein. Szilard visited the older man at his home in Princeton on March 25, bringing with him a letter of introduction to Roosevelt he had drafted for Einstein's signature. The letter pointed out to FDR that Szilard had been one of those who had urged Einstein in 1939 to propose that the government launch an atomic program. Now, Einstein asked the president to see Szilard and consider his recommendations. Although secrecy did not permit discussion of these recommendations in the letter, mention was made of Szilard's great concern about "the lack of adequate contact between scientists who are doing this work and those members of your Cabinet who are responsible for formulating policy."[29]

When no reply came from the White House, Szilard sent the Einstein letter to Eleanor Roosevelt and asked to meet with her. She agreed but set a date for early May, by which time FDR had died. Szilard then tried to see Truman, using political contacts a Met Lab member had in Kansas City. He did get an interview on May 25 with Matthew J. Connelly, Truman's appointments secretary, but was told that the president preferred that he confer with Byrnes, then at his home in Spartanburg, South Carolina.

Szilard, accompanied by Met Lab associate director Walter Bartky and Harold C. Urey, a Nobel laureate chemist working on the Manhattan Project at Columbia University, showed up at Byrnes's door on May 28. Unaware that Byrnes was to become secretary of state, the three men speculated on the train going down that perhaps he was in line to head the postwar atomic program. Szilard handed him the Einstein letter, an enclosure, and a revised version of the memorandum of March 12. Before Byrnes could finish reading the material, however, Szilard began lecturing him on the danger of an arms race with the Soviet Union if the United States used the bombs against Japan. By this time Szilard had moved to still another position: now he advocated forgoing even a test, let alone using the bomb, as a means of keeping the secret until the United States had decided upon comprehensive nuclear policies.

The meeting went badly. Szilard's flamboyant behavior offended Byrnes, as did his proposal that scientists such as himself be included in cabinet-level deliberations. "His general demeanor and his desire to participate in policy making," Byrnes later wrote, "made an unfavorable impression on me."[30] Szilard must have come across as an impractical professorial type, insisting on *what* should be done utterly without regard for how to go about doing it. When the scientist spoke of keeping the program secret while at the same time plunging ahead on research, for instance, Byrnes reasonably pointed out that Congress was unlikely to continue appropriating huge sums for a project without being told its purpose.

Byrnes made an equally unfavorable impression on Szilard. He revealed himself as woefully uninformed about the prospects of nuclear energy for peaceful purposes, and seemed unconcerned about the prospects of an arms race because, Szilard recalled him saying, "General Groves tells me there is no uranium in Russia." According to Szilard, what disturbed him most was Byrnes's attitude that a demonstration of the atomic bomb might make Russia "more manageable" in Eastern Europe. Szilard said he shared Byrnes's concern about Soviet behavior, but that he was "completely flabbergasted by the assumption that rattling the bomb might make Russia more manageable."[31]

What Byrnes actually said is unknown as we have only Szilard's version as he remembered it years afterward. Some writers have quoted the physicist's reconstructed exchanges as though they constituted verbatim dialogue. In an account based on interviews with all three scientists in 1957, Alice K. Smith wrote merely, "He [Byrnes] appeared to view the bomb as a nice thing to have on your hip when you met the Russians and was worried about justifying the expenditure of two billion dollars." The visitors spent most of the time trying to fill him in about the potential uses of atomic power. "There was little chance to discuss the contents of the March memorandum," Smith concluded, or Szilard's most recent idea of holding off even on a test so as to fool the Russians into thinking the program had failed.[32] Nothing came of the session in any case, except that both Szilard and Byrnes parted with a low opinion of the other's thinking.

Two days later Szilard was back in Washington arguing about the bomb with Oppenheimer, who was there for the May 31 meeting of the Interim Committee. In his recollection of this conversation, Szilard had Oppenheimer saying, "The atomic bomb is shit." When asked what he meant, Oppenheimer allegedly replied: "Well, this is a weapon which has no military significance. It will make a big bang—a very big bang— but it is not a weapon which is useful in war." Oppenheimer nonetheless favored dropping the bomb on Japanese cities after disclosing such intent to the Soviets.[33]

Szilard's memory for exact dialogue may again be questioned, unless Oppenheimer changed his mind overnight. The next day at the committee meeting he argued that a *demonstration* would produce a big bang that would not be useful in ending the war, which is why he thought it necessary that the bomb be used against cities in order to show its tremendous destructive power.[34] Whatever actually passed between them, Szilard once again failed to gain a convert.

Over the past eighteen months Szilard had moved from urging that the bomb be used, to assuming with apprehension that it would be used, to opposing even a demonstration, and now in the Franck report to advocating a demonstration for representatives of the United Nations from which the Japanese would be excluded. Szilard was "always stimulating," a colleague has recently written of him, "but also often very annoying because he would change his mind very often and without warning."[35] He had argued each position with great ardor, at times alienating those he wished to persuade. One did not have to question his passionate quest for peace to regard him and those he influenced as sincere gadflies, at home in their laboratories or classrooms but quite lost in the real world. The Franck report exhibited the same lack of concern for feasibility as Szilard had in argument. Consider the proposal to stage a technical demonstration, thereby enabling the United States to say, "You see what sort of a weapon we had but did not use." How would the American people, especially those with loved ones in the armed forces, respond to such a message? If Japan refused to surrender, would they be willing to watch casualties mount while American officials sought UN sanction for using the bomb? What if such action were vetoed by the Soviets, who had no interest in seeing the war end before their entry activated the Yalta Far Eastern accord? And finally, why would a bomb too small to shock Japan into surrender so impress observers that even the most despotic governments would open their borders for inspection teams to rove freely about?

The idea of a technical demonstration was attractive to the Scientific Panel as well, according to Compton. "We were determined to find, if we could," he later wrote, "some effective way of demonstrating the power of the atomic bomb without loss of life that would impress Japan's warlords." After discussions lasting several days, even the most optimistic member gave up "hope for finding such a solution." "Our hearts were heavy" as they completed their report on June 16, Compton remembered, but they consoled themselves with the expectations that military use would save many lives and bring closer the time when "war would be abandoned." Szilard himself later told an interviewer: "I think it is clear that you can't demonstrate a bomb over an uninhabited island. You have to demolish a city."[36]

After endorsing the panel's conclusion that there was no acceptable alternative to combat use of the bomb, the Interim Committee at its June 21 meeting took up the question of disclosure to the Allies. Under terms of what became known as the Quebec Agreement, signed by Roosevelt and Churchill in August 1943, the United States was obligated to secure British assent before using the bomb against a third party—that was taken for granted. Informing the French and Chinese seemed pointless. The real issue was whether to tell the Soviets at the Big Three conference only three weeks away. Earlier, on May 31, the committee at Byrnes's insistence had voted against such disclosure.

The group reversed itself after lengthy discussion. Minutes of the meeting do not disclose who said what so it is not clear whether Byrnes had come around on his own or was persuaded by the arguments of others to drop his objection. In any event the committee agreed unanimously to recommend that the president, "if suitable opportunity arose," inform the Soviets that "we were working on this weapon with every prospect of success and that we expected to use it against Japan." He might also say that he hoped the matter would be discussed "some time in the future" with a view toward ensuring that "this weapon would become an aid to peace." If the Russians should press for details, he should reply that "we were not ready to furnish more information at present."[37]

During the following days one committee member, Undersecretary of the Navy Ralph A. Bard, expressed misgivings about dropping the bombs on Japanese cities in several conversations with Stimson's deputy, Harrison. On June 27 he put his thoughts in a memorandum, which he told Harrison represented an effort to "think out loud" rather than to mark out a course of action.

Ever since he had become involved in the program, Bard wrote, he had been bothered by the idea of dropping atomic bombs without warning. In recent weeks he had the growing feeling that Japan was searching for some way out of the war. He suggested that after the Big Three conference a meeting should be arranged with the Japanese, who would be told about the bomb and Russia's impending entry into the war. This, together with whatever assurances the president wished to give about treatment of the emperor and of the Japanese people, might persuade them to surrender. No one could tell whether such an approach would work, but "The only way to find out is to try it out." Harrison immediately forwarded a copy of Bard's memorandum to Stimson, and one to Byrnes a few days later.[38]

Yet another myth that has flourished in much of the literature about the bomb is that Bard resigned from government as an act of conscience when his suggestions were not followed. A touching story, but false. He had announced his resignation a month earlier, not in protest but because of his more mundane "desire . . . to free himself of the routine of the job." As he had agreed to stay on until July 1, Forrestal recommended that he continue to serve on the Interim Committee until he left. On the evening of June 21, six days before Bard even composed his memorandum, Forrestal hosted a dinner aboard the presidential yacht *Sequoia* "in honor of Ralph Bard, retiring Under Secretary of the Navy."[39]

When Bard at Forrestal's suggestion secured an interview with Truman before leaving office, he raised the issue of using the bomb. "The question," he later recalled Truman as saying, "was whether we wanted to save many American lives and Japanese lives or whether we wanted . . . to win the war by killing all our young men." Bard, who believed that bombardment and naval blockade alone would choke Japan into surrender, said he told the president that only the army favored an invasion because it wanted to get "in on the kill." "For God's sake," Bard remembered pleading, "don't organize an army to go into Japan. Kill a million people? It's ridiculous."[40]

That number again! Whether Truman actually cited it cannot be known, but Bard's account provides further evidence that such a figure was being mentioned at the time. It also shows that he shared the president's assumption that an invasion would produce enormous losses. And unlike Truman, Bard cannot be accused of later trying to inflate casualty estimates to justify using the bomb.

The day after Truman's conference with the joint chiefs, Stimson met with Grew and a member of the Navy Department designated by Forrestal, who was testifying before Congress. The main topic of discussion was finding a way "of inducing Japan to surrender without a fight to the finish." Grew read the draft he had prepared for Truman and informed the others that the president intended to hold off until the Big Three meeting. Unlike Grew, who wanted to issue the warning quickly, Stimson at this time preferred to wait until further conventional air raids and perhaps the atomic bomb had lent the greatest possible sanctions to the warning. His only deadline was November 1, because he thought the Japanese would fight to the finish once the invasion began. After the meeting he began working on his own memorandum to Truman, and continued to do so at his Long Island home over the next few days.[41]

When Stimson returned to Washington on June 24 he was informed by Harrison about recent events: the Scientific Panel's response to the Met Lab petition, the Interim Committee's confirmation of its earlier view about dropping the bomb without warning, and its new position on disclosure to the Soviets. The next day a British official showed him a memorandum Churchill and Roosevelt had initialed in September 1944 at the latter's estate in Hyde Park, the American copy of which had been misfiled. This agreement provided that when the bomb was ready, "it might perhaps, after mature consideration, be used against the Japanese, who should be warned that this bombardment will be repeated until their surrender." The memorandum was no bombshell to Stimson, implying as it did that the Japanese should be warned only *after* the first bomb was used that others would follow until they surrendered. That was just what he wanted to do.[42]

Stimson met with Grew and Forrestal on the twenty-sixth and immediately raised the subject of issuing a warning to Japan "after she had been sufficiently pounded possibly with S-1." He read the memorandum he had been working on and "both Forrestal and Grew said that they approved of the propsed [sic] step and the general substance of the letter." They concluded by appointing a subcommittee of representatives from War, State, and Navy to draft "an actual warning to be sent when the time came."[43]

Stimson's memorandum ran along the same lines as Grew's, with one exception. Grew's proposal to notify Japan that it would be free to choose its own form of government after certain conditions were met did not address the question of what would happen to Emperor Hirohito. Stimson wanted to "add that we do not exclude a constitutional monarchy under her present dynasty," because he thought "it would substantially add to the chances of acceptance." The secretary made an appointment with Truman for the following week to present the memorandum to him and to discuss the Interim Committee's recommendation that the Soviets be informed about the atomic bomb.[44]

Countdown

The tempo of activity in Washington quickened during the last weeks before the Big Three convened. Truman's decision that a warning to Japan would be issued at or shortly after the meeting intensified debate over treatment of Japan, particularly with regard to the emperor. Attitudes changed about whether to inform the Soviets about the bomb, but a final decision was deferred until the conference met. Truman's continued efforts to reconcile outstanding differences with the Soviets and to clear the way for their entry into the war against Japan yielded mixed results. Meanwhile, as scientists at Los Alamos worked to stage the nuclear demonstration on schedule, Leo Szilard at the Met Lab mounted a final effort to prevent the bomb from being used against Japan.

The committee formed by Stimson, Grew, and Forrestal to draft a warning to Japan began meeting on June 27, using Stimson's memorandum as a basis. The dilemma that quickly emerged was easy to state but difficult to resolve. The problem, one of the participants wrote, was how to arrive at terms "which might be *acceptable* to Japan and still *satisfactory* to us," because "no honest declaration can satisfy both views" (emphasis in original). He gave two examples:

a. Shall we play up our intention to punish war criminals, and please (in theory, at least) the US public, or play it down and tempt the Japanese leaders?

b. Shall we state a flat intention to allow the Japanese to retain the structure of a constitutional monarchy, and tempt the Japanese public, or state the opposite intention and please (again in theory) the US public, or leave the matter vague and impress neither side, probably?

The committee completed a draft on June 29 and the next day, Saturday, McCloy traveled to Stimson's Long Island estate to present it to
his chief.[1]

Stimson met with the president at 11 A.M. on Monday. He first showed
Truman the memorandum he had previously cleared with Grew and
Forrestal and the draft warning. In his covering letter, Stimson pointed
out that the warning had been "written without specific relation to
the employment of any new weapon." The paper would have to be
"revamped" to "conform to the efficacy of such a weapon if the warning
were to be delivered, as would almost certainly be the case, in conjunc-
tion with its use." This passage provides further evidence of the assumption that the weapon would be employed as soon as it was ready, as does
a document prepared by the Interim Committee that Stimson showed
Truman a bit later in the meeting. This was the draft of a presidential
statement to be issued "after the first bomb is dropped on Japan."

"The plans of operation up to and including the first landings have
been authorized," Stimson's memorandum began, "and the preparations for the operations are now going on." An invasion, however, would
require "a very long, costly and arduous struggle on our part" because
it would "cast the die of last ditch resistance" and result in an "even
more bitter finish fight than in Germany." The only way to avoid such
a carnage, Stimson went on, was through an appeal to reason. Japan
"is not a nation composed wholly of mad fanatics," he said, and "has
the mental intelligence" to recognize the "folly of a fight to the finish."
He therefore recommended that a "carefully timed" warning be issued
by the United States, Great Britain, China, and "if then a belligerent,
Russia," calling upon Japan to surrender.

Stimson included in his memorandum the "elements" of what he
thought the warning should contain. These included a description of
the enormous forces the United States and its allies had at their disposal
and of "the completeness of the destruction" employment of such power
would entail, as well as assurances that Japan would not be destroyed
as a nation and that a constitutional monarchy might be permitted. The
draft warning followed similar lines.

In view of subsequent allegations that retention of the emperor was
the sole obstacle to an early Japanese surrender, it is important to understand what Stimson proposed be done *to* Japan. He called for occupation
to ensure its "complete demilitarization," the elimination "permanently

[of] all authority and influence of those who have deceived and misled the country into embarking on world conquest," the economy to be "purged of its militaristic influences," and the loss of all overseas possessions. In short, although he did not propose to destroy Japan as a nation, the nation he envisaged would be radically different from the one that had attacked Pearl Harbor.

After discussing the memorandum and the proposed presidential statement, Stimson took up the Interim Committee's recommendation that the Soviets be informed about the atomic bomb. By then the meeting had run overtime, however, and Truman told Stimson that these matters were "so important" that he wished to meet again the following afternoon. Stimson noted in his diary that the president seemed favorably impressed by the memorandum and had pronounced it "a very powerful paper."

Stimson raised an awkward question before he left. Ending the war with Japan and deciding how to treat Germany would be major items on the agenda of the Big Three meeting, now only two weeks away. The War Department was deeply involved in both matters, he pointed out, yet he had not been invited to attend the conference. Was this because of the president's "fear that I could not take the trip"? Truman "laughed and said 'Yes,' that was just it; that he wanted to save me from over-exertion at this time." Stimson replied that the Surgeon General had assured him that his condition was sound and that while he did not wish to "push into" the presidential party, he thought the president should be able get advice from the War Department on the secretarial level. Truman "seemed to agree with me."[2]

The president's belated invitation surely owed more to embarrassment than to the news about Stimson's fitness. If he had wanted the secretary to attend the meeting, all Truman had to do was ask him whether his health would permit such a journey and act accordingly. A more likely explanation is that Stimson's positions toward Japan and Germany already were known, and that Truman did not think he would be of any particular value in negotiating with the Soviets. James Byrnes may also have used his influence to ensure that another voice would not be competing for Truman's ear. The treatment accorded Stimson at the conference sustains either or both interpretations.

The next morning, July 3, Byrnes took the oath as secretary of state in the White House Rose Garden. Byrnes had been something of a mentor to Truman during his first term in the Senate and had helped him win reelection in 1940. Byrnes not only was the more influential senator but also had gone on to serve on the Supreme Court and then had exercised such broad powers as head of the Office of War Mobilization that he became known as the "Assistant President for the home front." Led by Roosevelt to believe he would be the vice presidential candidate in 1944, he had asked Truman to make his nomination speech. Byrnes thought himself betrayed when FDR at the last moment had turned to Truman, although he professed to believe the latter's assurance that he had not pushed his own candidacy.[3]

To what degree a feeling of indebtedness caused Truman to make Byrnes his secretary of state—and next in line of succession to the presidency—cannot be known. Certainly he was more comfortable with his former colleague than he was with Stettinius, whose intelligence he questioned, let alone some professional diplomat such as Grew. Having witnessed the South Carolinian operate in the Senate, Truman admired his bargaining skills although not always his advice, as when he opposed sending Harry Hopkins to Moscow. The president seems to have had some reservations about Byrnes's personal loyalty, referring to him as "my able and conniving Secretary of State" only four days after the oath was administered.[4]

Byrnes probably harbored resentment at having been passed over for the vice presidency, especially since there had been wide speculation among insiders that Roosevelt would not live out another four years. Now a younger man of lesser stature and fewer gifts held the most powerful position in the world. An incident that took place during the swearing-in ceremony provides a possible clue to his attitude. "Jimmy kiss the Bible," Truman said after the oath was completed, which Byrnes did. He then passed it to Truman and asked *him* to kiss it. "The President did so as the crowd laughed." This gesture of easy camaraderie may also have been Byrnes's way of indicating that he considered himself an equal to the president rather than a subordinate. In any event, he assumed office with the reputation of being a "very experienced and shrewd negotiator," as a British observer put it, "with exceptionally sensitive antennae" to popular and congressional opinion.[5]

Byrnes's new role meant among other things that the struggle over whether to inform the Japanese that they might keep their emperor was not over, despite Truman's apparent agreement with Stimson's memorandum. At his first staff meeting, the day after he took office, Byrnes learned from Assistant Secretary of State Dean Acheson that the department was by no means united behind Grew. Someone—probably an opponent of retention who wanted to appeal to Byrnes's "sensitive antennae"—must have leaked, for the day after that, influential columnist Arthur Krock published a detailed account of the debate in which he wrote that "those in office who would preserve Hirohito see no point in the national debate on the subject which is sought by those who differ with them."[6]

On July 6, the day he and Truman left Washington for the summit meeting, Byrnes received from another assistant secretary of state, Archibald MacLeish, an impassioned memorandum warning that "those lives already spent will have been sacrificed in vain, and lives will be lost again in the future" if the imperial institution was permitted to survive.[7] Byrnes telephoned former secretary of state Hull to ask his views about the proposed draft warning, passages of which he read aloud. Hull, who Byrnes greatly admired, also disagreed with the retentionists on the ground that it smacked of "appeasement"—a provocative term to those who believed that appeasement of aggressors had brought about the war.[8]

On the afternoon of Byrnes's investiture, Stimson finished conveying to Truman the Interim Committee's proposal that the Soviets be told about the bomb. Truman should "look sharp," the secretary advised, and "if he found that he thought Stalin was on good enough terms with him," he should go ahead. Truman should tell him that "we were busy with this thing working like the dickens and we knew he was busy with this thing working like the dickens, and that we were pretty nearly ready and we intended to use it against the enemy, Japan." The president should go on to indicate that he hoped future consultations would convert this new force into an instrument of peace, but if Stalin pressed for details he should reply "that we were not yet prepared to give them." Truman listened attentively, according to Stimson, and then said "he thought that was the best way to do it."[9]

The discussion is illuminating. The secretary's suggestion that Truman raise the issue only if he thought Stalin "was on good enough terms with him," rather than at the outset or during some dispute, refutes the notion that either the Interim Committee (on which Byrnes sat) or Stimson at this point sought to employ "atomic diplomacy" to gain concessions. His statement about telling Stalin that "we knew he was busy with this thing working like the dickens" makes obvious the assumption that the Soviets had their own atomic program. And the latter part of this sentence, that "we were pretty near ready and we intended to use it against the enemy, Japan," permits little doubt that using the bomb was a foregone conclusion.

The next day, July 4, the British gave formal consent to dropping the bomb on Japan as required by the Quebec Agreement. In mid-June Groves had submitted to Stimson a draft message requesting their agreement, the key sentence of which read, "As you are aware we are now preparing to use such a weapon against Japan at an early date." On June 22 an official of the British Embassy gave Harvey Bundy a paper outlining London's views on use. Since definite conclusions about the weapon could only be drawn after it "had been used on a full scale in actual operations," the paper stated, "our service authorities were anxious to see it put to a practical test of that sort as soon as possible." Anglo-American discussions a few days later "led to the conclusion that the most appropriate manner in which to record British assent to our use of the weapon" was to make it part of the minutes of the Anglo-American Combined Policy Committee (a liaison group formed to deal with atomic matters), which was done on the fourth.[10]

Truman had hoped to eliminate obstacles to a "peaceful conference," as he put it, by coming to terms with the Soviets over Poland—the "test case"—and reparations from Germany. Both matters had been simmering since the Yalta conference. He also wanted Sino-Soviet negotiations completed to pave the way for Soviet participation in the war against Japan. After meeting with him aboard the presidential yacht on July 4, his personal advisers prepared a list of goals to be sought at the forthcoming conference. "The entry of Russia into the Japanese war" was the first item.[11] Truman succeeded in reaching agreement with regard to Poland, but negotiations on the other two issues bogged down.

On June 11, less than a week after Hopkins's last session with Stalin, the previously deadlocked tripartite commission (Harriman, British ambassador Clark Kerr, and Molotov) established to form a provisional government in Poland had reconvened in Moscow. Under its auspices, representatives of the puppet Lublin regime and those Poles designated by Hopkins and Stalin worked out an arrangement under which Lublin would hold fourteen of twenty positions in the new Polish Provisional

Government of National Unity (PPGNU), which was proclaimed on June 28. Truman immediately urged Churchill to join the United States in recognizing the PPGNU, arguing that delay would be pointless and "might even prove embarrassing to both of us." An unenthusiastic Churchill asked for a few days' delay to settle matters with the London Poles and, knowing full well the date's significance for Americans, wickedly suggested extending recognition on the fourth of July. The president thought it prudent to wait until the fifth.[12]

Truman's reluctance to recognize the PPGNU on Independence Day is understandable, for the new regime was neither independent nor the genuine coalition government he previously had called for. Lublin not only received more than twice the number of seats as the other parties combined but also held *all* the really important ones such as minister of the interior. Negotiations among the Poles had been conducted amidst reports of ongoing repression at home, and the Soviets conveniently began the trials of sixteen former leaders of the Polish underground who earlier had been spirited off to Moscow as saboteurs. Harriman reported that "all the non-Lublin Poles are so concerned over the present situation in Poland that they are ready to accept any compromise which gives some hope for Polish independence and individual freedom." When Clark Kerr asked for a "definite pledge" that free elections would be held as provided for in the Yalta accord, moreover, Molotov and the Lublin officials refused to do more than indicate general endorsement of the agreement. Truman accepted such a dismal settlement for the purpose of Big Three unity.[13]

German reparations proved less tractable. The Yalta agreement had stated that the Reparations Commission should consider in its "initial studies" the Soviet proposal of $20 billion. Roosevelt and other American officials had assumed that "initial studies" meant on-site inspections of German industry. Stettinius had conveyed this understanding by telephone to Edwin W. Pauley, whom Truman had named to head the American delegation. At Yalta, Stettinius said, the Soviets "thought 20 [billion] would be an appropriate starting figure. We couldn't take a position until we found out what the condition of German industry was. It might be 20, 30, 40, or even 10, but we were willing to start with that figure."[14] The Russians served notice that they intended to follow a different course by refusing to accompany the American delegation in a preliminary inspection tour of Germany.

When the Reparations Commission began its deliberations in Moscow on June 21, the Soviets bore out Churchill's prediction at Yalta that they would later insist the $20 billion figure was a commitment to be honored rather than a target to be sought. Assistant People's Commissar for Foreign Affairs I. M. Maisky presented without supporting data a statement based on that amount. Pauley's request for particulars went unanswered for several weeks. Finally, on July 3 he complained to Maisky that "we have not received a single figure." At Yalta, he pointed out, amounts discussed necessarily were "of a very general character" because none of the Allies had access to all of Germany. "Reasonably accurate estimates" could be made, however, now that a physical inventory of German assets was possible. Maisky showed no interest in making such an inventory.[15]

Suspicion grew that the Soviets were deliberately stalling. Reports had been reaching Washington that they were dismantling and shipping eastward everything they could from their occupation zone. Such removals were designated "war booty," moreover, and would not be counted as reparations. Just ten days before the summit meeting began, Soviet Marshal G. K. Zhukov announced that resources in the German lands turned over to Poland would not be "available" as a source of reparations. This territory contained 12 percent of Germany's capital assets and "a large part" of its food surpluses. Its millions of inhabitants had fled west "bringing their mouths with them," as Churchill put it.[16]

The commission adjourned without reaching agreement, and reparations would become one of the most contentious issues at the Big Three meeting. Truman approved Pauley's refusal to approve sums without an inventory of German industry as he was unwilling to have the United States pay reparations by proxy if the German economy had to be propped up because of excessive extractions. "Pauley is doing a job for the United States," the president noted in his diary en route to the conference.[17] Allegations that Pauley deliberately blocked accord because Truman sought to use reparations as a bargaining counter or to stall until the atomic bomb placed the United States in a stronger position are flatly contradicted by a British participant. "Mr. Pauley did not hide the fact that his desire was to leave Moscow . . . carrying with him as much as he could by way of results," the official reported. "His desire to score a quick personal success made him an obvious victim for delaying tactics, and Mr. Maisky did not hurry."[18]

Negotiations between the Chinese and the Soviets, which Truman also wanted out of the way before the summit meeting began, proved equally frustrating. At their first meeting in Moscow on June 30, Stalin informed Foreign Minister Soong that all outstanding issues had to be settled before a pact of friendship and mutual assistance could be signed. At a later session he handed Soong drafts of four agreements. One was the pact of friendship the Chinese coveted, but the other three called for such extreme concessions on the part of the Chinese that the foreign minister tried to hand them back before being persuaded to forward their contents to Chungking.

One draft Soong regarded as unacceptable provided for a Soviet military zone that would include not only Port Arthur but also Dairen, which the Yalta accord had said would be "internationalized." Another stipulated that the major connecting railways, including related timberlands, coal mines, and factories, would be owned and operated by the Soviet Union. The third provided for Chinese recognition of the independence of Outer Mongolia, a region within the Soviet sphere that had maintained de facto independence from China for decades. The Yalta accord regarding Outer Mongolia had stated merely that the status quo "shall be preserved," and Soong interpreted this to mean what it said: that his government would take no steps to alter the situation.[19] As British ambassador Clark Kerr put it, after talking with Soong, the Soviets "were trying to expand the text of the [Yalta] Agreement to their own advantage."[20]

Ambassador Harriman, with the approval of Truman and Byrnes, acted as unofficial adviser to Soong and reported back in messages headed "Personal and Top Secret for the President and Secretary of State." These messages reveal that Harriman repeatedly urged Soong to compromise. Regarding Port Arthur and Dairen, he told the foreign minister that he "was being unrealistic in not conceding more liberal rights and privileges to the Soviets." "I urged Soong not to come to an impasse with Stalin," Harriman stated, and "again pointed out the great advantages" to the Chinese in reaching agreement. Three days later he told Soong that "if he wished to make concessions to Stalin in return for other assurances on Stalin's part, I urged him to do so."[21] Although Soong wanted settlements, especially the treaty of friendship, he said his government would be overthrown if it became known in China that he had agreed to the other Soviet demands. He left Moscow on July 14 with nothing in hand.

Truman and Byrnes departed for the summit meeting amidst rumors that Japan was seeking peace. These led to growing demands that the president clarify unconditional surrender as a means of hastening an end to the war. On July 2, Senator Homer Capehart of Indiana announced unequivocally at a press conference that Washington had received a peace offer from Tokyo.[22] Although the State Department previously had denied such allegations, Grew, acting secretary again in Byrnes's absence, felt compelled to call his own press conference on the tenth.

"We have received no peace offer from the Japanese Government," he told reporters, "either through official or unofficial channels." Without giving specifics, he cited several instances where low-level Japanese diplomatic or military officials in neutral countries had made overtures. In no case had any of these individuals been able to "establish his authority to speak for the Japanese government." Grew dismissed such approaches as "familiar weapons of psychological warfare" designed to "divide the Allies and to produce division of opinion within the Allied countries." Japanese leaders, he said, would like nothing better than to "initiate a public discussion of the terms to be applied to Japan." He then referred to President Truman's previous assurances that unconditional surrender meant neither the destruction of Japan as a nation nor the enslavement of its people.[23]

Grew forwarded the text of his statement to Byrnes along with his reasons for making it. He wanted to stop the "growing speculation" as to whether the Japanese had made "a bona fide peace offer." He thought this was dangerous because it tended to undermine American morale and to create a belief in Japan that the American people were ready to compromise, "and all the Japanese have to do is to continue to fight." His second reason for speaking out was to create a situation in Japan whereby a presidential announcement on unconditional surrender "will have maximum effect." He also got in a plug for his own version of what the president should say, which he had given Byrnes a few days earlier.[24]

The statement Grew gave to the press reflected existing attitudes about what many historians refer to as "Japanese peace feelers," as though they were sanctioned by Tokyo, rather than the more accurate "peace feelers in neutral countries by low-level Japanese officials lacking authorization to negotiate."[25] Although most of the Japanese consular personnel and military attachés engaged in these activities claimed to have important connections in Japan, none was able to produce verification. Indeed, the more contacts made the less credible they became. If the Japanese government really had wanted to learn what terms might be offered, all it had to do was designate someone to speak in its behalf. When this did not happen, American officials naturally assumed that those involved were either sincere individuals trying to get talks started on their own or that they were being orchestrated by Tokyo as "weapons of psychological warfare."

Two days before Grew met with the press the Combined Intelligence Committee completed a report entitled "Estimate of the Enemy Situation" for the Combined Chiefs of Staff. The committee predicted that the Japanese would try to keep the Soviets neutral, "while at the same time making every effort to sow discord" between them and the western Allies. "As the situation deteriorates still further," the report continued, "Japan may even make a serious attempt to use the USSR as a mediator in ending the war." Tokyo also would put out "intermittent peace feelers" to "weaken the determination of the United Nations to fight to the bitter end, or to create inter-allied dissension." While the Japanese people would be willing to make large concessions to end the war, the committee concluded, "For a surrender to be acceptable to the Japanese army, it would be necessary for the military leaders to believe that it would not entail discrediting warrior tradition and that it would permit the ultimate resurgence of a military Japan."[26]

As if acting on cue, Japanese foreign minister Shigenori Togo on July 12 notified Ambassador Naotaki Sato in Moscow that the emperor wished to send a personal envoy, Prince Fumimaro Konoye, in an effort "to restore peace with all possible speed." Although he realized Konoye could not reach Moscow before Stalin and Molotov left for the Big Three meeting, Togo sought to have negotiations begin as soon as they returned.[27]

Through a process of code decryption known as the MAGIC intercepts, American officials in Washington were able to read what one of them referred to as "the long awaited Japanese peace offer" that same day. On the next, Deputy Acting Chief of Staff General John Weckerling prepared for transmittal to General Marshall the army G-2 (intelligence) interpretation of the Japanese message. Weckerling listed three possible constructions: that the emperor had intervened, that "conservative groups close to the throne" had won out over the militarists, or that the Japanese "governing clique" was making a coordinated effort to "stave off defeat" through Russian intervention and an "appeal to war weariness in the United States." He rated the first as "remote," the second a "possibility," and the last "quite probably the motivating force behind the Japanese moves." He added that Grew "agrees with these conclusions."[28]

Truman has been accused of deliberately prolonging the war even though he knew the Japanese were trying to end it. But as the Combined Intelligence Committee report and Weckerling's memorandum make clear, the various peace "feelers" and the proposed Konoye mission were seen at best as efforts to avoid the consequences of defeat through a negotiated peace and at worst as cynical efforts to exploit American war weariness. These documents were written for internal consumption at high levels, after all, not to fool the American public then or historians later. There was no evidence that the Japanese were prepared to surrender on anything resembling the terms even the most lenient American policy maker could support.[29]

Decryption of the Togo-Sato exchanges merely confirmed the view that Japan was trying to cut a deal that would permit it to retain its prewar empire intact. On July 11, the day before Togo informed Sato of the proposed Konoye mission, he had instructed the ambassador to convey the message to Molotov that Japan "has absolutely no idea of annexing or holding the territories occupied as a result of the war, out of concern for the establishment and maintenance of lasting peace."[30]

Sato's reply, though deferential in form, was scathing. Pointing out that the enemy already had wrenched away most of these territories by force, he asked how much effect such "pretty little phrases devoid of all connection with reality" could have on the Soviets. He reported that when he spoke about the statement to Molotov, "he heartily (word missing) and merely made a non-committal reply." It requires no great leap of the imagination to assume that the word missing was "laughed."

"If the Japanese Empire is really faced with the necessity of terminating the war," the ambassador argued, "we must first of all make up our minds to do so." Togo ignored Sato's advice, and informed him on July 17 that "we are not asking the Russians' mediation in *anything like unconditional surrender*"[31] (emphasis added). Sato spent the next several weeks unsuccessfully trying to convince his superiors that they were deceiving themselves in banking on Soviet intercession to end the war on relatively painless terms.

On July 10, the day Grew held his press conference about Japanese peace feelers, the Joint Chiefs of Staff approved an operation code-named "Pastel." This was a scheme to deceive the Japanese into thinking that the United States meant to invade Formosa and the northern home island of Hokkaido so that they would disperse their forces away from Kyushu. The plan also sought to persuade them that because of the heavy American losses sustained at Okinawa, the rotation of Pacific veterans, and the logistical difficulties of redeployment from Europe, the landings would not take place until the autumn of 1946.

Far from being optimistic about the imminence of Japanese capitulation, American military planners had submitted Pastel out of fear that even a "successful allied invasion of Japan" would not be sufficient. They raised the possibility that the "transfer of Japanese industry and government [to the mainland] and the presence of large ground forces in Manchuria and China, will permit continued resistance." The strategists sought to forestall such a move by lulling the Japanese into believing that any major assaults lay more than a year in the future.[32]

Meanwhile, Leo Szilard was busy at the Met Lab circulating a petition that called upon the president "to rule that the United States shall not, in the present phase of the war, resort to the use of atomic bombs."[33] This flat injunction against using the bomb generated a flurry of counterpetitions and aroused such controversy that Arthur Compton asked the new Met Lab director, Farrington Daniels, to conduct a survey of attitudes among the members.

Daniels reported back in a letter dated July 13. Of 150 respondents, 15 percent favored using the weapon in whatever manner would be "most effective in bringing about prompt Japanese surrender at minimum cost to our armed forces." Forty-six percent endorsed a "military demonstration" in Japan, followed by a renewed opportunity to surrender before "full use." Twenty-six percent opted for a demonstration in the United States attended by Japanese observers, followed by a renewed opportunity to surrender before "full use." Eleven percent wished to "withhold military use" and 2 percent wanted to maintain secrecy about the entire project. The poll revealed, therefore, that 61 percent favored military use of the bomb, though some of the respondents most likely assumed the targets would be military or air bases rather than cities.[34]

The furor his first petition had aroused and the lack of support for "no use" under any circumstances persuaded Szilard to revise his approach. His final draft, dated July 17, now called on the president not to use the bomb "unless the terms which will be imposed upon Japan have been made public in detail and Japan knowing these terms has refused to surrender." Even then, the appeal concluded, the decision should be made only in light of all the moral responsibilities involved. This version was circulated and was signed by sixty-eight members of the Met Lab, after which it was handed to Compton for transmittal to the president.[35]

Compton on July 24 gave the petition in a sealed envelope to Groves's assistant, Colonel K. D. Nichols, requesting that the envelope be opened only by someone authorized to read the president's mail. At Groves's request, Compton also included his own evaluation of the petition. He referred to the Scientific Panel's earlier recommendation that the bomb be used militarily, to counterpetitions Nichols previously had received from the Clinton Laboratory in Tennessee, and to the Met Lab poll, a copy of which he attached. With regard to the latter, Compton stated that his own preference coincided with the 46 percent who favored a military demonstration and, as far as he knew, that was the preference "in all informed groups where the subject has been discussed." Nichols on the following day gave all these documents to Groves, who held on to them until August 1, when he delivered them to Stimson upon his return from Europe.[36]

Some authors have ascribed great importance to this episode, depicting Groves as the villain who prevented Szilard's last-minute petition from reaching the president's attention.[37] No doubt Groves relished stymieing his longtime enemy, but the notion that his behavior could have had the slightest influence on events is impossible to credit. The documents could not have reached Truman before July 26 even if Groves upon receipt had forwarded them by air. That very day Truman issued the warning to Japan, the form of which had been cleared with the British and Chinese. By that time preparations for dropping the bombs already had gotten underway and could be countermanded only by the president himself if he deemed Japan's reply to the warning satisfactory.

There is no reason to believe that Szilard's petition would have had any effect even if Truman had seen it. It was, after all, an appeal endorsed by only a minority of scientists at a single facility. As none of its signers had any better knowledge of the Japanese situation than they could read in the newspapers, there was no reason to assign more weight to it than to the counterpetitions. Truman probably would have thought the warning he was about to issue met the criteria stated in Szilard's modified version anyway. And finally, in view of Byrnes's low opinion of Szilard after their encounter, the secretary almost certainly would have advised Truman to dismiss out of hand *anything* bearing the scientist's name.

Szilard himself did not really believe his petition would have any practical effect. "I knew by this time that it would not be possible to dissuade the government from using the bomb against the cities of Japan," he said later, "the cards in the Interim Committee were stacked against such an approach to the problem."[38] His main purpose, he wrote another scientist at the time, was to influence "the standing of the scientists in the eyes of the general public one or two years from now" by placing it on record that some of them opposed using the bomb.[39] Three days after Japan surrendered, Szilard wrote presidential secretary Matthew Connelly asking permission to make the petition public.

Meanwhile, scientists at Los Alamos were struggling to stage the atomic test by July 14, before the Big Three meeting began. On July 2, Oppenheimer informed General Groves by telephone that although that date was possible, the "wisest thing" was to schedule it for July 17. He thought the chances were good it could be brought off then, and everyone "ought to be able to go fishing on the morning of the 18th." Groves continued to press for the earlier date because, as he put it, "the upper crust wanted it as soon as possible." In a conversation later that afternoon, Groves asked Oppenheimer to tell his people that insistence on haste "wasn't his [Groves's] fault but came from higher authority." The next day Oppenheimer reported that technical problems made a test on the fourteenth out of the question.[40]

Finally, at 5:30 on the morning of July 16, the countdown began for the first atomic test in history. Groves, Bush, Conant, and others had traveled to Los Alamos and from there to the test site at Alamogordo to witness the event. At the word "now," as Groves's deputy Brigadier General Thomas F. Farrell wrote a few hours after the explosion, "The whole country was lighted by a searing light with the intensity many times that of the midday sun. It was golden, purple, violet, gray and blue. It lighted every peak, crevasse and ridge of the nearby mountain range with a clarity and beauty the great poets dream about but describe most poorly and inadequately." Then, after thirty seconds, there came a roar "which warned of doomsday and made us feel that we puny things were blasphemous to dare tamper with the forces heretofore reserved to the Almighty."

Although some may have felt blasphemous, others were triumphant. Farrell noted that Oppenheimer's face "relaxed into an expression of tremendous relief." Chemist George B. Kistiakowsky, "the impulsive Russian, threw his arms around Oppenheimer and embraced him with shouts of glee. Others were equally enthusiastic." "As to the present war," Farrell wrote, "there was a feeling that no matter what else might happen, we now had the means to insure its speedy conclusion and save thousands of American lives." Groves put it another way in his memorandum to Stimson two days later: "We are all fully conscious that our real goal is still before us. The battle test is what counts in the war with Japan." Neither made any mention of impressing Russia.[41]

With an estimated force of between fifteen thousand and twenty thousand tons of TNT, the blast exceeded the expectations of most. Oppenheimer had guessed only three hundred tons in a betting pool organized shortly before the test.[42] Still he was apprehensive that the plutonium bomb would not work in combat. Even before Groves arrived back in Washington, Oppenheimer called to leave word that he was "unconvinced that our present plans are right" and that he wanted to talk them over with the general.[43]

The components of *Little Boy*, except for the three U235 target pieces, had been transported by truck to a nearby air force base a few days before. From there they would be flown to San Francisco, then transferred to a naval vessel for shipment across the Pacific. The target pieces had been left behind because they were not yet finished and would have to be flown the entire way.[44] Oppenheimer and others at Los Alamos now wanted to distribute the U235 from the target pieces into several *Fat Man* bombs.

Groves telephoned Conant on July 19. As he put it to foil potential eavesdroppers, "the boys out there are discussing the advantages of murdering the L.B. and devoting all his clothes to the F. B. [*sic*]." Groves said he thought it would be a "terrible mistake," and Conant replied, "I agree with you 100%." An hour later Groves learned from another scientist at Los Alamos that a "considerable body of people" there sided with Oppenheimer.[45] Groves nonetheless informed Oppenheimer that there would be no change: "It is necessary to drop the first Little Boy and the first Fat Man and probably a second one in accordance with our original plans." Groves said that "as many as three of the latter *in their best present form* may have to be dropped to conform to planned strategical operations" (emphasis added).[46]

The next afternoon Oppenheimer defended his proposal over the telephone, saying, "It increases the number we can get out of it," and "reduces the unreliable feature we have discussed." He estimated such a procedure would take an additional six to ten days.[47] He was overruled. Work on the target pieces for *Little Boy* was completed on July 24, and two days later they were placed aboard separate aircraft for delivery to the island of Tinian in the Pacific. That same day a cargo plane bearing the plutonium core of *Fat Man* also took off.[48] Both types exploded, for better or worse, and whether acceptance of Oppenheimer's plan would have altered the course of events can never be known.

CHAPTER 6

Potsdam
Nearing Armageddon

Truman and Byrnes, aboard the heavy cruiser USS *Augusta,* arrived at the Belgian port of Antwerp on July 15. Truman had spent his days reading position papers and conferring with advisers; his evenings walking on deck, playing poker, or watching movies. After debarkation, the presidential party was driven to Brussels, where it boarded a plane for Berlin. Truman was struck by the devastation he saw from the air. The group then drove to Babelsberg, a residential area near Potsdam. What became the "Little White House" was a mansion Truman described as looking "just like the Kansas City Union station." Conference sessions would be held in Potsdam at the Cecilienhof, a palace once owned by the last German crown prince.

Originally scheduled to begin on July 16, the meeting was postponed a day pending Stalin's arrival. That first morning Churchill called on the president at the Little White House. Truman was modestly impressed by his visitor, finding him "a most charming and a very clever person" who "gave me a lot of hooey about how great my country is and how he loved Roosevelt and how he intended to love me, etc. etc." In the afternoon Truman toured the ruins of Berlin with Byrnes and Leahy. "Never did I see a more sorrowful sight," he wrote in his diary, "nor witness retribution to the nth degree."[1]

That evening Truman dined with Leahy, Harriman, Davies, and Edwin Pauley, who was there to discuss his problems with the Soviets over German reparations. After dinner, while having coffee, the group was interrupted by an aide who informed Truman that Stimson and Marshall were waiting in the library to see him on an important matter. He left the room, then Byrnes was sent for. When Truman returned,

Davies asked him, "Is everything all right?" "Yes," he replied, "fine." He then told the gathering about what Davies called "the terrible success." This was, of course, the atomic test in New Mexico.[2]

"Operated on this morning," began the message Stimson showed Truman and Byrnes. "Diagnosis not yet complete but results seem satisfactory and already exceed expectations."[3] The test had no relevance for *Little Boy*, of which there was only one. What it meant was that plutonium implosion was practical and that even if *Little Boy* and the first *Fat Man* failed to detonate over target, other plutonium bombs would follow in increasing numbers during the next months. Some were bound to work.

At noon on July 17, Stalin and Molotov arrived at the Little White House for a meeting with the president and Byrnes arranged by Davies, who had been given the rank of Special Ambassador. After preliminary talk about additions to the conference agenda and some banter about Stalin's habit of sleeping late, Truman, according to interpreter Bohlen's sketchy longhand notes, told Stalin "I am here to—be yr friend—deal directly yes or no—[I am] no diplomat" and a bit later "friends—all subject differences settle—frankly." That is what he thought Stalin wanted to hear: that the two of them could deal on a frank and friendly basis dispensing with the flowery language of diplomacy. "It pleased him," Truman later noted in his diary.[4]

The ensuing discussion ranged over a number of issues but most of the time was devoted to the related questions of Soviet entry into the war against Japan and its negotiations with China. Stalin repeated his earlier promise that Russia would be ready by mid-August, but that operations would not actually begin until Sino-Soviet agreements were completed. He said he had assured Foreign Minister Soong that the Soviets would recognize the Nationalist regime as the legitimate government of China, refrain from any interference in China's internal affairs, and acknowledge Chinese sovereignty over Manchuria. When Byrnes asked what differences remained, Stalin replied that the Chinese were trying to nullify the Yalta provision for recognizing Soviet "preeminent interests" regarding Port Arthur, Dairen, and the railways.

Truman, showing no interest in the composition of railroad boards or city councils, got to the point: what effect would Soviet conditions have on American rights in the port city of Dairen? Stalin answered that Dairen would be a "free port," to which Truman commented that this meant an Open Door. Byrnes then said that there would be no problem if the arrangements proposed by Stalin conformed to the Yalta accord, but if they exceeded that agreement there would be difficulty. When Stalin protested that Soviet desires in reality were more "liberal" than the Yalta agreement, Truman and Byrnes both informed him that the United States' "main interest" was in a free port at Dairen.[5]

Truman and Byrnes afterward told Leahy that they believed Sino-Soviet agreements could be reached only "through radical concessions by China," but that Stalin would enter the war on August 15 "whether or not such concessions are made, and will thereafter satisfy Soviet demands regardless of what the Chinese attitude might be."[6] Despite this assessment, Truman's diary entry about his talk with Stalin brimmed with enthusiasm. "He'll be in the Jap War on August 15th. Fini Japs when that comes about." "I can deal with Stalin," he wrote, "He is honest—but smart as hell." And he told Stimson at dinner that evening that "he thought that he had clinched the Open Door in Manchuria."[7]

Truman's satisfaction even in the face of Sino-Soviet stalemate points to an obvious conclusion. His top priorities were Soviet entry into the war against Japan and an Open Door in Manchuria. He had received Stalin's promises on both, the latter's qualification about reaching accord with China before going to war notwithstanding. As Truman had made clear to the Chinese in June, he expected them to have to make concessions in return for Soviet recognition and noninterference in China's internal affairs. He told Davies "he could go home now if he had to, for he had obtained from Stalin a commitment that he would fight the Japs."[8] And this *after* word had been received that the atomic test had succeeded beyond predictions.

Truman and Byrnes briefly met again with Stalin and Molotov on the afternoon of July 18. Stalin gave Truman a copy of the letter Sato had sent to Molotov, asking the Soviets to receive Prince Konoye at the emperor's request. Stalin had told Churchill about it the day before, saying he was reluctant to inform the president as he did not wish to appear eager to act as an intermediary. Truman, unwilling to reveal that the United States had broken the Japanese diplomatic code, gave no indication that he already had seen the decrypted message to Sato instructing him to make the overture. He merely remarked that he had no respect for the emperor, but that the form of a reply "was a matter for the Generalissimo to decide." When Stalin suggested that he "lull" the

Japanese by informing them that their proposal was too vague to accept in its present form, Truman said that was satisfactory to him. Later that evening Stalin showed the president a copy of his reply.[9]

The news from Alamogordo and Tokyo's approach to Moscow intensified the struggle over when the warning to Japan should be sent and how it should be worded with regard to the emperor. Stimson, who had arrived the same day as the presidential party, prepared a memorandum for Truman on July 16 urging him to issue the ultimatum as quickly as possible. The punishment already being inflicted on Japan, the impending entry of Russia into the war, and Tokyo's appeal to the Soviets, he wrote, "impels me to urge prompt delivery of our warning." He referred specifically to the draft warning he had attached to his memo of July 2, which provided for retention of the Japanese imperial institution in the form of a constitutional monarchy.

If Japan should reject the ultimatum, Stimson counseled, then the "full force of our newer weapons" should be brought to bear. During the course of using these weapons, by which time Russia might be in the war, a "renewed and heavier warning" to Japan should be sent. With regard to the Yalta Far Eastern accord, Stimson considered it of no concern provided the traditional American policies of an Open Door and Chinese sovereignty over Manchuria were maintained. He thought American occupation of the Japanese home islands should be limited to that necessary to demilitarize the society and to punish war criminals. If the Soviets sought a role after "creditable participation" in the war, he did not "see how we could refuse at least a token occupation."[10]

The retentionists received help from another quarter. At a meeting of the Combined Chiefs of Staff on July 16, British Field Marshal Sir Alan Brooke suggested that if a way could be found to communicate to the Japanese that the imperial institution would be retained, the emperor would be "in a position to order the cease-fire in outlying areas." If the dynasty were destroyed, on the other hand, the fighting might go on for "many months or years." Brooke suggested that an opportune time might be shortly after Russia joined the war.

One of the American chiefs, probably Marshall, replied that considerable thought had been given this matter and one possibility was to issue an ultimatum to Japan explaining "what the term 'unconditional surrender' did not mean rather than what it did mean." Leahy, an advocate of retention, said the matter was a political rather than a military one but that it would be "very useful" to have Churchill convey the British view to Truman.[11]

The prime minister did so two days later at lunch. Referring to the carnage an invasion would entail, Churchill asked whether some assurance could be given Japan that it might retain its military honor and national existence. Truman observed that the Japanese had no military honor after Pearl Harbor, but then spoke with feeling about the "terrible responsibilities that rested upon him in regard to the unlimited effusion of American blood."[12] Churchill's memorandum of the conversation refutes the view that casualty estimates for an invasion were so low that Truman must have had ulterior motives for using atomic bombs.

The same day that Stimson composed his memorandum and the Combined Chiefs met, Cordell Hull sent a message to Byrnes via the State Department. The draft warning had to receive the most serious consideration, Hull admitted, in view of its support by Stimson, Forrestal, and Grew. Still, he questioned the wisdom of notifying the Japanese "*now*" that they might retain the emperor (emphasis in original). The idea that such notification would produce surrender was an appealing one, but the truth was that no one knew how the Japanese would react. The military most certainly would try to prevent capitulation. If the offer were rejected the Japanese would be encouraged by it to fight on for greater concessions and there would be "terrible political repercussions" in the United States. "Would it be well," Hull concluded, "first to await the climax of allied bombing and Russia's entry into the war?" Whether he meant by the "climax of allied bombing" use of atomic weapons is not clear, but Byrnes assured him that the ultimatum would not be issued immediately and "when made, should not contain commitment to which you refer."[13]

The precise ingredients of Byrnes's opposition to notifying the Japanese they might retain their emperor can only be guessed. The allegation that he deliberately sought to prolong the war until the United States could use atomic bombs to awe the Russians is entirely unsupported by evidence. Probably he was most influenced by domestic political considerations, which always were of great importance to him. Regardless of what the experts might know of the emperor's largely ceremonial role, Byrnes was well aware that most Americans bracketed Hirohito with Hitler and Mussolini as the monsters responsible for killing and maiming American boys. Offering to retain the emperor would appear to constitute a betrayal of Roosevelt's legacy and might result in the "terrible political repercussions" Hull predicted.

Charles Bohlen, one of Byrnes's advisers, put forward another argument against modifying unconditional surrender. He had been present when Stalin had explained to Harry Hopkins and Ambassador Harriman his wish to destroy the imperial institution to prevent the Japanese from keeping "their military cards and, as Germany had done, prepare for future aggression." Harriman had replied that the United States remained committed to unconditional surrender. Offering to retain the emperor as an inducement to early capitulation at this late date, Bohlen warned, was sure to strike the Soviets as a perfidious attempt to deny them the results of Yalta and to maintain Japan intact as a counterweight against them in the Far East. Stalin reaffirmed his position during his second meeting with Truman and Byrnes when the latter asked him if there was any change in Soviet policy toward unconditional surrender. "No change," Stalin replied.[14]

Those historians who have characterized the refusal to give Japan assurances about the emperor as aimed against the Soviet Union have ignored the alternative. Bohlen surely was right in thinking Stalin would have considered it an act of betrayal. He had made just such accusations when the United States and Great Britain had tried to negotiate a German surrender on the Italian front shortly before Roosevelt's death, and was unlikely to accept American protests of innocence now. It was no coincidence that among those who wished to compromise on the emperor were such anti-Soviet hard-liners as Leahy, Grew, and Forrestal, while individuals more favorably disposed toward Russia such as Hull, Acheson (at the time), MacLeish, and Hopkins did not.[15]

Stimson discussed the proposed warning with Byrnes at the Little White House on the morning of July 17. Byrnes opposed issuing it immediately, as Stimson wanted to do, and "outlined a timetable on the subject warning which apparently had been agreed to by the President, so I pressed it no further." Stimson soon learned that his anticipated role as presidential adviser on political issues was largely an illusion. He was excluded from strategy meetings at the Little White House, and Byrnes turned down his request that McCloy be permitted to attend plenary sessions of the conference. He had to appeal to Truman that at least he be permitted to "drop in early every morning" to talk over what had been done the previous day. In fact he had become little more than a messenger with cabinet rank, delivering reports from Washington and relaying back instructions and inquiries about timetables.[16]

The same morning Stimson talked with Byrnes, General Marshall at a meeting of the Joint Chiefs of Staff questioned that part of the ultimatum providing that the Japanese might retain "a constitutional monarchy under the present dynasty." Relying on a report from the Joint Strategic Survey Committee he had just received from Washington, Marshall pointed out that some Japanese might interpret this to mean that the Allies intended to depose or execute Hirohito and replace him with another member of the imperial family. "Radical elements" would be repelled by an offer to retain the imperial system. Marshall suggested and the chiefs endorsed a more general statement: "Subject to suitable guarantees against further acts of aggression, the Japanese people will be free to choose their own form of government." The formula Marshall offered, though not his exact words, would appear in what became known as the Potsdam Declaration. It must be emphasized that the substitution was intended to hasten Japanese surrender, not to forestall it. In his memorandum forwarding the proposal to Truman, Leahy wrote that "such a statement . . . would be more likely to appeal to all elements of the Japanese populace." He added that "from a strictly military point of view" nothing should be said or done that would interfere with using the emperor to "direct a surrender of the Japanese forces in the outlying areas as well as in Japan proper."[17]

Stimson at first concurred with the Joint Chiefs of Staff revision, and so informed Truman. A few days later the secretary reverted to his original position that mention should be made of the imperial dynasty. On July 24, while discussing with the president dates when atomic bombs would be available, he made his final pitch. It was too late. Truman told him that the text of the ultimatum already had been transmitted to Chiang and would be issued as soon as he approved it. Stimson could only ask that assurances be given the Japanese through diplomatic channels if surrender hinged on that one point. Truman agreed. Two days later Chiang radioed his endorsement, suggesting only that his name precede Churchill's in the document. Truman and Byrnes released the ultimatum at once, and within hours its text was being broadcast to the Japanese.[18]

The Potsdam Declaration of July 26 very closely resembled the draft Stimson had given Truman before they left Washington, except that reference to the imperial system had been omitted. After alluding to the "prodigious" forces now arrayed against Japan and to the terrible destruction that had been visited upon Germany, the ultimatum called upon Japan to decide whether it would continue to be controlled by the "self-willed militaristic advisers" who had brought it to the "threshold of annihilation," or whether it would "follow the path of reason."

"Following are our terms," the declaration went on. "We will not deviate from them. There are no alternatives. We shall brook no delay." These terms included eliminating the authority of those who had led Japan "into embarking on world conquest," Allied occupation of Japan proper, carrying out of the Cairo Declaration limiting Japanese sovereignty to the four main islands, disarmament of Japanese military forces, and the punishment of "all war criminals."

Acceptance of the ultimatum meant that Japanese military forces would be permitted to return home to resume their peaceful lives, the Japanese would not be "enslaved as a race or destroyed as a nation," freedom of speech, religion, and thought would be established, and eventually Japan would be permitted to participate in world trade. Occupation forces would be withdrawn once Allied objectives were achieved and "there has been established in accordance with the freely expressed will of the Japanese people a peacefully inclined and responsible government." The document ended by calling upon the Japanese government to proclaim now the "unconditional surrender of all the Japanese armed forces" or face "prompt and utter destruction."[19]

The Potsdam Declaration added little to what already had been conveyed to the Japanese through presidential speeches and Office of War Information broadcasts. A few Japanese officials at the time and some later American authors (including this one in a previous book) interpreted the reference to unconditional surrender of "all the Japanese armed forces" rather than of the government itself as a softening of terms. It was not. Truman had used the phrase in his V-E Day speech and it had appeared in numerous propaganda messages.[20] Nor did the document indicate any lessening of resolve to punish war criminals and to drastically alter or eliminate those institutions deemed responsible for Japanese aggression. How the Allies intended to treat Hirohito and the imperial system was left unanswered.

The Soviets did not learn of the declaration until hours before its release. Byrnes forwarded a copy to Molotov, and refused the foreign minister's request to hold it up two or three days. The next day he told Molotov that he had declined to consult the Soviets because they were not then at war with Japan and he wished to spare them embarrassment if word leaked that they had helped compose the document.[21] A more likely reason is that he and Truman wished to avoid delay haggling over revisions the Soviets inevitably would have suggested. Truman told Davies on July 25 that he knew the Russians were displeased, but that there was no time to confer with them because he wanted Churchill to sign the declaration before leaving for London that day to await the results of general elections. His concern, justified as it turned out, was that Churchill "might not come back."[22]

Truman and Byrnes had gone to Potsdam intending to carry out the Interim Committee's recommendation to inform the Soviets about the atomic bomb. Stimson first raised the issue with Churchill on July 17 after informing him of the successful test in New Mexico. The prime minister was "greatly cheered up," Stimson noted, "but was strongly inclined against disclosure."[23]

Truman discussed the matter with Churchill the next day at lunch. According to the report Churchill sent the War Cabinet that afternoon, Truman "seemed determined" to tell the Soviets and "said he thought that the end of the Conference would be best." Churchill replied that if "he were resolved to tell it might be better to hang it on the experiment," of which he had just gotten word. That would provide a more suitable answer if the Soviets asked why they had not been told earlier. "I shall inform Stalin about it," Truman noted in his diary that evening, "at an opportune time."[24]

Stimson underwent a change of heart about disclosure and the prospects of international control soon after arriving at Potsdam. Depressed by reports of the Soviets' conduct in areas they occupied and by his own observations (Potsdam was in the Soviet zone), he began to doubt whether cooperation over the long run would be possible with such a repressive police state. As usual, he worked out his thoughts in a memorandum. Perhaps, he speculated, it might be wiser to use the American advantage to prod the Soviets into liberalizing their political order in exchange for nuclear information. He showed this paper to Harriman on July 20. The ambassador, who had spent several years observing Soviet oppression firsthand, may have been amused that Stimson had done such an about-face after only a few days. In any event, he said he strongly doubted the Soviets would undertake reform whatever the inducements. Stimson nonetheless gave Truman a copy, and a few days later the president said he "agreed with it" without indicating he intended to follow any particular course of action.[25]

At the end of the plenary session on July 24, Truman took a step that has remained controversial ever since. Leaving the American interpreter behind, he casually walked around the conference table to where Stalin was standing with his interpreter, V. N. Pavlov. The president told Stalin that the United States had "a new weapon of unusual destructive force." Showing no emotion or curiosity, the Generalissimo said that he was pleased and hoped the United States would make "good use of it against the Japanese." Churchill, who later found himself near Truman as they waited for their cars to be brought around, asked the president, "How did it go?" "He never asked a question," Truman replied.[26]

The frequent interpretation of this episode is that by failing to use the word "atomic" Truman meant to deceive Stalin into thinking he was referring only to some conventional weapon. That way the Soviets would be kept unaware until the bombs were used against Japan, yet he could later claim he had been a good ally in informing them. "Technically," as one account has it, "he forestalled a Russian charge that the United States and Britain had not dealt frankly."[27] Since Truman previously had told Churchill, Stimson, and others that he intended to tell Stalin about *atomic* bombs, presumably he and Byrnes cooked up the scheme at the last moment.

This version rests on two very dubious assumptions. The first is that Truman thought Stalin would fail to realize what he was talking about, even though American officials believed that the Soviets had long since learned about the atomic program through espionage and that they had one of their own. That Truman and Byrnes nonetheless expected to dupe Stalin into concluding that the president acted as he did merely to report a larger blockbuster or a more effective incendiary is not credible. The second is that Truman somehow knew that Stalin would refrain from asking about the nature of the weapon, which is very unlikely.

A less conspiratorial rendition of events better fits the known evidence. Since the entire purpose of disclosure was to earn Stalin's trust, it was important to avoid the impression that American officials viewed the new weapon as a bargaining lever. This accounts for Truman's earlier inclination to tell the Soviets at the end of the conference rather than during it. His informal, man-to-man approach, therefore, makes more sense if viewed as an effort to act in a friendly manner instead of being part of a subterfuge, the response to which he could not have foreseen. It also had the advantage of circumventing the abrasive Molotov, who might be expected to pursue the subject aggressively.

Had the president pursued the conversation in the face of Stalin's apparent indifference, he would have run the risk of encouraging inquiries he did not wish to answer. There had been concern, during the weeks before Potsdam, over how to respond should the Soviets press for details or ask to be taken in as partners. The Interim Committee and Stimson had recommended that the president say no more than that the United States was not yet ready to discuss specifics. Truman understandably was relieved that Stalin spared him any such embarrassing questions, as his comment to Churchill indicates.

"Byrnes said that everything was fine tonight," his aide noted later that evening, "but by tomorrow he thinks the importance of what Truman told Stalin will sink in and well may it."[28] The secretary's attitude obviously was based on the belief that Stalin knew about the atomic program or there would have been nothing to "sink in." Byrnes subsequently assumed that the Soviets had interpreted Truman's words correctly and even hoped it would be a factor in negotiations. He told Davies on July 28 that "the knowledge of the atomic bomb" had been "reported to them."[29] That Truman, who was Byrnes's source for the discussion with Stalin, thought otherwise is unlikely. Neither was inclined to raise the issue with Stalin again because to do so might elicit unwanted requests to send technical observers or to be taken into partnership.

On July 21 Stimson had received by courier a memorandum from General Groves giving a lengthy, graphic account of the explosion at Alamogordo. The secretary first showed it to Marshall, then went to the Little White House to read it to Truman and Byrnes. Stimson recorded in his diary that the president was "tremendously pepped up" by the report, which he said "gave him an entirely new feeling of confidence."[30] As though the promise of ending the war against Japan were not reason enough for enthusiasm, some writers have placed this response entirely within the context of relations with the Soviets. Now American officials could get tough as they had wished to do all along.

A staple in the "get tough" literature has been a comment Truman allegedly made at Potsdam: "If it [the atomic bomb] explodes, as I think it will, I'll certainly have a hammer on those boys." This first appeared in a book about Truman written by a former White House staff member, Jonathan Daniels. Daniels, who had heard of it secondhand, stated specifically that Truman had been referring to Japan but went on to suggest that he *may* have had the Soviets in mind as well.[31] Some enterprising authors have converted Daniels's speculation into an apparent statement of fact by rendering the quotation as follows: " 'If it explodes,' Truman remarked, 'I'll certainly have a hammer on those boys' (the Russians)."[32] Readers who assume that authors use quotations properly have no defense against this sort of thing.

Accounts emphasizing Truman's showdown mentality also omit mention of an encounter he had with Stalin at dinner the evening Groves's report arrived. Davies noticed that the president engaged Stalin in a protracted conversation, even keeping Churchill standing to propose a toast. After the dinner, Davies asked him what he was telling Stalin that took so long. Truman replied that he was trying to convince the Generalissimo how much the United States wanted "peace with friendship and neighborliness." "I spread it on very thick," Truman said, "and I think he believed me. I meant every word of it."[33]

The news from Alamogordo did not incline Truman toward staging any showdowns, but it did have bearing on the stalled Sino-Soviet negotiations and by extension Soviet entry into the war against Japan. In a series of memoranda intended for Byrnes's eyes, State Department Far Eastern expert John Carter Vincent warned that Soviet demands in Manchuria threatened the American Open Door policy and that acquiescence would cause trouble at home. Vincent wrote on July 23 that since the Yalta accord already recognized Soviet special interests there, "present differences" with China might be regarded as minor. "But the situation is not likely to be so regarded by the American public," he wrote, "a large section of which is profoundly interested in China and in safeguarding the American position in China." Such people would be not only critical of what had been done at Yalta but also "highly critical" of any concessions beyond that. He attached to his memorandum a draft of a protocol that would affirm Stalin's oral assurance that the Open Door would be preserved.[34]

Vincent's caveat had special relevance for Byrnes in the event Stalin reneged on his promise. Byrnes had accompanied Roosevelt to Yalta and, upon his return to Washington, had pronounced the conference an unalloyed triumph for American principles. He had lobbied so hard for acceptance of the agreements made there that one journalist had dubbed him the "Yalta Legman."[35] Always sensitive to public opinion, he must have been horrified by the specter Vincent raised. The Far Eastern accord had been kept secret but would have to be revealed someday. To be criticized for having endorsed arrangements that compromised the venerable Open Door policy was a sufficiently unappetizing prospect. Now, as secretary of state, to incur blame for having pressed the Chinese to compromise further to meet Soviet demands must have been unthinkable. Truman shared the predicament to a lesser degree because he had been part of the Roosevelt administration.

The Chinese added their voices. On July 19 foreign minister Soong sent an urgent message to Ambassador Harriman. Having consulted with Chiang and other government leaders, he stated, "I am convinced that we have gone as far as we possibly could in meeting Soviet demands." The next day Chiang personally appealed to Truman to intercede with Stalin because China already had gone beyond Yalta and further concessions were impossible.[36] Had Truman and Byrnes nonetheless pressured them into giving up more, it is improbable that Chiang and Soong in defending themselves would have refrained from making known who was responsible.

Truman faced an agonizing choice. To stand by the Chinese would perpetuate the Sino-Soviet deadlock and risk delaying Soviet entry into the Pacific war if Stalin meant what he said about not commencing operations until negotiations were completed. To abandon the Chinese might make the administration an accomplice to subverting the Open Door in Manchuria. The president was sufficiently distressed to ask Stimson to confer with Marshall about whether "we needed the Russians in the war or whether we could get along without them." The general's reply was that Soviet troop buildups along the border already had served the purpose of pinning down Japanese forces in Manchuria. He added, however, that even if Japan surrendered before Russian entry, nothing could prevent the Soviets from invading Manchuria and getting "virtually what they want in the surrender terms."[37]

Marshall's analysis, coupled with the successful atomic test, made Soviet help appear less crucial though still desirable in Truman's mind. Besides, there was the chance that Stalin would moderate his demands to prepare the way for Soviet entry. Truman therefore notified Chiang that "I asked that you carry out the Yalta agreement, but I have not asked you to make any concession in excess of that agreement. If you and Generalissimo Stalin differ as to the correct interpretation of the Yalta agreement, I hope you will arrange for Soong to return to Moscow and continue your efforts to reach understanding."[38]

Some, ignoring the very real issues Vincent had raised, have alleged that Truman sought to drag out Sino-Soviet negotiations to delay Soviet entry into the war. Byrnes, who for personal reasons if nothing else was unlikely to have countenanced further dilution of the Open Door anyway, did hope for that result as a dividend. He told James Forrestal as much, and as his aide noted in a frequently quoted passage, "JFB still hoping for time, believing after atomic bomb Japan will surrender and Russia will not get in so much on the kill, thereby being in a position to press for claims against China." Those who cite these words to support the "delay" thesis invariably neglect to cite the preceding sentence in the same document. Truman, the aide wrote, "Hopes Soong will return to Moscow and agreement can be reached with Stalin."[39] And the president, in the final analysis, determined American foreign policy.

Truman later denied he had any desire to keep the Soviets out of the war and said he was unaware of such intent on Byrnes's part. *After* learning of the successful atomic test, he told Eisenhower and Davies, among others, how pleased he was by Stalin's renewed pledge to join the war against Japan. He said the same thing in letters to his wife: "I've gotten what I came for," he wrote, "Stalin goes to war with no strings on it . . . I'll say that we'll end the war a year sooner now, and think of the kids who won't be killed. That is the important thing now." In another letter, two days later: "Then I want the Jap War won and I want both of 'em [the Soviet Union and Great Britain] in it." How, in the face of such evidence, authors can claim Truman no longer wanted Soviet entry is something of a mystery. While it might be argued that he had an ulterior motive for misleading the others, why he would want to deceive Bess on this matter is difficult to fathom.[40]

Concurrent with these diplomatic maneuverings, final preparations were being made to use atomic bombs against the Japanese should they reject the Potsdam Declaration. On July 21 Harrison notified Stimson that "Patient *[Little Boy]* progressing rapidly and will be ready for final operation first good break in August." Asked for more definite dates, Harrison replied two days later that there was "some chance" it would be ready by the third, a "good chance" by the fifth, and "barring unexpected relapse almost certain by August 10."[41]

Stimson then asked when the first plutonium *Fat Man* would be available and "the approximate time when additional weapons of this kind would be ready." As it was a "matter of greatest importance here," Stimson requested an answer as quickly as possible. The first would be available August 6, Harrison replied, the second on the twenty-fourth. "Additional ones ready at accelerating pace from possibly three in September to we hope seven or more in December."[42] Stimson's query and the projected timetables clearly indicate that although American officials hoped that Japan would surrender after one or two bombs were used, they had to proceed on the assumption that the invasion scheduled for November 1 would still prove necessary.

Truman in his memoirs claimed that after consulting with the Joint Chiefs of Staff he approved on July 25 the directive for using atomic bombs against Japan. "I had made the decision," he wrote. "I also instructed Stimson that the order would stand unless I notified him that the Japanese reply to our ultimatum was acceptable."[43] Such a recollection testifies both to his deliberateness in conferring with the chiefs and to his decisiveness afterward. The problem with it is that there is no record of any such meeting, nor did any of the chiefs refer to one in their diaries or memoirs. There also is no indication that Truman even saw the directive at the time. Instead, the evidence strongly suggests that the decision to drop the bombs already had been made before the Potsdam conference, and that what is usually referred to as the "historic" directive was an afterthought of no real consequence.

On July 18 Groves notified Marshall that he had met with General Carl A. Spaatz, newly appointed commander of the United States Strategic Air Forces in the Pacific. Spaatz, soon to leave Washington to assume his command, was scheduled to meet with General MacArthur in Manila on August 1. "In view of the successful results of our field test," Groves reported, and the "imminence of the use of the atomic fission bomb in operations against Japan, 5 to 10 August," it seemed to him essential that Spaatz inform MacArthur "as to the plans for the use of the bomb." Groves stated that he had given Spaatz the "necessary background information and the general plan of the proposed operations" and, with Acting Chief of Staff Handy's approval, had asked him to disclose the plan to MacArthur.[44]

Spaatz had second thoughts. History would record that a unit of his command had dropped the first atomic bombs on populated cities. He was unwilling to take responsibility for these cataclysmic acts on the basis of nothing more than informal discussions with Groves and Handy. He therefore resorted to the time-honored military tradition of covering his rear in the event there were recriminations and fingers pointed later. "I haven't got a piece of paper yet," Handy recalled him saying, "and I think I need a piece of paper." Handy agreed.[45]

Following a meeting with Groves on Saturday, July 21, Handy sent a message to Marshall requesting authorization of a directive for Spaatz. On Sunday Marshall instructed Handy to prepare a draft for approval by Stimson and himself. Handy sent Groves a copy of Marshall's reply on Monday morning. "I assume that you will inform Mr. Harrison, confer with Colonel [John N.] Stone [a courier Air Forces Chief of Staff Arnold was sending] immediately upon his arrival," Handy wrote, "and then bring over a tentative directive for us to consider."[46]

On Tuesday, July 24, Colonel Stone in a long memorandum notified Arnold that the "plan and schedule for initial attacks using special bombs have been worked out." He reported that the gun-type uranium bomb would be ready between August 1 and 10, and that "plans are to drop it the first good day following readiness." He went on to list and describe the military value of four target cities, and pointed out that all "are believed to contain large numbers of key Japanese industrialists and political figures who have sought refuge from major destroyed cities." He provided details on how the bomb would be dropped and current estimates as to when the plutonium bombs would be available. Stone's memorandum was shown to Truman without any request for approval of the plans, and later "recovered from the President and burned."[47]

Later that day Handy radioed Groves's draft directive "for Marshall's eyes only" to save time. Drawn up as an order from Handy to Spaatz, it stated that the 509 Composite Group would deliver its "first special bomb" as soon as weather permitted after about August 3 on one of four targets: Hiroshima, Kokura, Niigata, or Nagasaki. Additional bombs would be used when available. Dissemination of all information about the operation was reserved to the president and the secretary of war. The order was issued "by direction and with the approval of the Secretary of War and the Chief of Staff, U.S.A.," and instructed Spaatz to person-ally deliver copies to MacArthur and Admiral Nimitz. Harrison sent a separate message to Stimson, saying he thought it "most important" that the directive be approved by the next day, "even if it is necessary to modify it later." Stimson did so, and Marshall notified Handy that "S/W approves Groves directive."[48]

The directive did no more than put in writing what Groves had told Spaatz a week earlier on July 18. It was drawn up not at the initiative of Stimson or Marshall, let alone Truman, but because Spaatz insisted he have his "piece of paper" and Handy sought to oblige him. Had Spaatz been informed only that he "might" be ordered to use the bombs if Truman so decided, there would have been no complaint to raise because those orders would have constituted the written directive he sought.

Marshall's initial reply to Handy and his message endorsing the draft indicate that Stimson's authorization was deemed sufficient without reference to the president. Nowhere in his diary does Stimson mention requesting Truman's approval of the directive, a most unusual omission if such approval constituted "the decision" to drop atomic bombs. The reason there was no need to secure Truman's permission to issue the directive is because it was, by that time, a mere formality to placate Spaatz.

Truman's own diary entry for July 25 has contributed to the confusion over what actually happened. "This weapon is to be used against Japan between now and August 10," he wrote. "I have told the Sec. of War, Mr. Stimson, to use it so that military objectives and soldiers and sailors are the target and not women and children."[49] His allusion is to a conversation he had with Stimson the previous day (they did not meet on the twenty-fifth) before the draft directive reached Potsdam. Truman's words do not refer to a decision about *whether* to use atomic bombs, as the quotation out of context might make it appear, but to which cities should be hit.

Stimson had shown the president a telegram from Harrison "giving the dates of the operations." Truman said that he was "highly delighted" because they fit in with his plans to issue the Potsdam Declaration. After expressing his concern over giving assurances about the Japanese emperor, Stimson "again gave him my reasons for wanting to eliminate one of the proposed targets." This was the ancient city of Kyoto, once the capital of Japan and now a cultural and religious center. Stimson had turned down several requests by the Target Committee to include Kyoto and he wanted the president's support, which he got with "the utmost emphasis." That Truman's comment about using the bombs, cited in the previous paragraph, pertained only to target choice is confirmed by his next sentence, ending "we . . . cannot drop this terrible bomb on the old capital [Kyoto] or the new."[50]

There is additional evidence that the decision to drop the bombs had been made well before the order was drafted. On July 19, the day after he met with Spaatz, Groves told Oppenheimer, "It is necessary to drop the first Little Boy and the first Fat Man and probably a second one in accordance with our original plans."[51] On the twenty-first Harrison notified Stimson, "Complicated preparations for use are proceeding so fast we should know not later than July 25 if any *change* in plans" (emphasis added). That is why he later urged Stimson to approve the directive by that date even if it had to be revised later. Handy was even more explicit. One of the reasons he gave Marshall for sending the draft by radio instead of by courier was the "necessity for not interrupting preparations for use." Finally, there is Admiral King's recollection that on July 18 Marshall informed the other chiefs that the bombs *would* be used, without inviting discussion. King insisted he was never consulted.[52]

In 1951 Truman's former assistant press secretary, Eben A. Ayers, initiated a search for any written record of Truman's decision to drop the bombs. This search, conducted not only in the Truman papers but also in the Manhattan Engineer District records then located at the Atomic Energy Commission and those at the Department of Defense, proved fruitless. Consultation with the historian of the Manhattan Project was equally unavailing. This led Ayers to conclude, he later wrote, that "it was entirely an oral decision reached at conferences between the President, Stimson and others at Potsdam."[53] Yet neither Truman's diary nor those kept by such key figures as Stimson and Leahy make any reference to what would have been momentous "conferences."

No one yet has found the documents Ayers sought. Barring new revelations, it may fairly be concluded that the only decision regarding atomic bombs made at Potsdam was not to stop the machinery that went into motion immediately after the successful test at Alamogordo. Perhaps Admiral Leahy's aide, George M. Elsey, said it best during a later interview. Among the top officials, including "the President himself," there "was never any question but what it would be used." "The big question was not whether the bomb was going to be used," he recalled, "the big question in those spring and summer months of '45 was 'Will the bomb work?' *That* was the question" (emphasis in original). If Truman's "decision" has to be dated, June 1, 1945, is as good a choice as any. That is the day he told Byrnes, in response to the latter's report that the Interim Committee recommended using the bombs against Japanese cities without warning, that "regrettable as it might be, so far as he could see, the only reasonable conclusion was to use the bomb."[54]

CHAPTER 7

Japan Unbowed

An Office of War Information transmitter began broadcasting the text of the Potsdam Declaration by short-wave radio within three hours of its release on July 26. It was aired frequently thereafter, leading a British official to warn that such repetition would give the impression that the Allies were "anxious" for peace and would offer better terms if the Japanese held out longer. He cited as evidence a Japanese broadcast contrasting the "softening attitude of the Allies" with the "stiffening attitude of Japan."[1]

Japanese officials began discussing the declaration on the morning of July 27, even before the translation was completed, and several meetings at the highest levels were held during the day. Foreign Minister Togo and Premier Suzuki advocated a policy of delay. They wished to send a noncommittal reply, or none at all, to buy time to seek favorable clarifications of terms, particularly with regard to the emperor, and to pursue Soviet mediation. Army and navy hard-liners vehemently disagreed. They found a number of the conditions totally unacceptable and insisted that anything less than an immediate, defiant rejection would sorely damage military and civilian morale.

A compromise was reached. The premier managed to get reluctant approval to refrain from answering the declaration pending the outcome of overtures to the Soviets. Because the fact that the Allies had issued an ultimatum could not be kept secret, Suzuki proposed to issue an expurgated version of it as a news item merely reporting enemy propaganda. Those parts would be excised that might appeal to peace sentiment in Japan, such as assurances that the Allies did not intend to enslave the people or destroy the nation and that military personnel would be free to return home after being disarmed.

In making his case for withholding comment, Suzuki used the Japanese word *mokusatsu*, which literally means to "kill it with silence," but which has harsher connotations such as to "treat it with silent contempt." Someone leaked the premier's phrase to the press, with the result that on Saturday morning several newspapers used it to describe the government's official position toward the declaration. Nor was that all. The militarists, reneging on the fragile understanding reached the day before, pressured Suzuki into appearing at a press conference that afternoon to denounce the ultimatum: "I believe the Joint Proclamation by the three countries is nothing but a rehash of the Cairo Declaration. As for the government, it does not find any important value in it, and there is no other recourse but to ignore it entirely and resolutely fight for the successful conclusion of this war." Japanese radio broadcasts and newspaper items thereupon began referring to the declaration as "insolent," "unforgivable," and "ridiculous."[2]

Truman has been criticized for not seizing upon the ambiguity of *mokusatsu* to inform the Japanese through diplomatic channels that they might retain the emperor. Had he done so, some have claimed, the war might have ended without further bloodshed.[3] But even if there had been any doubts over the Japanese reply—there were none—Suzuki's press conference and the subsequent media coverage would have dispelled them. Several minor Japanese officials in Switzerland, who themselves interpreted the response as rejection, reported to the Office of Strategic Services that Suzuki's words were for public consumption and that he would convey his "real" position through other means.[4] This interpretation was discredited when Japanese authorities continued to seek Soviet mediation and made no inquiries to Washington about the emperor as Ambassador Sato had been pleading with them to do.

Signaling Tokyo then or later that the imperial institution might be preserved would have played directly into the hands of the Japanese militants. The very notion of surrender was anathema to them, as were prospects of foreign occupation, punishment of war criminals, and the planned extermination of the warrior tradition. At best, hard-liners argued, the bloodbath at Okinawa would cause the United States to shrink from incurring the even heavier losses an invasion of the home islands would entail. They claimed that such apprehensions lay behind the Potsdam Declaration and would lead to further concessions the longer Japan held out. At worst, if an invasion were launched, Japanese defenders would inflict such terrible punishment that more lenient conditions would be offered at that time. Had Truman made an overture regarding the emperor, he would have appeared as a supplicant for peace, thereby bearing out the militants' most optimistic prediction.[5]

Meanwhile, formal sessions at Potsdam had been suspended following Churchill and Eden's departure for London to be present when the election returns were completed. While awaiting Japan's reply to the ultimatum, Truman learned that Churchill would be replaced by Clement Attlee and Foreign Secretary Eden by Ernest Bevin.

The first plenary session of the conference following the recess met after Attlee and Bevin returned on July 28. If Stalin hoped that Labour Party leaders would be more sympathetic to Soviet aspirations than Churchill and Eden had been, he was to be disappointed. Bevin's first words upon his arrival reportedly were "I will not have Britain barged about." He acted in such a way that evening, repeatedly questioning Stalin's remarks in an aggressive manner. When the latter made a vaguely worded proposal that would have conferred legitimacy on Soviet-controlled governments in eastern Europe, for instance, Bevin replied that in order to be "perfectly straight with the House of Commons" he would not "quote things in words of doubtful meaning."[6] Following the meeting Stalin developed a "cold" that resulted in another suspension of plenary sessions, this time until July 31. His cold may have been a device to avoid having to deal with the truculent Bevin while working out compromises with the more accommodating Americans.

Most disputed issues until this point in the conference had been settled or referred to the Council of Foreign Ministers, the organization of which Truman had proposed on the opening day. Several matters were not disposed of so easily, and there seemed to be agreement—at least between the Soviets and Americans—that they be resolved before the meeting adjourned. These included reparations from Germany, the western boundary of Poland, and joint recognition of the governments of Italy (occupied by the British and Americans), Romania, Hungary, and Bulgaria (occupied by the Soviets).

At noon on July 29, Molotov visited the Little White House to confer with Truman and Byrnes. They first discussed the western boundary of

Poland. At Yalta, Roosevelt and Churchill had refused to accept Stalin's proposal that Poland be awarded German territory up to the Oder-western Neisse rivers to compensate for loss of its eastern lands to the Soviets. To obscure this disagreement, the phrase "substantial accessions of territory" had been used in place of specific boundaries.[7] The Briefing Book Paper on Poland drawn up for the Potsdam Conference stated that the United States should be prepared "with reluctance" to support Polish claims up to the Oder-eastern Neisse but not beyond.[8] Byrnes handed Molotov a paper to that effect during the meeting. When the foreign minister protested that Stalin probably would find the proposal unsatisfactory, Truman replied that it represented "a very large concession on our part."

Aside from its obvious implications for Poland and Germany, location of the border directly affected the matter of German reparations. The Soviets already had declared that assets in territories administered by the Poles would not be available for extractions. The farther west the boundary line, therefore, the smaller the German economic base that would have to provide for a population swollen by those who had fled or been evicted from the lost homeland.

Byrnes next turned the discussion to reparations. Although Molotov had offered to lower Soviet claims by $2 billion, the Americans still opposed setting sums before a physical inventory because they did not want to end up having to foot the difference should the amounts exceed Germany's capacity to pay. Byrnes asked whether the Soviets had considered his earlier proposal that each nation take what it chose from its own zone, with imbalances being made up by the exchange of goods. This plan, devised by Assistant Secretary of State William L. Clayton, provided that Germany would be treated as a whole on matters such as transportation and communication. Molotov said he had no objection "in principle," but tried to pin down Truman and Byrnes on specific figures with regard to capital equipment the Soviets would receive from the industrial Ruhr, which lay in the British zone. Again the Americans were unwilling to discuss amounts prior to a systematic assessment of usable German assets, but Soviet consent "in principle" to the Clayton plan marked a step forward.[9]

Toward the end of the meeting, Molotov asked that when Sino-Soviet negotiations were completed the United States and its allies formally request Russia to declare war against Japan. This was not, as some have claimed, an offer to join the conflict immediately. Truman later referred to Molotov's proposal as a "cynical diplomatic move to make Russia's entry at this time appear to be the decisive factor in bringing about victory." American forces had borne the brunt of the fighting against Japan for nearly four years. Truman and Byrnes at this late date had no intention of making a public appeal for what was expected to be a token contribution—especially one that would be amply compensated by the Yalta agreement. After talking with Attlee, Truman had Byrnes draft a note to Stalin suggesting that the Soviets base their entry on the Moscow Declaration of October 30, 1943, and on portions of the as yet unratified United Nations Charter.[10] No one believed this bit of jockeying would have even the slightest effect on the course of events: the Soviets would join the war when they thought it was in their interests to do so with or without an invitation.

The next day Byrnes met with Molotov before the scheduled foreign ministers' meeting. He made three proposals that, he emphasized, the United States regarded as inseparable. First he offered to recognize Polish administration of the area east of the Oder-western Neisse. Next he recommended that the Council of Foreign Ministers begin drawing up peace treaties for Italy and the former German satellite states of Romania, Bulgaria, and Hungary. This was a kind of mini-package whereby in exchange for Soviet recognition of Italy, the United States and Great Britain would confer quasi-legitimacy—though not official recognition—on the Russian-dominated regimes in Eastern Europe.

Finally, Byrnes offered the Soviets 15 percent of the Ruhr's industrial equipment free and 25 percent to be exchanged for foodstuffs and raw materials from their zone. Molotov said that the Soviets should get 25 percent without exchange. When Byrnes protested that the British would not accept such a figure, Molotov replied that if so Russia should get percentages of equipment from all the western zones rather than just from the Ruhr. He suggested 10 percent outright and 15 percent in exchange. Despite Byrnes's objection that these figures were too high, Molotov said he was encouraged that progress was being made.[11]

Averell Harriman later remarked that Byrnes regarded himself as the mediator between Great Britain and the Soviet Union. "He seemed to go with the idea, as he had always done in the Senate," Harriman recalled, "when there was a controversy, that he would pour oil in the waters." A recent author, Kai Bird, apparently never having heard of the old saying about pouring oil on troubled waters, actually has used Harriman's remark to show how pugnacious Byrnes became after learning of the successful atomic test![12]

Harriman was right, and the British were displeased at what was being done behind their backs. "Jimmy B. is a bit too active," one member of their delegation complained, "and has already gone and submitted various proposals to Molotov which go a bit beyond what we want at the moment."[13] Byrnes and Molotov spent most of the foreign ministers' meeting that day trying to persuade a recalcitrant Bevin to accept what they already had decided.

Stalin recuperated from his cold sufficiently to have a plenary session scheduled for July 31. Byrnes talked with Molotov privately before the meeting. The United States had gone as far as it could to accommodate the Soviets, he said, and pointed out again that he and Truman regarded the three proposals as inextricably linked. He later claimed that this time he warned Molotov that unless the Soviets approved the package in its entirety, "the President and I would leave for the United States the next day."[14]

Truman opened the plenary session that afternoon by calling on Byrnes to present the American propositions. The secretary did so, again stressing their linkage. Stalin expressed disapproval of "such tactics" and declared that the Soviets would vote on each proposition separately. Only the paper on reparations provoked extended debate as it turned out. Byrnes had offered the Soviets 7.5 percent of surplus industrial equipment from the western zones free and an additional 12.5 percent in exchange for raw materials. Stalin said he had no quarrel with the idea of each nation taking reparations from its own zone, but he thought the Soviets should receive higher percentages from the west. Over Bevin's objection that the American figures already were "very liberal," agreement was reached whereby in exchange for dropping their claims on shares of German gold and investments abroad, the Soviets would receive the 10 and 15 percent figures Molotov had suggested to Byrnes the day before.[15]

Most of the time during the final two sessions on August 1 was spent preparing the conference protocol and communiqué. One discussion during the first meeting bears mention. Truman "after a long study of history" had become enamored of a plan to internationalize certain inland waterways in Europe bordering on two or more states as well as those passages known as "straits." He had raised the issue three times, only to have Stalin refuse to discuss it because of "differences." Now Truman asked that at least mention be made in the conference documents that the subject had been considered. When Stalin refused, the president appealed to him: "Marshal Stalin, I have accepted a number of compromises during this conference to conform to your views, and I make a personal appeal now that you yield on this point." "Nyet," Stalin burst out without waiting for the interpretation and, in English: "No, I say no!" An angered Truman muttered to his aides, "I cannot understand that man."[16]

Truman *had* made a number of concessions to Stalin during the conference. Those who claim he grew "tougher" after Alamogordo emphasize his expressions of confidence upon hearing the news and upon his few sharp exchanges with Stalin. They ignore the more important reality that on several important issues he retreated from positions agreed on before the atomic test took place. Acknowledging the Oder-western Neisse line is a case in point. This boundary, which Roosevelt had refused to accept, involved an additional area of 8,100 square miles (with a prewar German population of 2.7 million) beyond what the State Department had recommended Truman might concede "with reluctance."

Truman and Byrnes also softened conditions under which Soviet puppet regimes in Eastern Europe, particularly those of Bulgaria and Romania, might be recognized. A month before Potsdam, the United States had notified the Soviets that recognition would not be conferred until these governments conformed to the requirements of the Declaration on Liberated Europe promulgated at Yalta. Truman's haste to recognize the Communist-dominated government of Poland in early July indicated that cosmetic changes in the other states would be sufficient. At Potsdam the United States retreated from insisting on "supervision" of elections to the mere "observation" of them. "As long as American observers were present," one scholar has written, "Washington would not significantly object to rigged elections in Eastern Europe."[17]

With regard to reparations, although Truman and Byrnes all along had refused to accept any arrangements that might result in having to feed a starving Germany because of excessive extractions, they did accept over British protests the percentages of industrial equipment to be made available to the Soviets that Molotov originally had proposed.

Truman in his memoirs, published during the 1950s, claimed he realized at Potsdam that the Russians "were planning world conquest."[18]
Such an exaggeration may be attributed to his desire to defend his
presidency against right-wing charges then being made that he had been
duped by the Communists, or worse. During and after the conference he
said no such thing, instead likening Stalin to a shrewd horse-trader with
whom he could get along. "I like Stalin," he wrote his wife shortly before
he left Potsdam, "He is straightforward. Knows what he wants and will
compromise when he can't get it." Years later he privately identified
himself as a "Russophile" at the time of Potsdam, and wrote of Stalin
that he "liked the little son of a bitch."[19]

The diaries and journals of Joseph Davies provide valuable witness
to the conduct of Truman and Byrnes during the conference. Davies,
who attended the plenary sessions and talked with both men daily, was
quick to discern signs of hostility toward the Soviets from whatever
quarter. On July 21, the day Harrison's lengthy report on the atomic explosion arrived, Davies after a conversation with Stimson about Russia
"thought I detected a change in his attitude from what he had evinced
in Washington." Complaining about anti-Soviet sentiments within the
American delegation, Davies went on to write, "About the only ones
here who are steady are the President himself, Byrnes, Clayton, and
[James C.] Dunn. It is disheartening."[20]

Davies expressed no disagreements with American bargaining positions, nor did he notice any escalation of terms after the detailed report
from New Mexico arrived. Davies himself suggested to Byrnes on July 22
that he propose the Clayton plan to Molotov as a possible way to end
the deadlock over reparations. "It might work," Byrnes told him, "and
he was going to try it out. He was 'fed up' with everlasting bickering
with Molotov." The next day Byrnes discussed the new approach with
the Soviet foreign minister for the first time.[21]

Davies registered disapproval over only two aspects of Truman and
Byrnes's behavior. He regretted that they had not consulted the Soviets
before issuing the Potsdam Declaration, even though he seems to have
accepted Truman's explanation that British elections necessitated its
release before Churchill went out of office. "There is danger there," he
noted.[22]

He regarded as far more important the failure to offer the Soviets
partnership in the atomic program. Byrnes repeatedly had complained

to him about the difficulty in negotiating with the intractable Molotov over reparations. Davies grew horrified when, a few days after Truman's approach to Stalin, Byrnes said, "He thought that the knowledge of the atomic bomb, which had been reported to them, would have some effect and induce them to yield and agree to our position." The next day, when Davies warned Byrnes that such a stance might lead to an arms race, the secretary in a colossal example of short-sightedness replied that "he had considered such possibilities, but Molotov was impossible to deal with."[23] Soviet acceptance of the Clayton plan "in principle" that afternoon must have convinced Byrnes of his wisdom.

As the Potsdam Conference neared its end, the Japanese foreign office continued to press Ambassador Sato to secure Soviet approval of the proposed Konoye mission. Sato remained pessimistic. On July 27 he informed Tokyo, "Any aid from the Soviet Union has now become extremely doubtful." He referred to a Soviet broadcast indicating that for the first time Stalin had taken part in discussions "regarding the war in the Far East," which he regarded as ominous.[24]

The next day Foreign Minister Togo asked him to arrange an interview after Molotov returned to determine the Soviet attitude toward the Potsdam Declaration and to find out whether it had been issued in response to the Japanese overture. If it had, the Japanese could only conclude that Stalin was responsible since they were unaware their codes had been compromised. Without waiting, Sato replied that "you must believe" Stalin had revealed the Japanese request to the Allies, and that the declaration in turn "most certainly" had been shown to him.[25] Americans reading these messages would have had to conclude that even the "peace" faction in Tokyo was still hoping that Soviet mediation would enable Japan to obtain a negotiated peace despite growing evidence that Stalin was actively collaborating with its enemies.

Exclusive reliance upon the MAGIC intercepts of diplomatic traffic to evaluate Japanese attitudes toward peace is misleading in any event. Suzuki and Togo did not control the situation, and the reason they were unable to convey any specific proposals to the Soviets through Sato was because they knew the army was monitoring their messages. Intercepts of Japanese military communications, designated ULTRA, told a very different story. "ULTRA did portray a Japan in extremity," Edward J. Drea has written, "but it also showed that its military leaders were blind to defeat and were bending all remaining national energy to smash an invasion of their divine islands." And, as he points out, even the most confidential messages between them "gave no hint of surrender."[26]

Japanese Imperial General Headquarters had correctly guessed that the next Allied operation after Okinawa would be against southern Kyushu and was making every effort to bolster its defenses. In addition to frantic construction of fortified emplacements on the few beaches where the Japanese knew invaders would have to come ashore, reinforcements were arriving almost daily. By July 21, ULTRA intercepts placed the number of Japanese defenders at about 455,000, and more units were on the way. That source led to estimates that the Japanese would have more than ten thousand aircraft available in all of Japan, about two thousand of which were kamikaze, together with a formidable array of special weapons such as flying bombs and suicide submarines.[27] The kamikazes were especially worrisome. They had taken a dreadful toll of men and ships at Okinawa, and would be even more effective operating off the shores of Japan. Prospects were that the Kyushu operation would be not just "another Okinawa" as Truman feared but something even bloodier.

When the president had discussed expected invasion casualties with the Joint Chiefs on June 18, Marshall's estimate for the first thirty days had been based on the assumption that the Japanese would have about 350,000 men in place. To Truman's inquiry about the prospects of reinforcements from the other home islands, the general replied that "it was expected that all of the communications with Kyushu would be destroyed."[28] He had been assured that naval and air operations would virtually seal off the island and even restrict troop movements overland from north to south. By July 21, therefore, with ULTRA estimates of Japanese forces already increased by 105,000, Marshall's earlier casualty projection was obsolete and would be totally irrelevant by invasion day, scheduled for November 1. On July 24, at a tripartite military meeting, he told the Soviets and British that there were "approximately 500,000 troops in Kyushu" and that "the most noticeable movements of Japanese troops have been towards Kyushu." It is inconceivable that he failed to inform Truman about the Japanese buildup when they met the next day to discuss "the tactical and political situation."[29]

Yet another myth that has long flourished among certain historians about using atomic bombs is that Truman knew such use was unnecessary because several of his highest military advisers had assured him that Japan would surrender before the invasion was scheduled to take place. Such a claim, of course, strengthens the thesis that the weapons were employed for political purposes. The problem with it is that no one yet has produced any documentary evidence. Efforts to create substantiation where none exists have resulted in some gross distortions of the historical record.

General Marshall firmly believed an invasion would be necessary if the war were to be ended in the foreseeable future. He had told Truman at the June 18 meeting that "air power alone was not sufficient to put the Japanese out of the war," just as it had been "unable to put the Germans out." General Ira Eaker, representing General Arnold for the air force, had agreed with this. Marshall had said that if the invasion were put off much beyond November 1, bad weather might delay the operation "and hence the end of the war" for up to six months.[30]

Marshall and Stimson worried that public and military morale would disintegrate if the war dragged on too long. Marshall had asked Hollywood director Frank Capra, who had made the widely shown "Why We Fight" series, to make two more films to educate American servicemen on the need to finish the war against Japan. One was to be titled "Two Down and One to Go," the other "On to Tokyo." As Marshall's principal biographer has pointed out, "There is no evidence that at any time his thinking or plans were influenced by any possible political effect use of the bomb might have on the Russians." Stimson, having been profoundly moved by the despondence among soldiers he had visited at a redeployment center in March, had concluded that failure to use any means necessary to end the war before an invasion "deserved punishment."[31]

Navy Chief of Staff King also had supported an invasion at the June 18 meeting with Truman. Immediately following Marshall's comments about the inadequacy of bombing to force surrender, King had said "he agreed with General Marshall's views and said that the more he studied the matter, the more he was impressed with the strategic location of Kyushu, which he considered the key to the success of any siege operations."[32] King never suggested that he conveyed to Truman any change of mind regarding this evaluation.

General Arnold had been on a tour of Pacific bases when Marshall sought his views in preparation for the Joint Chiefs of Staff meeting with Truman. Arnold later wrote that by then General Curtis LeMay, who commanded the B-29s fire bombing Japanese cities, convinced him Japan would be so devastated by October 1 that it "couldn't continue fighting." Yet even after LeMay's briefing, Arnold's first recommendation in his reply to Marshall was: "Continue with our present plans and occupy Kyushu to get additional bases for forty groups of heavy bombers."[33] At the meeting, Eaker stated that he "agreed completely" with Marshall's views and that he had just received a cable from Arnold which "also expressed complete agreement."[34]

As with King, Arnold at no time claimed to have informed Truman that he had revised his opinion since the June 18 meeting or that he opposed using atomic bombs on any grounds. During one Combined Chiefs of Staff meeting at Potsdam he reported on LeMay's estimates about the damage that would be done by October 1, stating that Japan "will become a nation without cities" and "will have tremendous difficulty in holding her people together for continued resistance to our terms of unconditional surrender."[35] He and other air generals previously had said the same thing about Germany. Marshall later recalled that conventional bombing had "destroyed the Japanese cities, yes, but their morale was not affected as far as we could tell at all."[36]

Admiral Leahy is often cited as having protested to Truman on military and moral grounds against use of atomic bombs. His diaries make no mention of any such protest, a curious omission in view of the subject's importance. Leahy did denounce using atomic bombs in the final paragraphs of his memoirs, published in 1950, calling it "barbarous" and of "no material assistance in our war against Japan." The Japanese were "already defeated" and "ready to surrender," he wrote, because of conventional bombing and naval blockade. "I was not taught to make war in that fashion," he declared, "and wars cannot be won by destroying women and children." How he thought women and children would have fared had LeMay gone on for months "driving them back to the stone age" he did not say.[37]

Leahy nowhere indicated in his book that he conveyed such sentiments to Truman before the bombs were used. One inventive author, Gar Alperovitz, has tried to make it appear he did by braiding together snippets from the admiral's condemnation of them with a quotation from an earlier page in which he wrote that he "acquainted Truman with my own ideas about the best course to pursue in defeating Japan as fully as I had done with President Roosevelt." The passage in question clearly refers to the period immediately following Roosevelt's death, hence his use of the word "acquainted." Leahy wrote that he had expressed his preference for bombing and blockade over invasion without even suggesting any mention of the bomb, which had yet to be tested. The admiral at no time contended that the siege would compel Japan to surrender before the scheduled invasion, only that it would do so eventually and was worth the wait.[38]

Leahy's indignation about the bombs came later, and may have had something to do with fear that they would reduce his beloved navy to a marginal role. During the months before their use he had confidently predicted as a "munitions expert" that they would not work, and even after the test at Alamogordo he referred to them as a "professor's dream."[39] Averell Harriman remarked at a roundtable discussion years later, "I remember that great genius, Admiral Leahy, saying that he would guarantee that the bomb wouldn't go off," to which John McCloy replied, "Yeah, I remember that." Two days after Hiroshima, Truman told aides that "the admiral said up to the last that it wouldn't go off."[40]

Of all the high-ranking officers who were in Germany at the time of the Potsdam Conference, only Dwight D. Eisenhower, then Supreme Commander, Allied Expeditionary Forces (in Europe), later professed to have spoken out against using the bomb. In his *Crusade in Europe*, published in 1948, Eisenhower recalled that when Stimson told him about it, he said he hoped "we would never have to use such a thing against any enemy" because he did not want the United States to be the first to use "something as horrible and destructive as this new weapon was described to be." He admitted, however, "My views were merely personal and immediate reactions; they were not based on any analysis of the subject."[41]

Eisenhower's recollection of this discussion grew more vivid with the passage of time. By 1963, when his *Mandate for Change* appeared, he now remembered telling a "deeply perturbed" Stimson that "dropping the bomb was completely unnecessary."[42] That same year he provided an interviewer with an even more colorful account. "We'd had a nice evening together at headquarters in Germany," he recalled. Then, after dinner, "Stimson got this cable saying the bomb had been perfected and was ready to be dropped. The cable was in code . . . 'The lamb is born' or some damn thing like that."

Eisenhower said he listened in silence as Stimson outlined the plans for use, but when asked his opinion replied that he was "against it" because "the Japanese were ready to surrender and it wasn't necessary to hit them with that awful thing" and because he "hated to see our country be the first to use such a weapon. Well . . . the old gentleman got furious." In this rendition, he had gone from merely expressing dismay to delivering such a forceful denunciation on moral and military grounds as to infuriate the secretary.[43]

Although Stimson was no longer alive to confirm or deny Eisenhower's later account, parts of it are demonstrably false and the rest of dubious authenticity. The first coded cable about the atomic test arrived at Potsdam on the evening of July 16, the second on the morning of the eighteenth. Stimson did not talk with Eisenhower until July 20 at a flag-raising ceremony in Berlin. General Omar Bradley also was there and Stimson noted in his diary simply that "I had a pleasant chat with each of them after the show was over."[44] None of Eisenhower's several versions of his debate with Stimson over the bomb has it occurring during this brief encounter.

Stimson next saw the general at his headquarters in Frankfurt on July 27. The secretary wrote in his diary that at lunch he had tried to convince Eisenhower of the importance of the latter's new job as military governor of Germany "because I knew that he was very much disappointed in having to do it." There is no mention of discussing the bomb. In a set of notes about Stimson's Potsdam trip, however, his aide wrote that the secretary, Eisenhower, and his deputy, General Lucius D. Clay, went to Eisenhower's quarters for lunch, where they "talked informally about civil affairs and General Groves' project."[45] As Stimson and Eisenhower had only two meetings during the Potsdam Conference, this had to have been the one in question.

Stimson's failure to note in his diary that he discussed atomic bombs with Eisenhower and Clay suggests two possibilities. One is that Eisenhower's protest against using them may have been so pungent and so obviously correct that the secretary was too embarrassed to set them down in writing. The other is that Eisenhower responded so mildly— Truman himself, after all, had referred to the bomb as "the most terrible thing ever discovered"—that Stimson saw no reason to allude to that part of their conversation. The latter is more likely, as Stimson had not hesitated in the past to record disagreements with others over the bomb.

Most important, even if the general had expressed disapproval at this meeting Truman could not have learned of it because Stimson left for the United States later that day. He did not see the president again until after the first bomb had been dropped.[46]

Authors of all persuasions have tended to accept uncritically one or another version of Eisenhower's alleged dissent. At times they have simply cited one another's books, which upon examination turn out to be based on the general's unsupported assertion. Those who seek to show that Truman knew there was no military reason for using the bombs have given it special emphasis.[47] The publication of Bradley's autobiography in 1983 appeared to corroborate Eisenhower's recollection and to shed new light on the subject. This volume not only had Bradley in the room when Eisenhower voiced his objections to Stimson but also had him present when the Supreme Commander confronted Truman personally at lunch in Berlin on July 20. This was something Eisenhower himself never claimed to have done.[48]

Although apparently written without knowledge that Stimson's aide had alluded to a discussion with Eisenhower about "General Groves's project" on July 27, a 1987 article on the subject offered a judicious analysis. Citing the testimony of several individuals who knew Eisenhower, the author contended that it would have been entirely out of character for this tactful general to have openly criticized on moral and military grounds a policy endorsed by Truman, Stimson, and Marshall. The essay went on to point out that although no one yet has found any contemporary evidence that Eisenhower opposed use of the bomb, there is some reason to believe he supported it—or at least led others to believe that he did. Writing to Eisenhower a few days after Japan's surrender, for instance, Bradley expressed gratification that the war was over, remarking, "It certainly didn't take long for the Japs to make up their minds after we started hitting them with atomic bombs." That Bradley would have written his friend and superior in such a vein had he thought Eisenhower opposed using the bombs as immoral and unnecessary must be doubted.

The article concluded that while the available evidence does not disprove Eisenhower's contention, it certainly raises grave doubts. What is not open to question is that Bradley's "autobiography" is a spurious source on the subject of Eisenhower and the atomic bomb. The writer who collaborated with Bradley on the volume wrote that section after the latter's death and with no prior consultation. He simply took on faith Eisenhower's own words about the meeting with Stimson and for good measure placed Bradley in attendance. He made up the alleged confrontation with Truman entirely on his own.[49]

Both of the top commanders in the Pacific supported the invasion of Japan's home islands, and neither at the time expressed any reservations about using atomic bombs. Admiral Chester W. Nimitz, Commander in Chief, Pacific Ocean Area, learned of the planned operations months earlier because the special bombing group would operate from within his jurisdiction. According to the courier who delivered Admiral King's letter stating that the first bomb was expected to be available in August, Nimitz read it and then said, "This sounds fine, but this is only February. Can't we get one sooner?" Far from opposing use of the bombs, after Hiroshima and Nagasaki he favored using a third on Tokyo.[50]

General Douglas MacArthur, Commander in Chief, Southwest Pacific Area, had long argued for an invasion of the Japanese home islands. Just prior to Truman's meeting with the Joint Chiefs of Staff on June 18, MacArthur had notified Marshall that "I most earnestly recommend no change in Olympic." At about that time he told General Arnold in Manila that bombing would help win the war, but "in the final analysis, the doughboys would have to march into Tokyo."[51] Although he probably was informed about the atomic program in 1944, he did not learn of the bomb's imminent use until Spaatz talked with him on August 1. Spaatz later told General Handy that he conveyed the message and "that's all I did." MacArthur thereupon responded with an hour-long lecture on the future of atomic warfare, not with any criticism of existing plans. He continued to urge that preparations for the invasion go forward even after the first bomb was dropped.[52]

Pending the discovery of new material, there is no reliable evidence that *any* high-ranking officer expressed moral objections about the bomb to Truman or gave him reason to believe that the military situation had changed appreciably—except that Japanese defenses were daily growing more formidable—since he had approved the Kyushu operation during his meeting with the Joint Chiefs of Staff on June 18. On July 24 he and Churchill had met with the Combined Chiefs of Staff to review and approve final invasion plans. Nothing said there or in the chiefs' report suggested any need for revision.[53] From the standpoint of what Truman had to go on at the time, later claims by various generals and admirals about what *they* thought are immaterial and in many cases obviously self-serving or motivated by devotion to their particular branch of service.

Information being received through intelligence channels likewise provided no basis for reevaluating earlier decisions. The Japanese foreign office continued to press Ambassador Sato to sound out Soviet intentions and to make sure he arranged a meeting with Molotov as soon as the latter returned to Moscow. Sato in turn grew bolder in trying to convince his superiors that the Soviets were far more likely to join the war against Japan than to act as its go-between.

"There is no alternative but immediate unconditional surrender," Sato informed Togo on July 31, "if we are to try to make America and England moderate and to prevent [Russia's] participation in the war." He warned that once in, the Soviets would "bring full and heavy pressure" on the other Allies with regard to Manchuria, China, and Korea, and that Stalin would proceed "in the hope of achieving his own demands." "Your way of looking at things and the actual situation in the Eastern Area," he stated bluntly, "may be seen to be absolutely contradictory."[54]

On August 1, the head of the Office of Strategic Services (OSS) in Switzerland, Allen Dulles, reported to Washington on his contacts with Japanese officials in Switzerland. Some were hopeful that Japan would capitulate within a week "unless resistance is too great." They urged that the Allies not take "too seriously" what was being said about the Potsdam Declaration over the Tokyo radio because that was merely "propaganda to maintain morale in Japan."

A naval officer who reportedly had direct radio contact with the Navy Ministry and Navy Chief of Staff told a different story. In June he had "suggested that Japanese naval circles in Tokyo" would be willing to surrender provided the emperor were retained and "they could save some face from the present wreckage." More recently, he was informed that "the Japanese Navy no longer is able to 'act alone.'" The acting director of the OSS merely passed Dulles's message along to the White House with the comment that he thought the president would be "interested," without implying there was anything in it he should see before his return.[55]

The Japanese government's failure to heed the advice of Sato and officials in neutral countries that it should surrender or at least make inquiries about the status of the emperor indicated that the die-hard militarists still dominated the situation. Meanwhile, ULTRA continued to identify new units arriving in Kyushu with dismaying frequency. On July 29, MacArthur's G-2 reported that "this threatening development, if not checked, may grow to a point where we attack on a ratio of one (1) to one (1) which is not the recipe for victory." Standard military doctrine called for a ratio of three to one in favor of the invaders. And Japanese prisoners of war, including the former adjutant to the assistant chief of staff of the navy, were "almost unanimous" in predicting to MacArthur's intelligence officers that an invasion would be necessary.[56]

There is no suggestion here that Truman was being kept informed on a daily basis either of the MAGIC intercepts or of the information gleaned by ULTRA. The point is that nothing from either source, or from OSS contacts, would have led anyone along the chain of information to perceive some sort of breakthrough that should be brought to his immediate attention. Indeed, reading the ULTRA reports would have strengthened his determination to avoid "another Okinawa," this one on a much larger scale. By the time the first atomic bomb was dropped, estimates of Japanese defenders in southern Kyushu had risen to 560,000, now 210,000 more than Marshall had assumed as a basis for the casualty figures he gave Truman on June 18. Projections of Japanese strength as of "X Day" (November 1) placed the number at 680,000, and a July 31 estimate of American battle and non-battle casualties ran as high as 394,859 *for the Kyushu operation alone.* This figure did not include those who would be killed outright, of course, for they would require no medical treatment. The president would have been even more impressed had he known that the actual number of Japanese troops was closer to 900,000.[57]

Atom Bombs and the End of the War

The gun-type uranium bomb, *Little Boy,* was fully assembled on Tinian by July 31 and ready for delivery any time thereafter. Actual use depended upon favorable weather because orders called for visual bombing to permit observation by scientific personnel. Hiroshima had been moved to the top of the list after General Spaatz reported that it appeared to be the only targeted city that had no prisoner of war camps in the vicinity.[1] Stimson, who had arrived back in Washington on the twenty-eighth, secured Truman's approval to release the presidential statement if *Little Boy* proved successful. The plutonium bomb, *Fat Man,* at that time was scheduled to be dropped about August 10. Although officials of the Strategic Air Forces on the scene had latitude with regard to timing, only a direct order from the president could cancel these operations.

Truman and his party flew from Berlin to England on the morning of August 2, where they boarded the *Augusta* anchored in Plymouth Harbor. The president, Byrnes, and Leahy lunched with King George VI aboard the H.M.S. *Renown* moored nearby. When talk turned to the atomic bomb and Leahy again expressed his opinion that it would not work, the king offered to make him a small wager. The admiral accepted.[2] That afternoon the *Augusta* got underway for Newport News, Virginia. Those who knew what was coming could only wait to learn when the first bomb fell and whether it performed to expectations.

Truman seems to have made only one significant decision during the voyage home. Sino-Soviet negotiations, suspended for the duration of the Big Three meeting, were to resume when Stalin returned to Moscow. Secretary Byrnes's musings to his aide and to Forrestal about his desire to delay settlement in order to keep Russia out of the war were not translated into policy. On July 28, the same day Byrnes talked with Forrestal, Truman had instructed the secretary of state to notify the Chinese that the United States wanted parleys to recommence as quickly as possible "in hope of reaching agreement."[3] As Byrnes had no separate pipeline through which to convey his preferences, Chinese officials could only assume the message meant what it said.

An early Sino-Soviet accord would serve several purposes. There was no guarantee that atomic bombs alone would force the Japanese to surrender. A Russian declaration of war would crush any hopes the Japanese had of mediation and would greatly augment the already massive forces arrayed against them. Besides, as General Marshall had pointed out, even if the United States compelled Japan to give up without Russian help, there was nothing to prevent the Russians from invading Manchuria and getting "virtually what they wanted in the surrender terms."[4] If this happened before they signed a treaty with the Chinese, Stalin would be under no obligation to observe the Yalta Far Eastern accord.

Ambassador Harriman stressed the advantages of a settlement regardless of its bearing on Russian entry into the war, "particularly the agreement that the Soviet Government will support the Chinese National Government as the unifying force in China."[5] In Harriman's judgment, however, Stalin was unlikely to soften the terms he had offered Soong during the first round of talks. A message from the American ambassador to China, Patrick J. Hurley, reinforced this view. Replying to Byrnes's July 28 cable urging the resumption of negotiations, Hurley reported that despite Chinese concessions on other matters Soong had been unable to obtain "any modification in regard to railroads and ports." Soong was so pessimistic that he threatened to resign as foreign minister because "this proposed agreement with Soviet will be destructive politically to the man responsible for it."[6]

Harriman believed there were only two ways to resolve the situation. Either Soong would have to give in to Soviet terms, "contrary to the interests of the United States," or the United States would have to notify the Soviets that it stood by China's interpretation of the Yalta agreement. He recommended that he be instructed to inform Stalin that Roosevelt had insisted that Dairen be internationalized as a free port, that the United States would not consent to its being included in the Soviet military zone, and that the United States proposed to have it run by a four-power commission if Stalin refused to accept Chinese administration. Harriman appended to his recommendations a draft understanding with the Soviets providing for an Open Door in Manchuria.[7]

Harriman's draft was identical to the one Far Eastern adviser John Carter Vincent had submitted earlier to Byrnes.[8] Both men stressed the domestic political backlash that was sure to erupt should the administration appear to have condoned any Sino-Soviet agreement that compromised the Open Door policy. No one yet has found a record of shipboard discussions between Truman and Byrnes on this matter, but neither was inclined to treat the matter lightly. They had told Stalin at their first meeting that a free port at Dairen was indispensable to the Open Door, and therefore constituted their "main interest" with regard to Sino-Soviet negotiations.[9]

On August 5, Byrnes approved Harriman's recommendations and draft understanding with only minor revisions. He requested that the ambassador try to obtain Stalin's formal acceptance of the understanding immediately so that it could be published along with the Sino-Soviet treaties. "This would go far to dispel misunderstanding," Byrnes stated, "as our public opinion is much opposed to any arrangements which might be construed to prejudice our historic open door policy." Regardless of his own predilections, therefore, his message to Harriman was intended to facilitate Sino-Soviet agreements, not to prolong them.[10]

The next day, August 6, while having lunch with enlisted men, Truman received a short message from Washington: "Big bomb dropped on Hiroshima August 5 at 7:15 P.M. Washington Time. First reports indicate complete success which was even more conspicuous than earlier test." Truman read it and said to the officer who had handed it to him: "Captain Graham, this is the greatest thing in history."[11] One historian has pronounced these words "vile," apparently deciding without evidence that Truman used the word "greatest" as in the sense of "Tastes Great!" rather than "most awesome."[12] An account based on witnesses suggests the latter: "The President seemed both excited and deeply moved. The sailors at his table fell silent, but for the moment he said no more."[13] In any event, the promise of shortening a bloody war affecting millions of people no doubt seemed more welcome to those involved than to those writing about it decades later.

Hiroshima housed the Second General Army Headquarters, charged with the defense of southern Japan, and was an important communications and transportation center. *Little Boy* exploded over the city shortly after 8:15 A.M., August 6, Japanese time. It had been set to detonate above the ground for maximum blast effect and minimum radiation dispersal.[14] The results were visually spectacular and physically devastating. First there was a huge, blinding flash, then roiling black clouds laced with flame rose in a mushroom shape to a towering height. Everything near the blast site was obliterated, and only the strongest buildings remained standing even miles away. The combination of intense heat, concussion, and raging fires killed between seventy-eight thousand and one hundred thousand inhabitants outright and wounded many thousands more.[15]

At 11 A.M. on the sixth, Washington time, the White House released the statement prepared for Truman by the Interim Committee. Announcing that an atomic bomb had exploded over Hiroshima, the statement declared, "The force from which the sun draws its powers had been loosed against those who brought war to the Far East." If the Japanese did not now accept the Potsdam Declaration, it continued, "they may expect a rain of ruin from the air, the likes of which has never been seen on this earth."[16] Mighty sea and land forces would follow this terrible assault from the air. Truman himself arrived in Washington on the evening of the seventh.

Officials in Tokyo began receiving reports that some catastrophe had struck Hiroshima within an hour of the blast, but did not learn until early the following day that "the whole city of Hiroshima was destroyed by a single bomb." The cabinet met that afternoon. Moderates such as Premier Suzuki and Foreign Minister Togo hoped to persuade the army and navy hard-liners to accept surrender, provided the emperorship and national polity remained intact, because they would lose no military honor in bowing to superior technology. The militants refused to back down. They questioned whether the bomb was nuclear and said that even if it were, the United States probably did not have sufficient fissionable material to build another or would refrain from using it because of hostile world opinion. They insisted on such concessions with regard to the method of surrender, occupation, and treatment of war criminals that the moderates knew it would be futile to transmit them. No decision was reached.[17]

Even Togo continued to hope at this late date that Soviet mediation would enable Japan to get better terms. On August 8 he informed Ambassador Sato in Moscow, "The situation is becoming more and more pressing, and we would like to know at once the explicit attitude of the Russians."[18] Sato did confer with Molotov that day but not about the proposed Konoye mission. Instead, the Soviet foreign minister informed him that "as of 9 August [Russian time], the Soviet Union will consider it is in a state of war with Japan."[19]

The wording of the Soviet declaration of war was misleading. After Japanese rejection of the Potsdam Declaration, it stated, the other Allies had appealed to Russia for help. And, "Loyal to its Allied duty the Soviet Government has accepted the proposal." There was no such proposal. Truman and Byrnes had refused Molotov's request for a formal invitation precisely because they feared the Soviets would use it to show their magnanimity in responding to the plea of their embattled allies. Molotov poured salt on the wound. He told Ambassador Harriman that although "at one time" it was believed that operations could not begin until after August 15, the Soviet government was now living "strictly" up to its original promise.[20]

The claim that Russia had acted out of the desire to be a good ally rather than to get in on the kill lacked all credibility. Truman told aides on August 9 that he had gone to Potsdam "entirely for the purpose of making sure" that the Soviets would enter the war on or before the fifteenth. Stalin had said he was "ready to go in," Truman continued, but that Soviet forces were not yet fully deployed. The president then told the group that news of Hiroshima "settled it for Stalin, and he said Stalin hastened to get in before Japan could fold up." He gave no indication that this move displeased him.[21]

Truman was right, but for the wrong reasons. Although he and others assumed the Soviets were aware of the American atomic program through espionage, they had no idea how well informed Stalin really was. The Soviet leader had learned in late June that a test was scheduled for about July 10 (it was postponed until the sixteenth because of technical difficulties). Truman's informal approach at Potsdam had confirmed its success. As Stalin also knew that preparations were being made to drop the bomb in the near future, his reply to Truman that he hoped the United States would make "good use of it against the Japanese" was more significant than the president realized.

Stalin wanted to avoid the possibility that Japan would surrender before a Russian declaration of war validated the Yalta Far Eastern agreement. His knowledge of American progress on the bomb and Tokyo's recent overture must have impressed him that time might be running short. On the day he arrived at Potsdam, he called the commander of Soviet forces in Manchuria, Field Marshal Alexander Vassilevsky, to ask if an offensive could be launched ten days before the scheduled date of August 15. He reluctantly accepted Vassilevsky's explanation that he needed more time.

On August 3, after Stalin had returned to Moscow, Vassilevsky reported that Soviet troops would be ready by August 5, but he requested a postponement of the offensive until the ninth or tenth because of weather. Stalin agreed. The decision to move against Japan earlier than the fifteenth, therefore, had been made in part because of atomic bombs but *before* the first one fell on Hiroshima. That event at most led the Soviets to declare war on the ninth (August 8, American time) rather than the tenth.[22]

Had Truman no longer desired Russian entry, as many writers have claimed, he behaved curiously when he learned of it at about 2:45 on the afternoon of August 8. He immediately had his press secretary announce that there would be a press conference at 3 P.M., and efforts were made to round up as many reporters as possible on such short notice.

When those who were available entered Truman's office, they found him seated at his desk flanked by Byrnes and Admiral Leahy. The usually formal president had assumed an uncharacteristic pose, with one leg thrown "carelessly" over the arm of his chair and his arm stretched across the back. He rose and said, "I have only a simple announcement to make. I can't hold a regular press conference today, but this announcement is so important I thought I would call you in. Russia has declared war on Japan. That is all." Truman "rocked with laughter," according to one account, as reporters rushed from the room for the nearest telephones. If this were merely a performance, it is not clear for whose benefit it was intended.[23]

Truman probably was neither surprised nor greatly disappointed by what had happened. Practically everyone, including Byrnes on at least one occasion, had predicted that Stalin would join the war when he thought it was in Russia's interest to do so. That he would risk the possibility of Japanese capitulation before Soviet entry activated the Yalta Far

Eastern accord was remote. And, although the Russians no longer were needed to prevent Japanese troops on the mainland from returning to the home islands, their declaration of war might provide the additional shock necessary to precipitate surrender. That they had apparently acted so hastily, however, heightened apprehensions about Stalin's intentions with regard to maintaining the Open Door in Manchuria.

The Supreme Council for the Direction of the War met at the Imperial Palace in Tokyo on August 9. By this time Soviet armies had plunged into Manchuria and were advancing against once-formidable Japanese forces that had been bled of men and equipment for use elsewhere. Soon after the session began word arrived that another atomic bomb had fallen on Nagasaki. Now the prospect of Soviet mediation had disappeared, and the argument that the United States either did not have any more atomic bombs or would refrain from using them because of world opinion had become irrelevant. There were reports that a third bomb would be used against Tokyo in a few days.

Still the hard-liners refused to compromise. In addition to retention of the emperor and the national polity, they demanded that foreign occupation of the home islands be limited to a few points and that Japanese military forces be permitted to preside over their own disarmament and trials of those accused of war crimes. They reaffirmed their confidence that the decisive battle on Japan's shores would inflict such terrible casualties that the Americans would offer more lenient terms. Acceptance of the Potsdam Declaration, they warned, meant the destruction of Japan as a nation and of the Japanese as a people regardless of enemy propaganda to the contrary.

The basic arguments remained unchanged during a cabinet meeting that afternoon and were restated in the emperor's presence at another Supreme Council meeting that began shortly before midnight. Several individuals were members of both groups. After two hours of wrangling Premier Suzuki took the floor. Stressing the need for speedy resolution, he said that to break the impasse it was necessary to seek the emperor's "decision."

Hirohito spoke briefly. As painful as it was, he said, he had concluded that the war must be brought to an end. Alluding to the argument that national survival could only be assured by a decisive battle in the homeland, he pointed out that preparations were behind schedule and would not "be adequate until after the middle of September." Despite his anguish over the sacrifices already made and the prospects of what was to come, "we must bear the unbearable." "I swallow my own tears," he concluded, "and give my sanction" to accepting the Potsdam Declaration on the basis proposed by Suzuki and Togo. Suzuki then stated, "His Majesty's decision should be made the decision of this conference as well." No one dissented.[24]

Neither the emperor nor the Supreme Council had the authority to make such a decision binding, but their combined influence was enormous. The cabinet met immediately afterward to ratify the "imperial decision." This was done unanimously. Identic notes were drafted to each of the Allies proclaiming Japan's acceptance of the Potsdam ultimatum "with the understanding that the said declaration does not comprise any demand which prejudices the prerogatives of His Majesty as a Sovereign Ruler."[25] These were sent to Sweden and Switzerland for transmittal early in the morning of August 10, and at 7:30 A.M. the Domei News Agency began broadcasting their contents.

MAGIC intercepts made the Japanese notes available in Washington almost immediately, but those handling the traffic did not think it necessary to awaken Truman and other top officials. Couriers delivered copies to the president, the secretaries of State, War, and Navy, and to the chiefs of staff at 7 A.M., or shortly thereafter.[26] Truman summoned Leahy, Byrnes, Stimson, and Forrestal for a meeting at nine to formulate a response.

Leahy was with the president when Byrnes arrived. Both favored retaining the emperor, and Leahy already had composed a draft reply to that effect. When the meeting got underway, Leahy argued that the question of retention was a minor matter compared with delaying victory. Stimson went further, saying that even if the Japanese had not raised the issue "we would have to continue the Emperor ourselves under our command and supervision" to secure the orderly surrender of widely scattered Japanese forces. That was the only way to "save us from a score of bloody Iwo Jimas and Okinawas all over China and the New Netherlands."[27]

Byrnes vigorously objected. He referred to statements about the emperor both Roosevelt and Truman had made and their frequent declarations of support for the unconditional surrender policy, which the Potsdam Declaration recently had reaffirmed. "I cannot understand why now we should go further than we were willing to go at Potsdam," he said, "when we had no atomic bomb, and Russia was not in the war." He emphasized that a retreat from unconditional surrender would invite charges of betraying a major war aim and result in Truman's "crucifixion."[28] He also may have had his own reputation in mind.

Forrestal proposed splitting the difference. Why not answer in such a way that would accommodate Japanese concerns about the emperor, at least temporarily, but that also would indicate determination to carry out the provisions of the Potsdam Declaration? The president approved and told Byrnes to prepare such a message. Byrnes suggested to Stimson after the meeting that the War Department begin working on a draft as well. Later that morning Byrnes read State's version to Stimson over the telephone and had a copy delivered by hand. Stimson found it preferable to the one he and his aides had composed.[29]

Byrnes's draft began by referring to Japan's reservation about retaining the emperor as sovereign ruler. It then stated the Allied position. "From the moment of surrender the authority of the Emperor and the Japanese Government to rule the state shall be subject to the Supreme Commander of the Allied powers," and demanded that the emperor and the Japanese high command sign surrender terms necessary to carry out the Potsdam Declaration. After directing the Japanese to assemble Allied prisoners for quick transport home, it repeated the declaration's provision that the "ultimate" form of government would be established "by the freely expressed will of the Japanese people." It concluded by asserting that Allied forces would remain in Japan until terms set forth in the declaration were achieved. Truman read it to the cabinet that afternoon, then sent it to the other Allies for approval.[30]

Historians Barton Bernstein and Walter LaFeber have claimed that in stipulating that the emperor must be subordinate to the Allied Supreme Commander and by failing to assure perpetuation of the imperial institution, Byrnes unnecessarily prolonged the war and caused the deaths of thousands of Japanese and some Americans.[31] The fact is that no one, save possibly Leahy who seemed unconcerned about the possibility of a resurgent Japan, favored accepting the Japanese condition about maintaining "the prerogatives of His Majesty as a Sovereign Ruler." Retentionists such as Stimson and Grew had advocated a thorough revamping of the imperial system to prevent future domination by the military. Stimson's remark during the meeting in Truman's office about retaining the emperor "under our command and supervision" and his preference for Byrnes's draft of the note over his own testifies to this consensus.[32]

The sole issue at hand was whether to depose the emperor, as Byrnes and others in the State Department wanted to do, or to keep him on to effect an orderly surrender and to serve as a transitional figure pending the establishment of a government representing "the freely expressed will of the Japanese people." Stimson had wanted to inform the Japanese only that "we do not *exclude* a constitutional monarchy under her present dynasty" (emphasis added). To now *guarantee* continuation of the institution without fundamental modification as the "ultimate" form of government would have gone well beyond what Stimson and other retentionists advocated. It also would constitute a public repudiation of the Potsdam Declaration issued only two weeks earlier, the Atlantic Charter, and numerous other statements made throughout the war favoring the right of peoples to choose their own forms of government.[33]

No American president could have approved such a blatant disavowal of stated principles so recently affirmed even if he had wished to do so, which Truman did not. "We told 'em we'd tell 'em how to keep him [the emperor]," he wrote in his diary, "but we'd make the terms." Byrnes's note did not represent the rear guard action of a frustrated abolitionist, therefore, but rather outlined the terms even the most ardent retentionists believed necessary to achieve a lasting peace. He had lost the argument and complied with the president's directive, however reluctantly.[34]

Byrnes came away from the White House meeting angered at being overruled, and he was especially incensed by what he regarded as Leahy's encroachment on his turf. "He said that Leahy still thought he was Secretary [o]f State, just as he had been under Roosevelt," Byrnes's aide noted, "and he had to show him differently." But Truman seems to have made up his mind to retain the emperor even before the Japanese message arrived. General Marshall, not given to idle speculation, said without equivocation on August 9 that "President Truman has no intention to oust the Emperor, rather his purpose is to use the imperial authority to induce all Japanese troops both at home and abroad to lay down their arms." Strict conditions would be imposed, however, "because of the impression throughout our country that the Emperor is one of the war criminals."[35]

Byrnes's initial position and Truman's decision reveal that other concerns took higher priority than their worry about Soviet intentions toward the Open Door in Manchuria and the postwar administration of Japan. The longer the war lasted the more territory the Soviets would occupy and the larger their claim to having contributed to Japan's defeat. Yet Byrnes argued against retaining the emperor, knowing this might prolong the war indefinitely. Even the compromise Truman endorsed ran the risk of rejection and assured delay at best.

Truman and Byrnes sought to protect American interests against possible Soviet intentions in two ways. By designating an American as Supreme Commander, they served notice that there would be neither zonal arrangements in Japan nor administration by an Allied condominium. With regard to protecting the Open Door, they instructed the Joint Chiefs of Staff to notify MacArthur and Nimitz that "the president desires" the occupation of Dairen and a port in Korea "immediately following the surrender of Japan if those ports have not by that time been taken over by Soviet forces."[36]

The impromptu meeting in Truman's office and the hasty drafting of a reply to Japan's note belie the notion that the president and his advisers knew that Japan was on the verge of surrender before the bombs were used and Russia entered the war. The truth is that even after these blows began to fall, there was no way to predict what effect they would have on Japanese determination to continue the war. There is abundant evidence to show that while American officials naturally hoped that capitulation would come sooner rather than later, especially after the first bomb was dropped, they were caught unprepared by the suddenness of the Japanese response and the form it took.

On August 7, the day after Hiroshima, Grew sent a memorandum to Byrnes opposing another official's recommendation that the emperor be tried as a war criminal. Grew wrote that he would support such a move should invasion prove necessary because of the "inevitable loss of life which will occur," but opposed it for the time being. Alluding to those in Japan who favored accepting the Potsdam Declaration, he said it was "possible although by no means certain that this movement may gain headway to the point where the advocates of peace will be able to overcome the opposition of the military extremists and their present control of the Emperor." The decision to try Hirohito, he warned, almost certainly would leak and would undermine the peace movement. He suggested that Byrnes talk the matter over with Stimson and Forrestal, as well as with the president, without conveying any sense of urgency about time.[37]

That same day General Marshall sent an "eyes only" message to MacArthur. Because military intelligence indicated so large a buildup of ground and air forces in Kyushu and southern Honshu, Marshall asked that MacArthur submit his personal estimate as to "possible alternate objectives to OLYMPIC."[38] Marshall's source was a Joint Intelligence Committee report that estimated the number of troops stationed in Kyushu had grown to 545,000. The document went on to describe other developments such as the release of 100,000 sailors from the Imperial Navy to bolster the ground forces. The result of all this was that defenses against invasion *already* were "in excess of that previously estimated as Japanese capability by OLYMPIC target date."[39] MacArthur replied that he opposed the "slightest notion of changing the Olympic operation," stating that intelligence in the past had invariably exaggerated enemy opposition and very probably now was being taken in by Japanese deception.[40]

Stimson met with the president on August 8 to show him photographs of the attack on Hiroshima and reports of the damage caused. The secretary also spoke in behalf of making it as easy as possible for Japan to surrender. He appears to have hoped that the Japanese would seek clarification of the Potsdam Declaration through one of their officials in a neutral country, at which time they could be notified that they might retain the imperial system in the form of a constitutional monarchy.

Toward the end of the session Stimson raised the matter of his health, which he thought might necessitate his resignation. Truman asked him to stay on so as to be "present when the war was over as he hoped it would be very soon, and he told me to take a month's rest when I wanted to but to come back to him when I could." "Very soon" apparently did not mean to the president soon enough to interfere with Stimson's vacation.[41]

The next day, by which time news of the strike on Nagasaki had arrived, Stimson wrote in his diary, "The bomb and the entrance of the Russians into the war will certainly have an effect on hastening victory." How much that effect would be "is impossible yet to determine." Noting that there "will be quite a little space before we intend to drop another" [then scheduled to be available about August 22], he expressed the desire that during the interval "something may be done in negotiating a surrender." His bags were packed and his car waiting the following morning when news of the Japanese peace offer "busted our holiday."[42]

Finally, although the Joint Chiefs of Staff had notified MacArthur and Nimitz on July 26 that "Coordination of plans for the procedure to be followed in the event of a Japanese governmental surrender is now pressing necessity," military planners in Washington had proceeded so leisurely that on August 2 they were only beginning to consider a list of "23 basic subjects on which there is no approved Governmental Policy," and by August 9 a member of the Strategy and Policy Group pointed out that "there is no approved surrender document, surrender proclamation, or General Order No. 1 in existence." Most telling of all, when Byrnes began drafting his reply to the Japanese peace offer on the morning of the tenth, he had to ask Stimson whether a Supreme Commander had been appointed yet. Stimson replied that he "thought" it would be MacArthur but that the navy wanted to have a dual command. Truman named MacArthur the following day.[43]

China approved Byrnes's proposed reply without reservation. London suggested only that the emperor be spared the humiliation of having to sign the surrender terms. The Russians proved less cooperative. An official of the American embassy delivered a copy of the draft to the Soviet foreign office during a meeting Molotov had called with Harriman and British Ambassador Clark Kerr to discuss the Japanese peace offer. Molotov already had informed the others that the Soviets found Japan's reservation unsatisfactory because it fell short of unconditional surrender and was too vague. He gave Harriman the "definite impression that he was quite willing to have the war continue."

After the draft reply arrived, Harriman explained that the United States was willing to maintain the emperor in a reduced role to bring about a quick and orderly surrender of all Japanese armed forces. Molotov raised no objection, but despite Harriman's plea for haste to stop the bloodshed replied that the Soviets would not respond until the following day. When Harriman insisted on an answer sooner than that, Molotov said he would do what he could.

Two hours later the foreign minister summoned Harriman and Kerr again. This time he read a statement that provided for a Soviet veto power over who would be appointed Supreme Commander, and later in the discussion raised the possibility of a joint Soviet-American Supreme

Command. The conversation grew hostile when Harriman pronounced both propositions unacceptable. The ambassador argued that America's right to name a Supreme Commander was unquestionable as it had borne the brunt of the war for four years while the Soviets had been involved for only two days. Molotov closed the meeting by requesting that Harriman relay the Soviet reply to Washington as written.

The impasse ended after Harriman returned to the embassy. Soviet interpreter V. N. Pavlov telephoned him to say that there had been a misunderstanding and that the Soviets only wished to be consulted on the appointment of a Supreme Commander without claiming the right of rejection. Another telephone conversation a few minutes later eliminated Harriman's remaining objection to the Soviet statement Molotov had handed him, and the ambassador transmitted it to Washington on the morning of the eleventh. Truman submitted Byrnes's note to the Japanese via the Swiss and released it over the radio in order to inform Tokyo as quickly as possible. The president had stated that he was prepared to go ahead without Soviet approval.[44]

General Marshall ordered the suspension of area bombing that afternoon, though not by design. Stimson and Forrestal had favored a bombing halt, but Truman wished to keep up the "present intensity" to discourage the Japanese from seeking further concessions. To Marshall's dismay, General Spaatz on Guam was being widely quoted in the press as having said that the "B-29s are not flying today." "This presents very delicate and critical problem to the president," Marshall notified Spaatz, because "Resumption of bombing would appear to indicate that preliminary negotiations had fallen through giving rise to a storm of publicity and confusing views." Marshall ordered Spaatz not to authorize any more missions until told to do so and not to make further press comments "of any kind." Truman later had an aide confirm Marshall's decision by telephone, and directed that leaflets containing the text of the Japanese peace offer and the American response be dropped instead. The reason the B-29s had not been flying, it turned out, was bad weather.[45]

In view of subsequent claims by some admirals and air generals that they knew atomic bombs were superfluous—often cited on faith by approving authors—it is important to understand what they were saying at the time.[46] Two days after Hiroshima, Arnold delightedly informed Spaatz, "Atomic bombing story received largest and heaviest smash play of the entire war with three deck banner headlines evening and morning papers." That same day Marshall rebuked Spaatz and bomber commander Curtis LeMay for telling reporters that because of the bomb "an invasion will not be necessary" and that conventional armies would become obsolete. "However good your intentions," Marshall warned, "you can do incalculable harm."[47]

On August 9, Spaatz and General Nathan Twining, commander of Twentieth Air Force, urged dropping a third on Tokyo. LeMay (who later claimed that atomic bombs "had nothing to do with the end of the war") and Admiral Nimitz concurred. Spaatz explained on the tenth that "the psychological effect on the government officials still remaining in Tokyo is more important at this time than destruction." The next day Arnold sent word to Spaatz that the recommendation was "being considered on a high level."[48]

Spaatz also asked that a "hardstand" with hydraulic lift for loading atomic bombs into aircraft be installed at Okinawa "ready for use not later than 15 September," an odd request if he thought Japan would surrender any moment. He pleaded on August 13 that "every effort be made to expedite delivery of [the third] atomic bomb." A few days after Japan surrendered, Arnold lamented to Spaatz that while he was "naturally feeling very good," it was, "shall I say, unfortunate that we were never able to launch the full power of our bombing attack with the B-29s" to convince "doubting Thomases" how devastating conventional bombing could be. Arnold obviously thought at the time that atomic bombs had ended the war and had denied the air force its opportunity to kill many more thousands of Japanese than had perished at Hiroshima and Nagasaki.[49]

General Marshall had been thinking along different lines while awaiting Tokyo's response to Byrnes's note. If the Japanese did not surrender after several atomic bombs, he reasoned, "we must prepare to continue a prolonged struggle to compel such action."[50] Conventional bombing, after all, had been destroying their cities for months. On the afternoon of August 13, General John E. Hull of the Operation Plans Division told one of Groves's assistants, Colonel L. E. Seeman, that "General Marshall feels we should consider now whether or not dropping them as originally planned, or [if] these we have should be held back for use in direct support of major operations," in other words, as tactical weapons against enemy troop concentrations before and during the invasion.[51]

Although Seeman and Hull discussed the danger posed to advancing forces by an unexploded or partially exploded bomb, neither mentioned the threat of radiation from a successful one. Tests conducted after Alamogordo, with which Seeman (and probably Hull) were familiar, indicated that little radioactivity would be released and that what there was would disperse quickly. Actually, winds had carried the fallout from the test shot well beyond the vicinity of ground zero. "As a result," as one scholar has written, "Manhattan Project scientists tragically miscalculated the radioactivity produced by the explosion."[52]

Whether or how the United States would have used other atomic bombs as they became available can never be known. During his meeting with the cabinet on the tenth, Truman had said he had given orders to stop the atomic bombing of cities because "the thought of wiping out another 100,000 people was too horrible."[53] Groves had notified Marshall earlier in the day that the timetable for shipping components for the next bomb had been advanced so that barring unexpected difficulties it would be ready for use by August 17 or 18. Marshall wrote in longhand on the bottom of the memorandum: "It is not to be released over Japan without express authority from the President," and the shipment was placed on hold.[54] Groves in turn called Oppenheimer in New Mexico on the eleventh to tell him to "ease up on the pressure" to produce more components. A bellicose Oppenheimer replied that as far as he was concerned, "until there is an official announcement that the war is over it is on."[55]

Truman grew impatient when the Japanese failed to respond during the next few days. Marshall ordered MacArthur and Spaatz on August 13 to resume conventional bombing: "The President directs that we go ahead with everything we've got." The next day Arnold informed Spaatz that "as of 1200 14 August the Japanese reply has not been received" and ordered him to "continue maximum effort operations until officially ordered to cease."[56]

Officials also began considering the resumption of atomic attacks. On August 13, Deputy Chief of Staff Handy notified Groves that he wanted "to know the availability of your patients together with the time estimates that they could be moved and placed." This request obviously pertained to using more bombs against Japanese cities, rather than as tactical weapons, because the next day Groves told one of Stimson's assistants that he had talked with Marshall and Handy about releasing the delayed shipment "and they decided to wait until tomorrow noon." Such a deadline would have been meaningless if the "patient" in question was intended for use in supporting the invasion planned for November.[57]

There is evidence that a third bomb might have been dropped on Tokyo as Spaatz, Twining, LeMay, and Nimitz had recommended. On August 9, General Marshall had stated that if Japan did not surrender "it was only a question of days for Tokyo to suffer the effects of the new explosive." On the fourteenth, after meeting with Truman about midday, a British official accompanying the visiting Duke of Windsor reported to London that the president had "remarked sadly that he now had no alternative but to order an atomic bomb to be dropped on Tokyo."[58] Such an operation could not have taken place until about August 22, the originally scheduled date, because of the hold order Marshall had issued on the tenth.

Truman's comment resulted from a misunderstanding. At 11:15 A.M. Washington time, Tokyo had informed its minister in Switzerland to forward to the United States upon receipt "supplementary wire 353," without indicating when it could be expected.[59] Instead of merely reporting that no reply to the Allied offer had yet arrived, however, Swiss officials sent the following message to Washington: "Very urgent 760. Japanese Legation reports that coded cables it received this morning do not contain the answer awaited by the whole world." This made it appear that what the Japanese legation *had* received amounted to a rejection of the Allied note, and the Swiss chargé had hurried over to so inform Truman shortly before he met with the Britons. Actually, the cables referred to consisted of the preliminary one previously mentioned and another demanding compensation for a Japanese hospital ship sunk by an American submarine.[60]

Truman's remark surely stemmed from his immediate frustration over what he regarded as a rebuff, and he may have revised his thinking upon reflection and discussion with individuals such as Stimson. The main reason for retaining the emperor, at least for the time being, was to use his authority to persuade Japanese forces at home and abroad to lay down their arms. Killing him and most of the imperial family would have produced chaos at best, and at worst would have provoked Japanese forces everywhere into a war of annihilation.

Meanwhile, Japanese officials had been meeting in various combinations to consider the Allied note. Militants argued for outright rejection because it contained no softening of the Potsdam Declaration terms they regarded as unacceptable: that Japan would be stripped of its overseas possessions, that the ultimate form of government would be decided by the people, that the enemy would preside over disarmament and war crimes trials, and that there would be an extended occupation of the sacred homeland. The hard-liners repeated their claims that Japan could obtain more favorable conditions after the decisive battle on its shores.

Even some of those who had earlier supported making the peace offer, most notably Premier Suzuki, found Byrnes's reply unsatisfactory. Several of the rejectionists had persuaded Suzuki that its failure to guarantee preservation of the imperial institution might mean the end of Japan's national polity, and that enemy control over disarming was intolerable to the military. Suzuki himself began to argue that they must seek clarification and that surrender was out of the question without formal concessions on these issues.

Moderates eventually prevailed upon the premier to withdraw his objections, pointing out that delay would cause unnecessary bloodshed and ran contrary to the emperor's wish to end the war. The deadlock continued even after Suzuki joined Foreign Minister Togo in favoring acceptance of the Allied note. The appearance of the leaflets Truman had ordered dropped hastened a climax. Peace advocates feared that unless something were done quickly, revelation of the negotiations might cause members of the armed forces to revolt against the government. They secured the emperor's permission to hold another imperial conference on the morning of August 14, Japanese time.

Suzuki opened the meeting and explained its purpose. He then called upon those who opposed accepting the Allied note to make their arguments in the emperor's presence. When they had finished, Hirohito stated that after careful study he considered the Allied note acceptable. He said he realized how difficult it would be for the armed forces to surrender and to see their homeland occupied, but he could not bear to have the war continue, bringing death to "tens, perhaps hundreds of thousands of people." He asked his ministers to prepare a reply to the Allies and an imperial rescript to be broadcast to the nation. Authorities loyal to the throne put down revolts by some army units and foiled efforts to seize the phonograph record containing Hirohito's speech.[61]

At 1:49 A.M. on the fourteenth, Washington time, American monitors picked up and relayed an announcement from the Domei News Agency:

"It is learned that an Imperial message accepting the Potsdam Declaration is forthcoming soon."[62] A crowd began forming outside the White House and reporters jammed the pressroom. Hours passed and no word came (except the misleading cable from the Swiss). Finally, at 1:24 P.M. Washington time, Tokyo sent "supplementary wire 353"—the surrender message—in English to Switzerland. Truman received notification in midafternoon. He promptly informed the Allies that the United States regarded the Japanese message acceptable and arranged for simultaneous release at 7:00 that evening.[63] The war was over, although formal surrender did not take place until September 2 in Tokyo Bay.

A Retrospect

Critics have condemned use of atomic bombs on a number of grounds. The most common is that since the United States ultimately permitted continuance of the emperorship in modified form, Washington should have signaled the Japanese its willingness to do so earlier. Such an approach, according to this view, might have ended the war months sooner. The obvious response is that considering the bitter struggle that took place within the Japanese government over the Allied note even *after* both bombs had been dropped and Russia had entered the war, the notion that comparable terms would have been agreed to before these cataclysmic events is far-fetched, to say the least. No American official, including even such ardent retentionists as Stimson and Grew, had advocated permitting the political structure to survive in anything like its present form.

The proposition that the Japanese would have capitulated in June or July if only Washington had extended a promise about the emperor rests on the fallacy that this was the sole obstacle to peace. Far from it. The very idea of surrender was alien to the Japanese samurai tradition. To give in without a last-ditch struggle, especially to racial inferiors, was virtually unthinkable. This attitude was most widely held in the army, which unlike the shattered navy remained largely intact. "Such a disgrace as the surrender of several million troops without fighting is not paralleled in the world's military history," the commander of Japanese forces in China protested to Tokyo, "and it is absolutely impossible to submit to the unconditional surrender of a million picked troops in perfectly healthy shape to the Chungking forces of defeated China."[1]

There was more. Reduction of the once mighty Japanese empire to the home islands, as the same general put it, "will take us back to the time when the race of Yamato was only 30,000,000 people." To those Japanese imbued with the warrior tradition, the announced goal of eliminating institutions that fostered militarism raised the appalling specter of turning Japan into an Asian Switzerland. Allied prosecution of war criminals was certain to heap dishonor on the army by revealing to the world the barbaric treatment Japanese forces had meted out to the luckless inhabitants of occupied areas. Finally, senior army men were well aware that there were many younger officers who were prepared to take any measures, including assassination, to prevent a humiliating surrender.

Giving assurance about the emperor should have been tried, it has been argued, whatever its chances of success. Quite aside from the fact that a number of individuals genuinely opposed retention as a threat to future peace, such a step was laden with risks. An American initiative would have enabled Japanese hard-liners to claim it showed a weakening of resolve and that continued resistance would wring further concessions. Stalin would have denounced it as a treacherous attempt to negate the Yalta agreement by striking a deal before Russia entered the war. Should it fail, as Cordell Hull had warned, there would have been "terrible political repercussions" in the United States. Small wonder that even though Truman on several occasions had said he had no objection to preserving the emperorship, he insisted that Tokyo make the first move.

The Japanese never indicated openly or in intercepted messages that retention of the emperor was the only prerequisite for surrender. In early July, Captain Ellis M. Zacharias, who as an "official spokesman" of the United States delivered radio broadcasts calling on the Japanese to capitulate, thought he detected a veiled statement to that effect in a speech Premier Suzuki had made. Zacharias thereupon published a letter intended for Japanese eyes in which he explained that unconditional surrender did not mean the end of the Japanese nation. If their "chief concern" was over the national structure and the status of the emperor, he wrote, "the way to find out is to ask." Their own ambassador in Moscow repeatedly said the same thing. No such inquiry was ever made.[2]

A variation on the "missed opportunity" theme is that by August 9, before the second bomb was dropped, "the decision to sue for surrender had become inevitable, though the tragedy's Japanese protagonists needed time to recite their lines." Although neither bomb may have been necessary, therefore, "certainly" the one dropped on Nagasaki was not.[3]

The decision in no way was inevitable because the lines changed drastically. Militants had argued that the Americans had no more atomic bombs or, if they had, would refrain from using them because of adverse world opinion. The second strike appeared to confirm the story that a downed American flyer had concocted for interrogators: the United States had a large number of such weapons and fully intended to employ them. Minister of War Anami, who previously had refused even to admit that the bomb dropped on Hiroshima was atomic, told the cabinet a few hours after Nagasaki that "the Americans appeared to have one hundred atomic bombs . . . they could drop three per day. The next target might well be Tokyo."[4]

A former official of the war ministry later stated that members of the imperial family, including the dowager empress (who began insisting that a "strong aerial shelter" be constructed in her palace for protection against a strike on Tokyo), "appeared to have been shaken extremely by the atomic bomb." He and others believed this "greatly influenced the minds of the advocates of peace." On the morning of August 14, he went on to say, an army field marshal told Anami that atomic bombs "had hardly any effect on the ground one foot below the surface." Obviously grasping an imaginary new straw, Anami urged the marshal, "Please explain about this to the Emperor without fail when you report to him, and make him understand that the atomic bomb is not such a dreadful weapon."[5] So much for merely reciting lines.

American officials had thought that two or more bombs might be necessary to compel surrender because they assumed Japanese hard-liners would try to minimize the first explosion or to explain it away as some sort of natural event such as an earthquake or a "huge meteor." That was one of the reasons for rejecting a demonstration.

The presidential statement released after Hiroshima emphasized that equally devastating bombs "are now in production and even more powerful forms are in development." As a member of OPD put it the next day: "Undoubtedly the biggest question in their minds is how many atomic bombs have we."[6]

Those who minimize the importance of the bombs in ending the war claim that the cumulative effects of battlefield defeats, conventional bombing, and naval blockade already had defeated Japan. Even without extending assurances about the emperor, all the United States had to do was wait—especially after Russia entered the war. The most frequently cited basis for this contention is the United States Strategic Bombing Survey, published in 1946, which stated that Japan would have surrendered by November 1 "even if the atomic bombs had not been dropped, even if Russia had not entered the war, and even if no invasion had been planned or contemplated."[7] Another source to the same effect, trumpeted as a "recently declassified" intelligence report (which actually has been available for nearly twenty years), has been offered by Gar Alperovitz and Kai Bird as additional evidence.[8] As both documents relied on information that became available only after the war ended, they are meaningless with regard to what Truman had to go on at the time.

Of course by any rational calculation Japan was a defeated nation by the summer of 1945. That was not the issue. The issue was how long Japanese militarists were willing to go on fighting in hope of obtaining a negotiated peace through Soviet intercession or, if that failed to materialize, through inflicting unacceptable casualties during the invasion they knew was coming. They held effective power over the government and were capable of defying the emperor, as they had in the past, on the pretext that his civilian advisers were misleading him.

American officials had two main sources for gauging Japanese intentions. MAGIC intercepts informed them that the foreign office continued to seek Russian mediation even after Hiroshima. ULTRA provided evidence of such an imposing buildup on Kyushu that General Marshall began to consider using atomic bombs as tactical weapons in support of the invasion and to question whether it should be mounted there at all. Neither source gave reason to believe that surrender was imminent before the bombs were used.

The War Department Military Intelligence Division reported to Marshall on August 12 that the Japanese still were able to "drag out negotiations for the purpose of obtaining more favorable terms." Their suicide planes and remaining naval elements "have a considerable capacity for inflicting damage on Allied transports and naval craft," and "Large, well disciplined, well armed, undefeated ground forces have a capacity to offer stubborn fanatic resistance to Allied ground operations in the homeland and may inflict heavy Allied casualties." Even atomic bombs, the report predicted, "will not have a decisive effect in the next 30 days."[9]

Concern persisted until the very end that Japanese armed forces might go on fighting regardless of what the government did. On August 11, the assistant chief of staff for army G-2, Major General Clayton Bissell, asked Marshall to make certain that surrender terms included a provision that the Japanese army must immediately begin transmitting all messages in plain text. Although many army codes could be deciphered in days or hours, Bissell pointed out, others had not been broken at all. Forcing the Japanese army to communicate in the clear would "minimize the risk that Japanese armed forces might, without our advance knowledge, issue orders to repudiate the surrender."[10]

During the days before the surrender, there were indications that some elements within the armed forces did intend to disregard peace negotiations. An intercepted communication of August 11 proclaimed, "The Imperial Army and Navy shall by no means return the sword to the scabbard, even though this should mean the total annihilation of the armed forces of the entire nation." That same day the commander of defenses on Kyushu stated, "The plans of the Southern Army have changed in no way whatsoever," and told subordinates to "obey only his orders." As late as August 14, a joint message from the navy vice minister and the vice chief of the naval general staff announced that the navy was determined "to prosecute our holy war to the last man."[11]

A year after V-J Day, the OPD prepared for Secretary of War Robert P. Patterson a top secret report entitled "Military Use of the Atomic Bomb." The study emphasized that before the bombs were used most American military leaders had assumed that Japan would hold out at least until the end of 1945, *after* the invasion had gotten underway. Only General Arnold had put forward the "comparatively optimistic Army Air Forces point of view that the Japanese might be forced to surrender during the month before the invasion of Japan—that is, during October 1945." Considering their previous estimates, the report ended, "military leaders could hardly avoid concluding that the use of the atomic bomb had materially hastened V-J Day."[12]

Statements made by Japanese officials at the time substantiate this conclusion. When informed that a new type of bomb had destroyed Hiroshima, Hirohito had replied that "we must put an end to the war as speedily as possible so that this tragedy will not be repeated." Foreign Minister Togo on August 10 informed commanders overseas that the government had made a peace offer because of "various foreign and domestic circumstances." The next day he explained that the "circumstances" alluded to "of course include the problem of the atomic bomb."[13] Hirohito's Imperial Rescript proclaiming surrender referred to "a new and most cruel bomb," the power of which was "incalculable," and said that it would cause the "obliteration of the Japanese nation" if the war continued. Premier Suzuki was even more explicit. The Japanese war "aim," he stated, had been "lost by the enemy's use of the new-type bomb."[14]

Some authors have claimed that atomic bombs merely provided the "excuse" for Japan's surrender. If they resulted in an earlier capitulation than otherwise would have been the case, however, providing the excuse is indistinguishable from providing the reason. Leon Sigal, although acknowledging that the bombs gave "the emperor a new sense of urgency about ending the war" and provided "those who wanted to sue for peace a pretext for involving him in the policy process," nonetheless concludes, "In the end it was his [Hirohito's] intervention not the atomic bombings or Soviet entry that was decisive." But if the bombs caused the emperor to intervene, as he says, then surely they *were* decisive.[15]

In a recent essay entitled "Hiroshima: A Strategy of Shock," Lawrence Freedman and Saki Dockrill provide copious evidence through statements made at the time that the atomic bombings caught Japanese policy makers "off guard" and that "despite the best efforts of the hardliners, they never recovered their balance." Soviet entry into the war, although constituting yet another heavy blow, caused no such shock. The Japanese army, having for months observed Soviet troop buildups along the Manchurian border, had long believed that Russian entry was merely "a matter of time." Without denying other factors, these authors conclude that "the events from 6 to 9 August 1945 helped to expedite the Japanese decision-making process, which was notoriously slow and time-consuming, and finally led to Japan's decision to terminate the war."[16]

Some accounts, if only by omitting evidence to the contrary, have conveyed the impression that American officials knew beforehand the effects radioactive fallout would have on the inhabitants of bombed cities. They did not. Studies made before and after the New Mexico test indicated that the threat was minimal, which is why General Marshall believed that invading forces could safely cross target areas if atomic bombs were used as tactical weapons.

Earlier experiments (propelling radioactive materials into the air by conventional explosives) and the test explosion itself caused Oppenheimer and others to assume and to report upward that there were two sources of danger: one in the cloud produced by the explosion—hence a peril to those in aircraft flying nearby—and the other on that portion of ground actually touched by the fireball. Measurements taken after the test shot led to the mistaken conclusion that radioactive particles in the cloud would quickly disperse over a wide area, thereby presenting little hazard to those on the ground. Exploding the bombs several thousand feet in the air would minimize the zone affected by the fireball. "With such high firing heights," Oppenheimer wrote on July 23, "it is not expected that radioactive contamination will reach the ground." As one Manhattan Project scientist later put it, the assumption was that "Any person with radiation damage would have been killed with a brick first."[17]

American officials privy to the scientists' calculations were shocked and angered, therefore, when two days after Hiroshima, newspapers carried a story warning that the long-range effects of radiation would be worse than the blast itself. The account relied on an interview with Columbia University professor Harold Jacobson, a former employee of the Manhattan Project.[18]

Groves immediately called Oppenheimer in New Mexico about Jacobson's statement. "This is of course lunacy," Oppenheimer responded. Measurements made after the test explosion indicated that "there would be no appreciable activity on the ground and what little there was would decay very rapidly." He said he was willing to be quoted, which is what Groves did (omitting the charge of lunacy) in a memorandum to the press put out that afternoon by the War Department Bureau of Public Relations. An individual who talked with Marshall the next day reported that the general "was sharply critical of Dr. Harold Jacobson of Columbia University" for making what Marshall believed were irresponsible statements.[19]

Groves on August 11 notified Admiral Nimitz that he had ordered General Farrell on Tinian to send three groups of scientists and technicians to Japan assuming surrender was forthcoming: one for Hiroshima, one for Nagasaki, and another to ascertain "Japanese activities in the field of atomic weapons." The groups dispatched to the bombed cities should enter with the first American soldiers, Groves stated, "in order that these troops will not be subjected to any possible toxic effects although we have no reason to believe that such effects actually exist." Marshall so informed MacArthur the next day.[20]

When reports began arriving from Tokyo that apparent survivors of the blast were dying mysteriously, Groves and others still discounted Jacobson's prediction. A flurry of stories in the American press and on the radio about the mounting toll of casualties led Groves on August 24 to inform Marshall that the inspection teams "are moving into Japan" with the occupying forces. "Although we felt that Japanese casualties from radioactivity were unlikely," Groves wrote, "it is most important, for the future of the atomic bomb work as well as for historical reasons, that we determine the facts."

The next day he placed several telephone calls to a physician at the atomic facility in Oak Ridge, Tennessee. The doctor assured Groves that those afflicted probably suffered from delayed thermal burns rather than radioactivity, and belittled the reports from Japan as "a good dose of propaganda." What bothered Groves most was the unwarranted allegation that American scientists, and by implication policy makers, had known all along what would happen. "That, of course, is what does us the damage."[21]

The gravest charge against Truman and his advisers is that they employed atomic bombs primarily as a diplomatic weapon to intimidate the Soviet Union, not to end a war they knew was all but over. They could have secured Japan's surrender any time during the summer of 1945, had they wished, merely by giving assurances about the emperor. They did not because they wanted the war to continue until they could demonstrate the awesome power of the new weapons. The strikes on Hiroshima and Nagasaki, according to Charles L. Mee Jr., constituted nothing less than "wanton murder." Alperovitz recently has charged, "Every new fragment of secret information suggests the Hiroshima decision was totally unnecessary." The "new fragment of secret information" he referred to, it should be added, was declassified in 1978.[22]

Those responsible for this monstrous crime, according to the conspiracy thesis, sought to conceal their real motives by pretending that they acted to spare the lives an invasion would cost. In reality they knew that by August Japan was on the verge of surrender regardless of guarantees about the emperor, and that Soviet entry into the war almost certainly would have ended it very quickly. Even in the unlikely event that an invasion had to be launched, moreover, casualty estimates projected by military planners were far lower than the bloated figures these officials later cited to fool the gullible. A few writers such as Alperovitz and Bird hint darkly that the cover-up is still going on and that the truth is gradually emerging thanks only to their own unceasing efforts to bare the "secrets that have been kept from the American people." The "secrets" they have revealed thus far have consisted of documents that have been available to the public for decades.[23]

As shown in previous chapters, the "evidence" for this alleged conspiracy ranges from insinuations and unsupported allegations to glaring distortions of the historical record. These latter include, among others, presenting statements made about the enormous leverage atomic bombs would provide against the Japanese as though they actually referred to the Soviets, citing obsolete casualty estimates that never were conveyed to Truman in the first place, and falsely claiming that numerous top-level army and navy officers had pleaded with him not to use the bombs.

That newspaper and magazine editors would publish these sensational charges without attempting to verify their reliability is understandable, if not especially commendable. They make good copy. That presumably knowledgeable historians should treat them with respect, given the practices used to uphold them, is more disturbing. Perhaps this phenomenon stems from a sense of egalitarianism: that all interpretations are created equal and only a scoundrel would call into question the procedures used to support them. Perhaps it derives from the fondness many academics seem to have for tales of conspiracy in high places.[24]

Until newly found documents show otherwise, the available evidence points to the unremarkable conclusion that Truman approved using the bombs for the reason he said he did: to end a bloody war that would have become far bloodier had an invasion proved necessary. A cessation of hostilities, after all, was not the ultimate goal, as some historians seem to assume. Truman was well aware of what Germany had done in a relatively short time after its defeat in the Great War, and he was determined not to accept terms with Japan that would provide what he referred to in one of his speeches as a "temporary respite." Such a settlement, however tempting after years of fighting, would constitute a betrayal of sacrifices already made and of future generations who might have to wage the next war.[25]

What often goes unmentioned is that fighting still was going on in the Philippines, China, and elsewhere, and that thousands of prisoners of war were condemned to live and to die in unspeakable conditions as long as the war continued. Fear also existed that the Japanese would slaughter their captives if the sacred homeland were invaded. Truman was commander in chief of American armed forces and had a duty to the men under his command not shared by those who were free to propose alternatives while bearing no responsibility for the consequences. Or by those passing moral judgment years later. One can only imagine what would have happened had tens of thousands of young Americans been killed or wounded on Japanese soil, and then it became known that the president had chosen not to employ weapons that might have ended the war months earlier.

To say that Truman used the bombs to save American lives is not to imply that he and the men around him were unmindful of the implications nuclear weapons would have on world affairs and on relations with the Soviet Union in particular. The problem was how to deal with this unprecedented new force while trying to cope with a bewildering variety of war-related issues that clamored for attention on a daily basis. In hindsight it is easy to say that the quest for neutralization through international controls should have rendered any other considerations inconsequential. All but the most credulous, however, had strong reservations about trusting the despotic Soviet government to act in good faith on a matter of such potential danger. The possibility of using America's nuclear advantage in the short run to secure other goals naturally appealed to politicians frustrated by what they regarded as Russia's obstructive behavior.

Stimson's rapidly changing and at times contradictory attitudes during this period best illustrate the quandaries involved. He had advised Roosevelt in December 1944 that "it was essential not to take them [the Soviets] into our confidence until we were sure to get a real quid pro quo for our frankness," and had said the same thing to Truman as late as June 6, 1945. Yet as he had written in his memorandum to the president of April 25, he also recognized that "modern civilization might be completely destroyed" unless nuclear weapons were brought under control, and had grown horrified when it appeared that relations with the Soviets might break down over a comparatively minor issue such as Poland.

During his June 6 meeting with Truman, Stimson had recommended that there be "no revelation" about the atomic program until the first bomb had been dropped on Japan. If the Soviets should bring up the subject and ask to be taken in as partners, he proposed, Truman should make the "simple statement that we were not quite ready to do it." Within a month he had reversed himself, now advising the president to tell Stalin at the Potsdam Conference and to assure him that the United States meant to hold later negotiations in order to "make the world peaceful and safe rather than to destroy civilization."

While at Potsdam, "very much impressed on this visit with the atmosphere of repression that exists everywhere," Stimson had experienced another conversion.[26] He began to argue that the promise of nuclear partnership be withheld from the Soviets not merely to gain some specific diplomatic concession but to compel a radical, democratic reorganization of their entire system without which he believed agreements would be worthless. He held to this view for several weeks after returning from Potsdam.

By the end of August, after a good deal of reflection and a series of long talks with John McCloy, Stimson changed his mind yet again. He concluded that efforts to modify the Soviet political structure were doomed to failure and that the threat of atomic bombs dwarfed all other issues. He therefore began working with McCloy on a proposal urging the president to approach the Soviets directly, and as quickly as possible, to bring them into a working partnership. Failure to do so, he believed, would lead to a potentially catastrophic arms race.

Secretary Byrnes had followed a different course. Like Stimson, he had reversed himself between June and early July on the matter of disclosure to the Soviets. The reason for his change of mind is not clear; probably it was because he thought it might provide an advantage in negotiations at Potsdam. At the conference, assuming that Stalin understood Truman's reference to a new weapon meant the atomic bomb, Byrnes had expressed hope that this knowledge would expedite Soviet acceptance of the American position on German reparations. Their agreement a few days later no doubt convinced him that the United States had acquired a valuable new bargaining counter.

Whereas Truman upon his return to Washington told people how well he had gotten along with Stalin, Byrnes expressed bitterness over what he regarded as Soviet duplicity. He opposed making any approaches to them about atomic matters. On August 18 he told George Harrison to inform Oppenheimer that a Scientific Panel proposal about international agreement "was not practical" for the time being, and to urge the scientist "and the rest of the gang" to pursue their work "full force" including development of the "super" (hydrogen bomb). Harrison refused the latter request without the express approval of the president, which was not forthcoming.[27]

Byrnes during this period was preoccupied with the upcoming Council of Foreign Ministers' meeting, scheduled to convene in London the second week of September. There he would have to negotiate with the contentious Molotov on a number of unresolved matters left over from Potsdam and new ones as well. He disagreed with Stimson and McCloy over nuclear sharing, believing that if the United States made known such intent before the conference began, Molotov would have little incentive to compromise on other issues. The secretary therefore wanted to withhold any public mention of collaboration on atomic matters at least until after the meeting adjourned.[28]

An extended analysis of Byrnes's conduct at the London Conference is beyond the scope of this volume. Suffice it to say that he had no intention of even mentioning the bomb himself, let alone threatening anyone with it, but he expected Molotov to raise the question of nuclear sharing. If the Soviet foreign minister had done so, Byrnes told Stettinius during the latter part of the conference, he would have replied, "You don't exchange scientific secrets with us and until we can have a complete arrangement we won't give this thing out." He also said he would have assured Molotov, "I can pledge to you that the United States will never use this bomb at any time unless it is within the United Nations Charter signed at San Francisco and we will only use it in the case of an aggressor to keep the peace."[29]

Molotov not only failed to raise the matter of nuclear sharing but on several occasions made scoffing remarks about the bomb to show that the Soviets were unawed. He was even more unyielding in negotiations than usual, leading one of Byrnes's aides to write, "The demands and tactics of Molotov will make it extremely difficult for Council to get any work done at an early date."[30]

When Byrnes realized that the nuclear monopoly would have no softening effect on Molotov, he quickly reverted to form and began bargaining off the top of his head and retreating from earlier positions in order to make deals. He "took over and sailed off in a way that terri-fied us," a member of the British delegation recalled. Byrnes's attitude toward the Soviet puppet regimes in Romania and Bulgaria provides a case in point. The United States had refused to recognize these gov-ernments since before the atomic test on the ground that they did not conform to the Yalta Declaration on Liberated Europe. Now Byrnes let Molotov know that the United States would be satisfied with purely cosmetic changes, citing Poland as a precedent. The secretary made an extraordinary offer when Molotov still refused to budge. He said he was willing to sponsor a twenty-five-year treaty among the major powers "for the demilitarization of Germany" so that the Soviet Union could let "the small neighboring countries go along their paths of peace and democracy."[31]

Finally, when it appeared that deadlock over Bulgaria and Romania would scuttle the conference, Byrnes was ready to give in. He was prevented from doing so by John Foster Dulles, a Republican member of the American delegation. Dulles likened acceptance of the two regimes to appeasement of Hitler. If Byrnes offered to recognize them, Dulles said he would leave the conference and go public to block what he regarded as a shameful sellout. Byrnes backed off, and the conference broke up with few achievements.[32]

Byrnes consoled himself by blaming Molotov's intransigence, and concluded that the "only hope for next meeting to be held in M[oscow] where he can deal with Stalin."[33] He had done a complete turnabout on nuclear sharing by the time the conference met in December, now wanting it placed at the top of the agenda. He was so anxious to achieve diplomatic successes that the first proposal he made on the subject went beyond the administration's previously stated position by omit-ting a stipulation about proceeding in stages. Only after Acting Secretary Acheson informed him that powerful members of the Senate Special Committee on Atomic Energy had met with the president to insist that controls be established before disclosure did Byrnes submit the para-graph that he said "had been omitted by mistake."[34]

After observing Byrnes during the sessions in Moscow, American chargé George F. Kennan wrote at the time, "He plays his negotiations by ear . . . his weakness in dealing with the Russians is that his main purpose is to achieve some sort of agreement, he doesn't much care what. . . . He wants an agreement for its political effect at home. The

Russians know this." James Conant, a member of the American delegation, received much the same impression after a private talk with Byrnes about the likelihood of achieving progress on atomic controls. Conant, according to his biographer, concluded that Byrnes's primary motivations were "ambition and public relations." Overall, Byrnes was so accommodating that when Truman later read the accords signed in Moscow he complained in a memorandum that he was "tired of babying the Soviets." Such, then, was the extent of what some have called "atomic diplomacy."[35]

Truman, of course, bore final responsibility for American policies. He had assumed office without warning or preparation, at a time when he had to make numerous hard choices that Roosevelt had deferred. The new president inherited an assumption of use with regard to atomic bombs, as evidenced by the formation under FDR of a special bombing unit and the Target Committee, whose task it was to propose which—not whether—Japanese cities would be attacked. The Interim Committee Truman appointed at Stimson's suggestion had as one of its tasks preparation of statements to be released *after* the first bomb was dropped. The committee was not charged with making recommendations about use, although eventually it did so.

Relations with the Soviet Union had deteriorated badly by the time of Roosevelt's death. Following a brief, impulsive attempt to show his personal toughness—his confrontation with Molotov after only eleven days in office—Truman adopted the view put forward by some of his advisers that Stalin represented the faction in Moscow most desirous of cooperation. He thereupon dispatched Harry Hopkins, Roosevelt's closest confidant, to meet with Stalin personally.

Truman hastily accepted an agreement over the Polish provisional government that Hopkins and Stalin cobbled together, even though it provided for only token representation by non-Communists. He tried to clear away other disputes before the Big Three convened at Potsdam and sought to meet privately with Stalin before the conference to iron out differences. "I am not afraid of Russia," he had noted in his diary. "They've always been our friends and I can't see any reason why they shouldn't always be."[36]

During his first weeks in office Truman apparently agreed with Stimson's proposal to seek concessions from the Soviets on other issues in exchange for collaboration with them on nuclear matters. If so, he had abandoned the idea by early July when he extended formal recognition to the Communist-dominated Polish government less than two weeks before the first atomic test.

At Potsdam, Truman's statement to Churchill that he intended to tell Stalin about the bomb at the *end* of the conference shows that he had no intention of using it to influence negotiations. Even after Churchill persuaded him that the delay would prove difficult to explain, he waited until eight days after Alamogordo before informing Stalin. Had he intended at that point to play the nuclear card he certainly would have specified to Stalin that he was talking about atomic bombs, rather than speaking vaguely only about a "new" weapon.

Before the Potsdam Conference Truman had told several people that his first priority was to obtain a reaffirmation of Stalin's promise to join the Pacific war, which he did at their first meeting. He continued to express his desire for Russian participation even after the successful atomic test. There is no evidence that he shared Byrnes's wish to prolong Sino-Soviet negotiations in order to delay Russia's entry, nor did his communications with the Chinese and with Ambassador Harriman indicate such intent.

On September 5 Truman met with Stimson, who outlined his proposal for nuclear sharing and criticized Byrnes's position, which he said would place the United States "on the wrong path" that would "revert to power politics." A week later, at a longer session, the president read Stimson's memorandum on the subject while the secretary followed along on a carbon. "He said step by step as we went through it that he was in full accord with each statement that I made," Stimson noted in his diary, "and that his view on the whole thing was in accord with me. He thought that we must take Russia into our confidence."[37]

At a regular cabinet meeting on September 18, Truman announced there would be a special session three days later on the subject of nuclear sharing. He said his "present disposition was to disclose the principles of atomic energy to the Russians and others but not the method of making the bomb." Stimson spoke first at the later meeting, outlining the points he had made in his memorandum to the president. Acting Secretary of State Dean Acheson, Undersecretary of War Robert P. Patterson, and Secretary of Commerce Henry A. Wallace supported him. Forrestal led the opposition, arguing that the United States should retain its advantage and "exercise a trusteeship over the atomic bomb on behalf of the

United Nations." At the end of the session Truman invited those present to submit their views in writing. It must be emphasized that the subject of discussion was what Truman should propose to Congress, not what he should attempt to do unilaterally.[38]

Word of the special cabinet meeting leaked immediately, provoking a flurry of stories in the newspapers the next day. An allegation that Wallace had recommended turning over "the bomb" to the Soviets proved especially inflammatory, despite denials by Wallace and Truman. The president admitted such a meeting had taken place without divulging details, and said he would make his decision known in a message he intended to send to Congress.[39]

The furor afforded a preview of things to come. Especially ominous was Democratic Senator Tom Connally's response that "complete secrecy should be maintained regarding the atomic bomb." Connally was chairman of the Senate Foreign Relations Committee and a member of the Special Committee on Atomic Energy. One opinion poll taken that month indicated that 85 percent of the respondents opposed nuclear sharing with the Soviets.[40]

Truman submitted his program on the domestic and international aspects of atomic energy to Congress on October 3. A close reading of his recommendations about nuclear sharing reveals that he intended to follow Stimson's advice: after consultations with the British and Canadians, Truman proposed to approach "other nations" in order that "international collaboration and exchange of scientific information might safely proceed."[41]

A firestorm erupted. Everyone interpreted "other nations" to mean Russia. Did this imply, as some were quick to point out, that Truman intended to reveal the results of American research to the Soviets even before controls were established? At his first press conference following his message to Congress and thereafter, Truman tried to defuse the situation by emphasizing that he was referring to basic scientific research rather than the technical know-how required to construct atomic bombs. He had little success. Critics complained that because the United States was so far ahead, "exchange" was a euphemism for what would amount to a giveaway. They rejected distinctions between scientific and technical data, warning that whatever information was provided to the Soviets would hasten the day when they could build their own atomic bombs.

Truman retreated in the face of domestic opposition and British objection. After a conference with the British and Canadians in mid-November, the administration now advocated the creation of a UN commission to study and make proposals about the various aspects of nuclear energy. The commission should proceed in stages, the completion of one being a prerequisite for moving to the next. Meanwhile, the United States would retain its nuclear monopoly until an effective control system had been established and would divulge no technical information without proper safeguards. This was the proposal Byrnes put forward in Moscow (after rectifying his "mistake"). The program ultimately foundered because the Soviets refused to permit on-site inspection, which the United States deemed crucial.

Byrnes later wrote, "History will not disclose action by any government comparable to this generous offer." Many Americans considered it too generous. Within the context of ongoing friction in Europe, China, and elsewhere, the United States nonetheless offered to share highly valuable information it had devoted enormous resources to obtain provided only that verifiable controls be established for protection. Truman had referred to the American nuclear monopoly as a "sacred trust," which threatened no one. Surely the Soviets were to blame for obstructing the establishment of a system that might have prevented the arms race that subsequently came to threaten the planet.[42]

The view must have been quite different from Stalin's perspective. This congenitally suspicious man could not have staked Soviet security on American statements of benign intent. Although he might assume that the United States would not launch an atomic attack over the composition of some regime in East Europe, what of the future? The American proposals must have impressed him as a scheme to retain permanent superiority. Even in the unlikely event he could have been satisfied that the United States would destroy or turn over to the UN *all* its existing bombs—rather than stashing some away in remote caverns— the fact remained that if a protracted conflict developed this nation alone possessed the knowledge to build new ones.

The failure of the American plan has provoked much speculation about what should have been done. If only the United States had approached the Soviets directly at an early stage, runs a common theme, satisfactory arrangements might have been made in an atmosphere of mutual trust. That is what some scientists and others had wanted to do.

Roosevelt had considered but rejected such an approach, as manifested in the Hyde Park Memorandum he and Churchill initialed in the autumn of 1944 and in his unwillingness to inform Stalin at the Yalta Conference. McGeorge Bundy surely is correct in criticizing FDR for not appointing something like the Interim Committee while there was time to consider alternatives in depth without the pressure of deadlines.[43]

Truman took office only a few more than ninety days before the first atomic test. The Interim Committee he appointed advised him in early July to tell Stalin about the bomb at Potsdam and to indicate that discussions about controlling this force for peaceful purposes would be held later. A specific program for nuclear sharing, which could not be justified as part of the war effort, would have to be worked out in cooperation with Congress after the fighting ended.

Some have contended that Truman deliberately misled Stalin at Potsdam by not stating specifically that he was talking about atomic bombs, thereby earning the latter's distrust and assuring the failure of arms control. "Very few turning points of history can be specified precisely," according to this view, but one "can be dated with extraordinary precision: the twentieth century's nuclear arms race began at the Cecilienhof Palace at 7:30 P.M., on July 24, 1945."[44]

Truman could not have anticipated Stalin's failure to inquire about the nature of the weapon. As he assumed the Soviets had an atomic program of their own, most likely he shared Byrnes's view that Stalin would understand once the news had time to "sink in." Byrnes, who learned of the exchange directly from Truman, told Joseph Davies a few days later without equivocation that Stalin had been informed about the atomic bomb and expressed hope that it would influence negotiations.

All the proposals to make an early approach to the Soviets had a common assumption: that Stalin would be so impressed he would be willing to open Soviet borders to roving inspection teams and to place its nuclear program under international supervision. "One thing is clear," as the Franck report put it, "any international agreement on prevention of nuclear armaments must be backed by actual and efficient controls. No paper agreement can be sufficient since neither this or any other nation can stake its whole existence on trust in other nations' signatures."[45]

No doubt an overture should have been made before the bomb became a reality, given the stakes involved. But the arms race did not begin at Potsdam or when the first bomb fell on Hiroshima. It began on February 11, 1943, when the State Defense Committee with Stalin's approval authorized a Soviet nuclear program. Stalin's deep distrust of the Western powers and his determination to prevent outside influences from contaminating the Soviet system made it highly implausible he would have agreed to such a radical abdication of national sovereignty, which even the most visionary plan required. Barring a near miraculous conversion on both sides, an earlier approach to the Soviet Union surely would have met the same fate as the one actually made.[46]

Introduction

1. William Appleman Williams, *The Tragedy of American Diplomacy*, 253–54; D. F. Fleming, *The Cold War and Its Origins*, vol. 1, 298–308.

2. Gar Alperovitz, *Atomic Diplomacy: Hiroshima and Potsdam, the Use of the Atomic Bomb and the American Confrontation with Soviet Power.*

3. The quoted phrase can be found on the back of the 1985 edition of *Atomic Diplomacy*. Lasch's words are in his introduction to Gar Alperovitz, *Cold War Essays*, 12.

4. The second edition is by Penguin Books, New York, 1985; the third edition is by Westview Press, Boulder, Colo., 1995. Subsequent citations of *Atomic Diplomacy* refer to the second edition. The Smith quotation is from the *New York Times Book Review*, August 18, 1985. The reception accorded the original version of *Atomic Diplomacy* is treated more fully in my *The New Left and the Origins of the Cold War*, 63–64.

5. Walter LaFeber, *The American Age: U.S. Foreign Policy at Home and Abroad*, vol. 2, 447.

6. Barton J. Bernstein, "A Postwar Myth: 500,000 U.S. Lives Saved," 38–40. See, for instance, Alperovitz's "Why the United States Dropped the Bomb," 22–34.

7. Interview with Ralph A. Bard, quoted in Nuel Pharr Davis, *Lawrence and Oppenheimer*, 247.

8. See the *New York Times* "Week in Review" section for published passages of the original *Enola Gay* text and for portions of letters written during the controversy. All quotations citing the text are from this source.

9. Dennis Warner and Peggy Warner (with Commander Sadeo Seno, JMSDF [Ret.]), *The Sacred Warriors: Japan's Suicide Legions*, 288, 289. Drea's book is *MacArthur's Ultra: Codebreaking and the War against Japan*; Skates's is *The Invasion of Japan: Alternative to the Bomb.*

10. See chap. 7 of the present work for a full discussion of the false claims that Leahy and Eisenhower protested directly to President Truman.

Chapter 1

1. Because Roosevelt spoke from notes but did not read them, his wording appears in slightly different variations according to what attending reporters

took down. This version is from Samuel I. Rosenman, ed., *The Public Papers and Addresses of Franklin D. Roosevelt*, vol. 12, *1943: The Tide Turns*, 39. Churchill's remark is from the *London Times*, January 27, 1943.

2. Robert E. Sherwood, *Roosevelt and Hopkins: An Intimate History*, 696.

3. Raymond G. O'Connor, *Diplomacy for Victory: FDR and Unconditional Surrender*, 37–38.

4. The Roosevelt quotation is from Papers Relating to the Foreign Relations of the United States, *Conferences at Washington, 1941–1942, and Casablanca, 1943*, 506. The notes Roosevelt used for the press are from pages 836–37. Volumes in this series hereafter will be referred to as FRUS, along with the conference name or, if one of the annual series, the year and volume number.

5. Maurice Hankey, *Politics, Trials, and Errors*, 31.

6. The exchange of messages is in Sherwood, *Roosevelt and Hopkins*, 972–73.

7. Churchill suggested that "we release a statement to the effect that the United Nations are resolved to pursue the war to the bitter end, neither party relaxing its efforts until the unconditional surrender of Germany and Japan has been achieved." FRUS, *Casablanca*, 635.

8. *London Times*, January 27, 1943.

9. Hanson W. Baldwin, *Great Mistakes of the War*, 14. The most detailed critique is Anne Armstrong, *Unconditional Surrender: The Impact of the Casablanca Policy upon World War II*; Hankey's *Politics* also is highly critical.

10. The best defense of the unconditional surrender formula remains O'Connor's *Diplomacy for Victory*. See also John L. Chase, "Unconditional Surrender Reconsidered," in Robert A. Divine, ed., *Causes and Consequences of World War II*, 183–201; John P. Glennon, "This Time Germany Is a Defeated Nation: The Doctrine of Unconditional Surrender and Some Unsuccessful Attempts to Alter It," in Gerald N. Grob, ed., *Statesmen and Statecraft in the Modern West: Essays in Honor of Dwight E. Lee and H. Donaldson Jordon*, 109–51; and Paul Kecskemeti, *Strategic Surrender: The Politics of Victory and Defeat* (Stanford: Stanford University Press, 1958). The Roosevelt quotation is in Elliott Roosevelt, ed., *FDR: His Personal Letters, 1928–1945*, vol. 2, 1485–86.

11. As quoted in Robert Dallek, *Franklin D. Roosevelt and American Foreign Policy, 1932–1945*, 349.

12. The best account of the Darlan deal is in Stephen E. Ambrose, *The Supreme Commander: The War Years of General Dwight D. Eisenhower*, chap. 9. The Roosevelt quotation is on page 131.

13. O'Connor, *Diplomacy for Victory*, 2–5.

14. *Public Papers and Addresses*, vol. 13, *Victory and the Threshold of Peace*, 210; O'Connor, *Diplomacy for Victory*, 5.

15. At times FDR invented a fairly lengthy dialogue between the two men.

See press conference of July 29, 1945, cited in *Public Papers and Addresses*, vol. 13, *Victory and the Threshold of Peace*, 210.

16. As quoted in Dallek, *Franklin D. Roosevelt*, 472–73.

17. Roosevelt, *FDR: His Personal Letters*, vol. 2, 1420.

18. Rosenman, *Public Papers and Addresses*, vol. 13, 65.

19. Meeting of the Combined Chiefs of Staff with Roosevelt and Churchill, February 9, 1945, FRUS, *The Conferences at Malta and Yalta, 1945*, 826.

20. Rosenman, *Public Papers and Addresses*, vol. 13, 570–86.

21. The Cairo Declaration is in *Department of State Bulletin* 9 (1943), 393; the "genie" quotation is from Thomas A. Bailey, *A Diplomatic History of the American People*, 760.

22. *Public Papers of the Presidents: Harry S. Truman, 1945–1946*, 2.

23. War Department intelligence staff comments on "Ending the War with Japan," attached to Marshall memorandum to Stimson, June 15, 1945, George A. Lincoln Papers, United States Military Academy, West Point, New York. Hereafter cited as Lincoln Papers.

24. The competing arguments, and those who made them, will be analyzed in subsequent chapters.

25. FRUS, *Conferences at Cairo and Teheran, 1943*, 71, 147, 152–55.

26. See Roosevelt-Stalin meeting, February 8, 1945, FRUS, *Yalta*, 766–71. The agreement is on page 984.

27. Roosevelt to Churchill, April 6, 1945, Map Room Files, Roosevelt Papers, Roosevelt Library, Hyde Park, N.Y.

28. Leslie R. Groves to Marshall, December 30, 1944, FRUS, *Yalta*, 383–84. See Groves's notation that "The Sec. of War and the President both read this paper and approved it."

29. Not all the scientists were as certain as the report implied. A week after it was shown to Roosevelt, Nobel Prize–winning physicist Ernest O. Lawrence wrote that despite "repeated assurances" that the gun-type bomb would work, "I should like nevertheless to see a trial at the earliest moment." Lawrence to Leslie R. Groves, Microfilm roll 1, "Correspondence (Top Secret) of the Manhattan Engineer District, 1942–1946," National Archives microfilm publication M1109, Washington, D.C., 1980. Hereafter cited as MED with microfilm roll number.

30. Harry S. Truman, *Year of Decisions*, 87.

Chapter 2

1. Truman, *Year of Decisions*, 9–10.

2. Winston S. Churchill, *Triumph and Tragedy*, 437.

3. For an excellent analysis of these discussions, see Russell D. Buhite, *Decisions at Yalta: An Appraisal of Summit Diplomacy,* chap. 3. The Roosevelt remark is in William D. Leahy, *I Was There: The Personal Story of the Chief of Staff to Presidents Roosevelt and Truman Based on His Notes and Diaries Made at the Time,* 315–16.

4. FRUS, *1945,* vol. 5, 129–30, 134–38, 140–44, and see Laurance J. Orzell, "A Painful Problem: Poland in Allied Diplomacy, February–July, 1945," 147–69.

5. FRUS, *1945,* vol. 5, 145–47, and Robert J. Maddox, "Roosevelt and Stalin: The Final Days," 118.

6. Albert Resis, ed., *Molotov Remembers: Inside Kremlin Politics,* 51.

7. Russell D. Buhite, "Soviet-American Relations and the Repatriation of Prisoners of War, 1945," 384–97. For Soviet charges about the negotiations in Italy, see FRUS, *1945,* vol. 3, 736–40.

8. Roosevelt to Churchill, March 29, 1945, FRUS, *1945,* vol. 5, 189–90; Roosevelt to Stalin, April 1, 194–96.

9. Roosevelt to Stalin, April 4, 1945, in FRUS, *1945,* vol. 3, 740–45; Roosevelt to Churchill, April 6, Map Room File, Roosevelt Papers.

10. The exchange of cables about Poland is in FRUS, *1945,* vol. 5, 196–98, 201–5, 213–16; about surrender negotiations in Italy, FRUS, *1945,* vol. 3, 749–51, 756.

11. The Churchill quotation is in *Triumph and Tragedy,* 437; the quotation about discouraging Churchill from going before Parliament is in a memorandum attached to FDR's cable of April 10, Map Room Files, Roosevelt Papers. Roosevelt's cable of the eleventh is in FRUS, *1945,* vol. 5, 210. The latter message often is cited as if it were FDR's last, considered testimony on relations with the Soviets rather than a specific effort to dissuade Churchill from doing something rash.

12. Truman to Churchill, April 13, 1945, FRUS, *1945,* vol. 5, 211–12.

13. Maddox, "Roosevelt and Stalin," 118.

14. Memorandum of telephone conversation between Stettinius and James C. Dunn, April 14, 1945, Calendar Notes, Stettinius Papers, University of Virginia Library.

15. Truman, *Year of Decisions,* 70–72.

16. Ibid., 10–11.

17. Bethe and Teller to J. Robert Oppenheimer, August 21, 1943, Box 20, Oppenheimer Papers, Library of Congress (hereafter referred to as LC).

18. Richard G. Hewlett and Oscar E. Anderson Jr., *A History of the United States Atomic Energy Commission,* vol. 1, *The New World,* 252–53, 314.

19. *Public Papers of the Presidents,* 2.

20. Wilson D. Miscamble, "Anthony Eden and the Truman-Molotov Conversations, April 1945," 167–80.

21. "Bohlen Memorandum of the White House Meeting," April 23, 1945, FRUS, *1945*, vol. 5, 252–55; the Stimson quotation is from a diary entry, April 23, Stimson Papers.

22. FRUS, *1945*, vol. 5, 256–58.

23. Truman's account of the meeting is in his *Year of Decisions*, 79–82. Bohlen's denial of the exchange is in Robert J. Donovan, *Conflict and Crisis: The Presidency of Harry S. Truman, 1945–1948*, 445n3. Leahy diary entry, April 13, 1945, Leahy Papers, LC.

24. W. Averell Harriman and Elie Abel, *Special Envoy to Churchill and Stalin, 1941–1946*, 454; and for Harriman's protest to Truman that he had been "too tough," see "Off the Record Discussion of the Origins of the Cold War," May 31, 1967, Mark Chadwin Files, Box 869, W. Averell Harriman Papers, LC. Hereafter cited as "Off the Record Discussion," Box 869, Harriman Papers.

25. Joseph E. Davies diary entry, April 30, 1945, Box 16, Joseph E. Davies Papers, LC.

26. Stimson diary entries, April 23–25, 1945; and Groves's account in "Report of Meeting with the President, April 25, 1945," in Box 1, Leslie Groves Collection, Marshall Library. See "Memorandum discussed with the President, April 25, 1945," Harrison-Bundy File, Folder 60, Manhattan Engineer District Records, NA.

27. Truman, *Year of Decisions*, 87. Gar Alperovitz, in *Atomic Diplomacy*, 111, and elsewhere, cited this remark in a paragraph devoted entirely to relations with the Soviet Union without even suggesting it may have referred to Japan. Lloyd C. Gardner similarly misused it in *Architects of Illusion*, 181.

28. Hewlett and Anderson, *The New World*, 314.

29. Leslie R. Groves, *Now It Can Be Told: The Story of the Manhattan Project*, 267. Minutes of the April 27 meeting are in Microfilm roll 1, M1109, MED.

30. See Groves memorandum to Marshall, June 30, 1945, proposing that Kokura, Hiroshima, and Niigata be spared conventional bombing and his memorandum of July 9 noting approval by the Joint Chiefs of Staff, both in Microfilm roll 1, MED.

31. Harrison to Stimson, May 1, 1945, Microfilm roll 1, MED; Stimson diary entry, May 1, Stimson Papers.

32. Stimson diary entries, May 2 and 3, 1945, Stimson Papers; Hewlett and Anderson, *The New World*, 344–45.

33. Stimson diary entry, May 3, 1945, Stimson Papers.

34. Entries of May 9 and June 7, 1945, *Interim Committee Log*, Xerox 1482/191, Marshall Library.

35. *Public Papers of the Presidents*.

36. Grew memorandum of conversation with Truman, May 7, 1945, Item 5-E–20, in Makoto Iokibe (ed.), "The Occupation of Japan: United States Planning Documents, 1942–1945." This is an enormous collection of documents on microfiche that hereafter will be referred to as *Occupation of Japan*, with item number.

37. How Zacharias came to write the statement is in his *Secret Missions: The Story of an Intelligence Officer* (New York: G. P. Putnam's Sons, 1946), 341–50; the entire text of his broadcast to the Japanese is on pages 399–401.

38. *New York Times,* May 10, 1945.

39. Joseph Grew-Leo T. Crowley Memorandum, May 11, 1945, and Truman's memorandum, same date, President's Secretary's File, Truman Papers. For evidence that what happened was a bureaucratic foul-up rather than an attempt to coerce the Soviets, see Grew-Crowley telephone conversation, May 12, vol. 7, Grew Papers; Minutes of Secretary's Staff Committee, May 14, Notter File, Box 304, Record Group 59 NA; and John G. B. Hutchins, Director-Russian Area, to Major General John Y. York Jr., Executive, The President's Soviet Protocol Committee, May 14, Lincoln Papers.

40. Davies Journal, May 2, 1945, Box 16, Joseph E. Davies Papers, LC; Molotov replied on May 9 that he was seeking settlements that would be in the interests of not only the Soviet Union and the United States but also "freedom loving peoples of the whole world."

41. Davies to Molotov for Stalin, May 14, 1945, and Davies journal entry same date, both in Box 17, Davies Papers. See also Truman diary entry for May 22, in Robert H. Ferrell, ed., *Off the Record: The Private Papers of Harry S. Truman*, 35.

42. For the inquiries Truman made about Hopkins, see appointment sheet entry, May 19, 1945, in Ferrell, ed., *Off the Record,* 31; Harriman later said that Truman "didn't like Hopkins. He didn't have much confidence in him." "Off the Record Discussion," Box 869, Harriman Papers.

43. The Truman quotation is from appointment sheet, May 18, 1945, in Ferrell, ed., *Off the Record,* 30; Leahy's quote is in a diary entry, May 20, Leahy Papers.

44. The Stettinius quotation is from Calendar Notes, April 13, 1945, Edward R. Stettinius Papers, University of Virginia. Hopkins's remark is in Truman, *Year of Decisions,* 31.

45. The Harriman and Bohlen statements are in Memorandum of Conversation, May 15, 1945, vol. 7, Grew Papers, Harvard. Anthony Eden shared this view. He told Forrestal and Leahy that "most of the difficulty" with the Russians was due to "Molotov's intransigence." Eden believed that "Molotov did not completely inform Stalin, and that when he did talk to him he talked with prejudice toward the British and the United States." Forrestal diary entry for April 21, Forrestal Papers, Firestone Library, Princeton University.

46. Truman's remark is in Report by [Lt.] Col. [Bernard] Bernstein, June 5, Book 852, 53–62, Henry J. Morgenthau Diaries, Roosevelt Library.

47. Truman diary entry for May 22, 1945, President's Secretary's File, Truman Papers.

48. Truman, *Year of Decisions*, 264.

49. The Yalta Far Eastern accord is in FRUS, *Yalta*, 984. Grew initiated a review of the Far Eastern situation on May 12 with a memorandum to Stimson and Forrestal asking their opinion on several aspects of the Yalta accord. For the results of this review, see Robert James Maddox, *From War to Cold War: The Education of Harry S. Truman*, 103.

50. Truman appointment sheet entry, May 21, 1945, in Ferrell, ed., *Off the Record*, 33.

51. Truman appointment sheet entry, May 19, 1945, and diary entry, May 22, in Ferrell, ed., *Off the Record*, 31–32, 35.

52. The Truman quotation is from his diary entry, May 22, 1945, in Ferrell, ed., *Off the Record*, 35; for Davies's access to the Map Room Files and being told by Truman about the atomic bomb, see journal entries for May 21 and 23, Box 17, Davies Papers. Truman's note to Churchill also is in this container.

Chapter 3

1. John J. McCloy diary entry, May 21, McCloy Papers, Amherst College Archives.

2. FRUS, *The Conference of Berlin (The Potsdam Conference)*, 1945, vol. 1, 32–33. Hereafter cited as *Potsdam Papers*, with volume and page number.

3. Hopkins-Stalin talks on Poland are in FRUS, *1945*, vol. 7, 314.

4. All quotations are from *Potsdam Papers*, vol. 1, 45–47.

5. Stettinius diary entries, May 26, June 1 and 2, *New York Times*, June 2 and 3.

6. FRUS, *1945*, vol. 1, 1171.

7. Eben A. Ayers diary entry, June 1, 1945, in Robert H. Ferrell, ed., *Truman in the White House: The Diaries of Eben A. Ayers*, 39.

8. Truman to Churchill, June 1 and 7, 1945, FRUS, *1945*, vol. 5, 314–15, 331–32.

9. Davies diary entry, June 4, 1945, Box 17, Davies Papers; Stimson diary entry, June 6, Stimson Papers; Truman diary entry, June 7, in Ferrell, ed., *Off the Record*, 44. On June 14, after reading the minutes of the Hopkins-Stalin talks, Truman informed Soong that "Stalin's assurances with regard to the sovereignty of China and Manchuria and elsewhere had been even more categoric than he had told Dr. Soong the last time he saw him." Grew memorandum of conversation, June 14, vol. 7, Grew Papers.

10. Davies diary entries, May 26 and 27, 1945, Box 17, Davies Papers.

11. Churchill to Truman, May 31, 1945, *Potsdam Papers*, vol. 1, 89.

12. Stimson diary entry, May 27, 1945, Stimson Papers. The secretary discussed the matter repeatedly with Marshall, McCloy, and others for the next few days. See especially McCloy's memorandum of conversation with Stimson and Marshall, "Objectives toward Japan and methods of concluding war with minimum casualties," following diary entry for May 29, 1945, McCloy Papers.

13. Hewlett and Anderson, *The New World*, 345.

14. All quotations in these paragraphs are from "Notes of the Interim Committee Meeting, Thursday, 31 May 1945," in Microfilm roll 4, M1109, MED.

15. Hewlett and Anderson, *The New World*, 358.

16. "Notes of the Interim Committee Meeting, Thursday, 31 May 1945," Microfilm roll 4, M1109, MED.

17. "Notes of the Interim Committee Meeting, Friday, 1 June 1945," Microfilm roll 4, M1109, MED.

18. Arthur Holly Compton, *Atomic Quest*, 238.

19. Interim Committee Log, entry for June 7, 1945, Xerox 1482/191, Marshall Library.

20. Stimson diary entry, June 6, 1945, Stimson Papers.

21. James F. Byrnes, *Speaking Frankly*, 262. Byrnes mistakenly refers to the Interim Committee meeting as having taken place on July 1.

22. Stimson diary entry, December 31, 1944, Stimson Papers. Stimson's memorandum on the meeting and one by Groves are in Microfilm roll 3, M1109, MED. Groves's file "Russian Activities" is in Microfilm roll 4, same source.

23. Memorandum of Sir John Anderson's talk with Joliot-Curie, 23 February 1945, Microfilm roll 4 , M1109, MED.

24. Alperovitz, *Atomic Diplomacy*, 192–93.

25. Otto Frisch, *What Little I Remember*, 159.

26. Hewlett and Anderson, *The New World*, 374–76.

27. The Byrnes quotation is from a diary entry, June 6, 1945, Box 17, Davies Papers; the Truman quotation from his diary, June 7, is in Ferrell, ed., *Off the Record*, 44.

28. Memorandum of conversation, June 9, 1945; Truman to Patrick J. Hurley, June 9, FRUS, *1945*, vol. 7, 896–98. See also Grew memorandum of conversation with Soong, June 11, vol. 7, Grew Papers. Messages to Churchill and Stalin are from June 15, Map Room Files, Truman Papers.

29. FRUS, *1945*, vol. 7, 901–4.

30. Diary entry, June 12, 1945, Box 17, Davies Papers.

31. Maddox, *From War to Cold War*, 18–23.

32. Truman appointment sheet, May 19, 1945, in Ferrell, ed., *Off the Record*, 30–31.

33. Grew memorandum of conversation, June 18, 1945, vol. 7, Grew Papers.

34. Leahy memorandum for the Joint Chiefs of Staff, June 14, 1945, attached to JCS 1388/1, Xerox 1567, Marshall Library; the Truman quotation is from a diary entry, June 17, in Ferrell, ed., *Off the Record*, 47.

35. Robert Joseph Charles Butow, *Japan's Decision to Surrender*, 99–100.

Chapter 4

1. Grew memorandum of conversation with the president, June 18, 1945, vol. 7, Grew Papers. Grew on June 16 had given Truman a telegram Stettinius had sent the day before, in which the secretary recommended that an ultimatum to Japan should "be made into a three or four power demand to be issued at or after the Big Three meeting." Grew memorandum of June 16, same source. When Truman on the eighteenth asked Grew to have the subject placed on the agenda for the summit, Grew noted, "the President had before him the secretary's telegram."

2. All quotations in these paragraphs are from "Extracted from Minutes of Meeting Held at the White House, 18 June 1945 at 1530," attached to JCS 1388/1, "Details of the Campaign against Japan," Xerox 1567, Marshall Library. Hereafter cited as "White House Meeting," Xerox 1567.

3. Leahy, *I Was There*, 384–85.

4. Larry I. Bland, ed., *George C. Marshall: Interviews and Reminiscences for Forrest C. Pogue*, 431–33. And see Thomas T. Handy, transcript of interviews February 28 and April 23, 1974, USAMHI. According to Handy, Marshall said later that "the president [FDR] had ruined Leahy." Roosevelt had referred to Leahy as "a kind of legman for me." The quotation about Leahy is from Grace Person Hayes, *The History of the Joint Chiefs of Staff in World War II: The War against Japan*, 726.

5. "White House Meeting," Xerox 1567.

6. Truman, "Special Message to Congress on Winning the War with Japan," June 1, 1945, *Public Papers of the Presidents*, 98.

7. "White House Meeting," Xerox 1567.

8. Unedited version of the "White House" meeting is Xerox 1537, Marshall Library.

9. John J. McCloy, *The Challenge to American Foreign Policy*, 40–42. McCloy gave a slightly different version to James Reston, who published it in his *Deadline: Memoirs*, 493–502. Although McCloy did favor issuing a warning to Japan, his accounts—especially the one he gave Reston—probably are more dramatic than what actually happened. Neither he nor Stimson mentioned it in their diaries, nor is there corroboration in the diaries or memoirs of the other participants.

10. Truman, *Year of Decisions*, 416–17; Henry L. Stimson and McGeorge Bundy, *On Active Service in Peace and War*, 619, give the figure as one million lives; Byrnes in *Speaking Frankly* writes of one million "casualties," 262.

11. JWPC 369/1, "Details of the Campaign against Japan," June 15, 1945, ABC File 384, RG 319, NARS.

12. Gar Alperovitz has put forward this argument in a number of journals and newspapers, each time claiming to have uncovered "new evidence" that turns out to have been known by other scholars for years. An example is "Why the United States Dropped the Bomb," 22–34. A similar thesis was put forward by Rufus E. Miles Jr., "Hiroshima: The Strange Myth of Half a Million Lives Saved," 121–40. Barton J. Bernstein relied on the JWPC estimate in, among other places, "A Postwar Myth: 500,000 Lives Saved," 38–40. His conclusion is less conspiratorial. He merely states that the "myth" helped deter Americans from asking "troubling questions" about the use of the bomb and that destruction of the myth "should reopen these questions."

13. King memorandum to Joint Chiefs of Staff, "Proposed Changes to Details of the Campaign against Japan," June 20, 1945, Xerox 1567, Marshall Library. King also pointed out that the statement in JCS 1388 that the highest casualties occur during the "assault phase" has not "been borne out in the latest operations in the Pacific where the Japanese have chosen not to defend the beaches."

14. The Joint Planners report of June 16 and Hull's "Amplifying Comments" of June 17 are in ABC File 384, RG 319, NARS.

15. Hull interview, Hull Papers, USAMHI. Army Deputy Chief of Staff Thomas T. Handy later said that an invasion would have been an "extremely expensive" operation. When the interviewer asked if it would be "something like Verdun," Handy replied, "And that's what we had in mind, all of us, and I think, if it hadn't been for the bomb we would have had to do it." Handy interview, April 23, 1974, USAMHI.

16. JCS 924/2, "Operations against Japan Subsequent to Formosa," August 30, 1944, ABC File 384, RG 165, NARS.

17. Hoover's memorandum, the Strategy and Policy Group's analysis of it, and Stimson's report to Truman of June 15, 1945, are all in Stimson "Safe File," RG 107, NARS.

18. MacArthur to Marshall, June 18, 1945, Xerox 1537, Marshall Library. The estimate from his headquarters, MacArthur stated, was "purely academic and routine and was made for planning alone. I do not anticipate such a high rate of loss." He submitted no alternate figure. Nimitz's estimate is in King memorandum to Joint Chiefs of Staff, June 20, Xerox 1567, same source.

19. The history of the Met Lab is treated thoroughly in Hewlett and Anderson, *The New World*, and see part 10, "Chicago Group," in "Notes of the Interim Committee Meeting, 31 May 1945," Microfilm roll 4, M1109, MED.

20. Hewlett and Anderson, *The New World*, 365–66.

21. The Franck report and Compton's letter are reprinted in Michael B. Stoff,

Jonathan F. Fanton, and R. Hal Williams, *The Manhattan Project: A Documentary Introduction to the Atomic Age*, 138–47.

22. The Scientific Panel's recommendations are reprinted in Stoff, Fanton, and Williams, *The Manhattan Project*, 149–50.

23. "Notes of the Interim Committee Meeting, 21 June 1945," Microfilm roll 4, M1109, MED.

24. For a favorable biography, see William Lanouette with Bela Szilard, *Genius in the Shadows: A Biography of Leo Szilard, the Man behind the Bomb*.

25. Lanouette, *Genius*, 237–42, 248–55.

26. "Notes of the Interim Committee Meeting, 31 May 1945," Microfilm roll 4, M1109, MED.

27. Szilard to Bush, January 14, 1944, in Spencer R. Weart and Gertrud Weiss Szilard, *Leo Szilard: His Version of the Facts; Selected Recollections and Correspondence*, vol. 2, 161–63.

28. The memorandum is reprinted in Weart and Szilard, *His Version*, 196–204.

29. Lanouette, *Genius*, 261–62.

30. James F. Byrnes, *All in One Lifetime*, 284–85.

31. Szilard's "Recollections," in Weart and Szilard, *His Version*, 181–85. An earlier version of Szilard's account of the meeting is in "A Personal History of the Atomic Bomb," 14–15.

32. Alice K. Smith, *A Peril and a Hope: The Scientists' Movement in America, 1945–1950*, 29.

33. Szilard's "Recollections," in Weart and Szilard, *His Version*, 185.

34. Hewlett and Anderson, *The New World*, 358.

35. Hans Bethe, in his review of a biography of Szilard, *Physics Today* (September 1993), 63.

36. Compton, *Atomic Quest*, 239–41; Weart and Szilard, *His Version*, 186. Szilard went on to say that the Japanese should have been notified to evacuate a city before dropping a bomb on it.

37. "Notes of the Interim Committee Meeting, 21 June 1945," Microfilm roll 4, M1109, MED.

38. Hewlett and Anderson, *The New World*, 370; the Bard memorandum is reprinted in Stoff, Fanton, and Williams, *The Manhattan Project*, 162. And see Interim Committee Log, entry for July 2, 1945, Xerox 14588/191, Marshall Library.

39. John McCloy to Stimson, June 1, 1945, Stimson "Safe File," RG 105, NARs; for the Forrestal dinner, see McCloy diary entry for June 21, McCloy Papers.

40. This account, based on an interview with Bard, is in Davis, *Lawrence and Oppenheimer*, 247. Bard presumably told Davis he had resigned over the issue.

41. Stimson diary entry, June 19, 1945, Stimson Papers.

42. Stimson diary entry, June 25, 1945, Stimson Papers.

43. Stimson diary entry, June 26 to June 30, 1945, Stimson Papers.

44. Stimson diary entry, July 2, 1945, Stimson Papers. A copy of his memorandum and cover letter to the president, both dated the second, are attached.

Chapter 5

1. General George A. Lincoln, Operations and Plans Division to Assistant Chief of Staff General John E. Hull, June 29, 1945, Lincoln Papers; and McCloy diary entry, June 30, McCloy Papers.

2. Stimson's account of the meeting is in his diary entry, July 2, 1945, Stimson Papers. A copy of his memorandum and the draft warning are included.

3. See Robert L. Messer, *The End of an Alliance: James F. Byrnes, Roosevelt, Truman, and the Origins of the Cold War,* chaps. 1 and 2. Messer also has a briefer account of the Truman-Byrnes relationship in Richard S. Kirkendall, ed., *The Harry S. Truman Encyclopedia,* 41–42.

4. Truman diary entry, July 7, 1945, in Ferrell, ed., *Off the Record,* 48.

5. The swearing-in story is in Walter Brown diary entry for July 3, 1945, Folder 602, James F. Byrnes Papers, Clemson University; the description of Byrnes by a British diplomat is reprinted in its entirety in James L. Gormly, "Secretary of State Byrnes: An Initial British Evaluation," 198–205.

6. Arthur Krock, "Our Policy toward the Emperor of Japan," *New York Times,* July 5, 1945.

7. FRUS, *1945,* vol. 6, *Japan,* 895–97.

8. Cordell Hull, *The Memoirs of Cordell Hull,* vol. 2, 1593–94.

9. Stimson diary entry, July 3, 1945, Stimson Papers.

10. Groves's draft and the British note are both in Item 5-F–2, *Occupation of Japan;* the quotation about recording British assent is in "Interim Committee Log," Xerox 1488/191, Marshall Library; and the Combined Policy Committee Notes are in *Potsdam Papers,* vol. 1, 941–42.

11. Memorandum for the President, July 6, 1945, Samuel I. Rosenman Papers, Truman Library.

12. *Potsdam Papers,* vol. 1, 733–34.

13. Harriman to Secretary of State, June 21 and 23, FRUS, *1945,* vol. 5, 352–60.

14. Memorandum of telephone conversation between Stettinius and Pauley, April 29, 1945, Calendar Notes, Stettinius Papers.

15. Pauley to I. Maisky, July 3, 1945, Clark Clifford Papers, Truman Library.

16. Harriman to Secretary of State, April 6, 1945, in Forrestal diary, vol. 2; *Potsdam Papers,* vol. 1, 756, 783; vol. 2, 842. Churchill quotation is from John L. Snell, *Wartime Origins of the East-West Dilemma over Germany,* 204.

17. Truman diary entry, July 7, 1945, Ferrell, ed., *Off the Record*, 49.

18. See Memorandum by a British Treasury Department official, July 16, 1945, *Documents on British Policy Overseas*, 327–28.

19. Harriman to Truman and Byrnes, July 8, 1945, Map Room Files, Truman Papers.

20. Clark Kerr memorandum to Eden, *Documents on British Policy Overseas*, 364–67.

21. Harriman to Truman and Byrnes, July 9 and 12, 1945, Map Room Files, Truman Papers.

22. *New York Times*, July 3, 1945.

23. *New York Times*, July 11, 1945.

24. Grew to Byrnes, July 13, 1945, vol. 7, Grew Papers.

25. Butow, in *Japan's Decision*, provides a convenient summary of the Japanese "feelers," in chap. 5, "Interlude in Switzerland: Peace Feelers through the Dulles Organization," 103–11. FRUS, *1945*, vol. 6, contains a generous sampling of Japanese messages to and from Tokyo, and periodic OSS reports are in Conway File, Truman Papers.

26. Department of Defense Press Release, September 1955, "The Entry of the Soviet Union into the War against Japan: Military Plans, 1941–1945," 88, found in Hanson Baldwin Collection, Marshall Library.

27. Togo to Sato, July 12, 1945, Folder 571, Byrnes Papers.

28. Weckerling to Handy, July 12 and 13, 1945, Microfilm roll 109, item 2581, Marshall Library.

29. Grew, often referred to as a "Japanist" because of his views, had told Truman on May 29 that attainment of American objectives meant "the destruction of Japan's tools for war and of the capacity of the Japanese again to make these tools. Their military machine must be totally destroyed and, so far as possible, their cult of militarism must be blotted out." Grew, Memorandum of Conversation, May 29, 1945, item 5-A–24, *Occupation of Japan*.

30. Togo to Sato, July 11, 1945, Folder 571, Byrnes Papers.

31. Sato to Togo, July 12, 1945, Folder 571, Byrnes Papers; Togo to Sato, July 17, MAGIC Summary, no. 1210.

32. See Joint Staff Planners report proposing Pastel and JCS approval, Box 24, Carl A. Spaatz Papers, LC.

33. Weart and Szilard, *His Version*, 209–10.

34. Daniels's letter is reprinted in Stoff, Fanton, and Williams, *The Manhattan Project*, 173.

35. Weart and Szilard, *His Version*, 211–12.

36. Hewlett and Anderson, *The New World*, 399–400; Compton's letter to Nichols is reprinted in Stoff, Fanton, and Williams, *The Manhattan Project*, 174.

37. See, for instance, Peter Wyden in *Day One: Before Hiroshima and After,* 179. Despite having written in a previous sentence that "Truman was already at Potsdam," Wyden nonetheless states that "Groves carefully routed it [the petition] through a circuitous obstacle course to be sure the President would be out of the country when it arrived in Washington." This makes no sense as Truman had departed ten days *before* Szilard even circulated his petition.

38. Szilard's "Recollections," in Weart and Szilard, *His Version,* 187.

39. Szilard to Oppenheimer, July 23, 1945, Box 70, Oppenheimer Papers, LC.

40. Groves diary entries, July 2 and 3, 1945, Groves Papers, NARS.

41. All quotations in the previous two paragraphs are from Groves's memorandum to Stimson, July 18, 1945, in Leslie Groves Collection, Box 1, Marshall Library.

42. Richard Rhodes, *The Making of the Atomic Bomb,* 656.

43. Groves diary entry, July 17, 1945, Groves Papers, NARS.

44. Rhodes, *Atomic Bomb,* 662; Hewlett and Anderson, *The New World,* 380.

45. Groves diary entry, July 19, 1945, Groves Papers, NARS.

46. Groves teletype to Oppenheimer, July 19, 1945, Microfilm roll 1, M1109, MED.

47. Groves diary entry, July 20, 1945, Groves Papers, NARS.

48. Rhodes, *Atomic Bomb,* 692.

Chapter 6

1. All quotations in the previous two paragraphs are from Truman diary entry, July 16, 1945, in Ferrell, ed., *Off the Record,* 50–53.

2. Davies diary entry, July 16, 1945, Davies Papers.

3. Another report, received on the morning of the eighteenth, indicated that the explosion was as powerful as that expected from *Little Boy,* previously referred to as the "big bomb." Both are in Microfilm roll 1, M1109, MED.

4. Bohlen's notes are in *Potsdam Papers,* vol. 2, 43–46; the Truman comment is in a diary entry for July 17, 1945, Ferrell, ed., *Off the Record,* 53.

5. All quotations in the previous two paragraphs are from Bohlen's notes, *Potsdam Papers,* vol. 2, 43–46.

6. Leahy diary entry, July 17, 1945, Leahy Papers.

7. The Truman quotations are from a diary entry, July 17, 1945, Ferrell, ed., *Off the Record,* 53.

8. Davies diary entry, July 18, 1945, Davies Papers.

9. Truman-Stalin meeting of July 18, 1945, *Potsdam Papers,* vol. 2, 86–87.

10. Stimson to Byrnes, July 17, 1945, with memorandum for Truman, July 16, *Potsdam Papers,* vol. 2, 753–57.

11. Meeting of the Combined Chiefs of Staff, July 16, 1945, *Potsdam Papers*, vol. 2, 35–38. The memorandum drawn up by the British chiefs and forwarded to Churchill on July 17 is reprinted in John Ehrman, *Grand Strategy*, 291.

12. Churchill memorandum of conversation, July 18, 1945, *Documents on British Policies Overseas* (London: Her Majesty's Stationery Office, 1984), 370.

13. Hull, *Memoirs*, vol. 2, 1593–94; Grew to Byrnes (transmitting Hull to Byrnes), July 16, 1945, and Grew memorandum of telephone conversation with Hull, relaying Byrnes's reply, July 17, *Potsdam Papers*, vol. 2, 1267, 1268.

14. Hewlett and Anderson, *The New World;* Byrnes later wrote in a chapter on Potsdam that Bohlen "was invaluable to me," Byrnes, *Speaking Frankly*, 67. Stalin's comment is in Walter Brown's diary, July 18, Folder 602, Byrnes Papers.

15. Stimson mentioned MacLeish, Acheson, and Hopkins as among those who had conducted "uninformed agitation against the Emperor" and "who know no more about Japan than has been given them by Gilbert and Sullivan's 'Mikado,'" diary entry, August 10, 1945, Stimson Papers; Truman met with Hopkins several times after the latter's return to Moscow and had asked him to serve as an adviser at Potsdam. Hopkins was too ill to make the trip but submitted some memoranda, Harry to Bess Truman, July 3, 1994, in Robert H. Ferrell, ed., *Dear Bess: The Letters from Harry to Bess Truman, 1910–1959*, 516.

16. The Stimson quotation is from his diary entry, July 17, 1945, Stimson Papers; on the nineteenth he noted that Byrnes had told him McCloy could not attend the plenary sessions. "So my meeting with him was rather a barren one," Stimson wrote. "He gives me the impression that he is hugging matters in this Conference pretty close to his bosom, and that my assistance, while generally welcome, was strictly limited in the matters in which it should be given"; not until July 23 did Stimson, after complaining, receive permission to visit the Little White House every morning.

17. "Military Aspects of Unconditional Surrender Formula for Japan," JCS 1275/5, in CCS 334, Joint Chiefs of Staff, Marshall Library; Leahy memorandum of July 18, Verifax folder 12S, same source.

18. "I concur in the revised form of paragraph (12) suggested by the Joint Chiefs of Staff in their memorandum to you of 18 July 1945," Stimson notified Truman on July 20, *Potsdam Papers*, vol. 2, 1271–72; on July 24, however, he told the president that insertion of a statement about the emperor "might be just the thing that would make or mar their acceptance," diary entry, July 24, Stimson Papers; for the delay in securing Chiang's approval, see Truman, *Year of Decisions*, 390.

19. *Potsdam Papers*, vol. 2, 1474–76.

20. In his propaganda broadcasts to the Japanese, Captain Zacharias read the text of Truman's May 8 speech in its entirety on three occasions and repeatedly stressed that unconditional surrender was purely a military act. All his broadcasts are reprinted in his *Secret Missions*, 399–424.

21. Byrnes-Molotov meeting, July 27, 1945, *Potsdam Papers*, vol. 2, 449–50. See also Walter Brown diary, July 27, 1945, Folder 54 (1), Byrnes Papers.

22. Davies diary entry, July 25, 1945, Davies Papers.

23. Stimson diary entry, July 17, 1945, Stimson Papers.

24. Churchill memorandum of conversation, July 18, 1945, *Documents on British Policies Overseas*, 370; Truman diary entry, July 18, in Ferrell, ed., *Off the Record*, 53–54.

25. Stimson diary entries, July 19, 20, and 23, Stimson Papers; his memorandum is reprinted in *Potsdam Papers*, vol. 2, 1155–57.

26. Truman, *Year of Decisions*, 416; Churchill, *Triumph and Tragedy*, 669–70.

27. Hewlett and Anderson, *The New World*, 394.

28. Walter Brown diary entry, July 24, 1945, Folder 602, Byrnes Papers.

29. Davies journal entry, July 28, Davies Papers. Byrnes said much the same thing on at least two other occasions so there was no misunderstanding on Davies's part, see his journal entries for July 29 and August 1.

30. Stimson diary entry, July 21, 1945, Stimson Papers; Groves's memorandum, dated July 18, is in Leslie Groves Collection, Marshall Library.

31. Jonathan Daniels, *Man of Independence*, 151.

32. A recent example of twisting Daniels's observation is in Mary Beth Norton et al., *A People and a Nation: A History of the United States*, vol. 2, 795.

33. Davies journal entry, July 21, 1945, Davies Papers.

34. Vincent memoranda, July 17, 19, and 23, all in Folder 569(2), Byrnes Papers. Vincent during the McCarthy period was accused of being a Soviet agent. If so, he cleverly concealed his loyalties in these papers by urging that the United States take a strong stand against the Soviet Union.

35. "Yalta Legman," *Newsweek*, March 19, 1945, 52.

36. Soong's message in Hurley to Byrnes, July 19, 1945; Chiang's in Hurley to Byrnes, July 20, both in Map Room Files, Truman Papers.

37. Stimson diary entry, July 23, 1945, Stimson Papers.

38. Truman to Chiang, July 23, 1945, FRUS, *1945*, vol. 7, 950.

39. Walter Brown diary entry, July 24, 1945, Folder 602, Byrnes Papers; Forrestal diary entry, July 28, vol. 2, Forrestal Papers.

40. Truman to Bess Truman, July 18 and 20, in Ferrell, ed., *Dear Bess*, 519–20. On August 9, 1945, reporter Ernest B. Vaccaro, who had accompanied the presidential party to and from Potsdam, published a bylined article entitled "Russian Entry into War Revealed as Truman's Chief Aim in Berlin," in the *New York Times*. "As vital as was, and is, his interest in bringing harmony to the European scene," Vaccaro wrote, "the president repeatedly told newsmen

en route with him aboard the cruiser Augusta that his main concern was to bring the Pacific war to a close 'with the least loss of American lives.' " Truman believed that Russian entry "might save hundreds of thousands of Americans from injury or death," Vaccaro continued, and "the results were evident in his demeanor on the way back."

41. Harrison to Stimson, July 21 and 23, 1945, both in Microfilm roll 1, M1109, MED.

42. Stimson to Harrison, July 23, 1945; Harrison to Stimson, same date, both in Microfilm roll 1, M1109, MED.

43. Truman, *Year of Decisions*, 421.

44. Groves to Marshall, July 18, 1945, Microfilm roll 1, M1109, MED.

45. Thomas T. Handy, Oral Interview, February 28, 1974, Handy Papers, USAMHI; Spaatz told an interviewer in 1962 that he "made further notification that I would not drop an atomic bomb on verbal orders—they had to be written— and this was accomplished." See David R. Mets, *Master of Airpower: General Carl A. Spaatz*, 303.

46. Marshall to Handy, July 22, 1945; Handy to Groves, July 23, both in Microfilm roll 1, M1109, MED.

47. Stone memorandum to Arnold on "Groves Project," July 24, 1945; and Colonel H. M. Pasco, Acting Secretary, General Staff to Groves, July 27, both in Microfilm roll 1, M1109, MED.

48. Handy to Marshall, July 24, 1945; Harrison to Stimson, July 24; Marshall to Handy, July 25, all in Microfilm roll 1, M1109, MED.

49. Truman diary entry, July 25, in Ferrell, ed., *Off the Record*, 55–56.

50. Stimson diary entry, July 24, 1945, Stimson Papers.

51. Groves to Oppenheimer, July 19, 1945, in Microfilm roll 1, M1109, MED. "It may be that as many as three of the latter [*Fat Man*-type bombs] in their best present form may have to be dropped to conform to planned strategical operations."

52. Harrison to Stimson, July 21, 1945; Handy to Marshall, July 24, both in Microfilm roll 1, M1109, MED. And see Thomas B. Buell, *Master of Seapower: A Biography of Fleet Admiral Ernest J. King*, 491–96.

53. Eben A. Ayers to Gordon Dean, January 14, 1955; and Memorandum for Eben Ayers, October 17, 1951, both in Ayers Papers, Truman Library.

54. George M. Elsey, transcript of oral interview, vol. 3, 17–19, Truman Library; Byrnes, *Speaking Frankly*, 262.

Chapter 7

1. *Documents on British Policy Overseas*, 1251–52.

2. *Potsdam Papers*, vol. 2, 1293; and Butow, *Japan's Decision*, 142–49.

3. Alperovitz, in *Atomic Diplomacy,* 233, claims that Truman deliberately chose to interpret the phrase in its most abusive sense in order to prolong the war until atomic bombs could be used. That the president had even the foggiest notion what *mokusatsu* meant is, of course, absurd.

4. OSS Memorandum for the President, August 2, 1945, Conway File, Truman Papers.

5. Butow, *Japan's Decision,* 144.

6. Hastings Ismay, *The Memoirs of General Lord Ismay,* 403; Bevin's remark to Stalin is in *Potsdam Papers,* vol. 2, 469. After his return to Washington, Truman told aides that Bevin reminded him of John L. Lewis, a rough-and-tumble labor leader. "Stalin and Molotov, the president said, might be rough men, but they knew the common courtesies, but Bevin he said was entirely lacking in all of them—a 'boor' the president said." Eben Ayers diary entry for August 7, 1945, in Ferrell, ed., *Truman in the White House,* 60.

7. FRUS, *Yalta,* 980.

8. Briefing Book Paper, "Suggested United States Policy Regarding Poland," *Potsdam Papers,* vol. 1, 743–47.

9. Truman-Molotov meeting, July 29, 1945, *Potsdam Papers,* vol. 2, 471–76.

10. The Truman quotation is in *Year of Decisions,* 402; the note to the Soviets about entering the war is in folder 602, Byrnes Papers.

11. *Potsdam Papers,* vol. 2, 480–83.

12. Transcript of Harriman interview with Elie Abel, Abel File, Box 865, Harriman Papers. The book mentioned is Kai Bird, *The Chairman: John J. McCloy, the Making of the American Establishment,* 256.

13. David Dilks, ed., *The Diaries of Sir Alexander Cadogan, 1938–1945,* 777.

14. Byrnes, *Speaking Frankly,* 85.

15. Stalin's remark is in *Potsdam Papers,* vol. 2, 530; Bevin's, 532.

16. Robert Murphy, *Diplomat among Warriors,* 312. A bland version of the Truman-Stalin exchange is in *Potsdam Papers,* vol. 2, 584.

17. Lisle A. Rose, *After Yalta,* 48.

18. Truman, *Year of Decisions,* 412.

19. Truman to Bess Truman, July 29, in Ferrell, ed., *Dear Bess,* 522; Truman to Dean Acheson (unsent), March 15, 1957, in Ferrell, ed., *Off the Record,* 348–49.

20. Joseph E. Davies diary entry, July 21, 1945, Davies Papers.

21. Joseph E. Davies diary entry, July 22, 1945, Davies Papers.

22. Joseph E. Davies diary entry, July 27, 1945, Davies Papers.

23. Joseph E. Davies journal entry, July 28, 1945, and diary entry, July 29, 1945, both in Davies Papers.

24. July 27, 1945, Folder 571, Byrnes Papers.

25. July 30, 1945, Folder 571, Byrnes Papers.

26. Drea, *MacArthur's Ultra*, 204, 211.

27. Ibid., 215.

28. "Details of the Campaign against Japan," extracted from minutes of meeting held at the White House June 18 at 3:30 P.M., 4, Xerox 1564, Marshall Library.

29. Tripartite Military Meeting, July 24, 1945, *Potsdam Papers*, vol. 2, 346; Truman diary entry for July 25, 1945, in Ferrell, ed., *Off the Record*, 56.

30. "Details of the Campaign against Japan," Marshall Library, 1, 3–5.

31. Joseph McBride, *Frank Capra: The Catastrophe of Success*, 501; Forrest C. Pogue, *George C. Marshall: Organizer for Victory*, 499–502; Pogue, *George C. Marshall: Statesman*, 19, 25; and Stimson and Bundy, *On Active Service in Peace and War*, 632.

32. "Details of the Campaign against Japan," Marshall Library, 3–4.

33. H. H. Arnold, *Global Mission*, 564, 567.

34. "Details of the Campaign against Japan," Marshall Library, 5.

35. OPD, "Military Use of the Atomic Bomb," 27, Lincoln Papers.

36. Marshall, *Interviews and Reminiscences*, 423.

37. The Leahy quotations are from *I Was There*, 441. Leahy attributed no ulterior motives to Truman: "He did not like the idea, but was persuaded that it would shorten the war against Japan and save American lives." The LeMay quotation is from Fletcher Knebel and Charles W. Bailey II, *No High Ground*, 111.

38. Alperovitz, *Atomic Diplomacy*, 14–15; for the passage showing that Leahy was speaking in the context of naval blockade and conventional bombing rather than atomic weapons, see his *I Was There*, 385. It appears in his discussion of Truman's June 18 meeting with the Joint Chiefs of Staff.

39. Leahy, *I Was There*, 431.

40. The Harriman and McCloy quotations are from the transcript of "Off the Record Discussion of the Origins of the Cold War," May 31, 1967, Mark Chadwin Files, Box 869, Harriman Papers; Truman's quote is in Eben Ayers diary entry for August 8, 1945, in Ferrell, ed., *Truman in the White House*, 61.

41. Dwight D. Eisenhower, *Crusade in Europe*, 443.

42. Dwight D. Eisenhower, *Mandate for Change*, 312–13.

43. "Ike on Ike," *Newsweek*, November 11, 1963, 108.

44. Stimson diary entry for July 20, 1945, Stimson Papers.

45. Stimson diary entry for July 27, 1945; Colonel W. H. Kyle, "Notes on the Trip of the Secretary of War," July 6 to July 28, Reel 128, both in Stimson Papers.

46. The Truman quotation is in Ferrell, ed., *Off the Record*, 56.

47. Alperovitz, *Atomic Diplomacy*, 14, 16, 18; Rhodes, *Atomic Bomb*, 688. Alperovitz describes Eisenhower as "the triumphant Supreme Commander of the

Allied Forces in Europe and one of Roosevelt's most respected advisers," and Rhodes depicts him as a "hard and pragmatic commander," thereby lending authenticity to his alleged views. But Eisenhower never was one of Roosevelt's advisers; he had been overseas since 1942 and reported through Marshall. And precisely because he had served in North Africa and Europe, Eisenhower had no special expertise or sources of information about conditions in Japan, let alone how close it was to surrender.

48. Omar Bradley and Clay Blair, *A General's Life: An Autobiography by General of the Army Omar Bradley*, 445, 707.

49. Material in these two paragraphs is based on Barton J. Bernstein, "Ike and Hiroshima: Did He Oppose It?" 377–89.

50. The Nimitz quotation is in Knebel and Bailey, *No High Ground*, 90. For Nimitz's concurrence in using a third atomic bomb against Tokyo, see Commanding General 313th Bomb Wing to General Nathan Twining, August 9, 1945, and Twining to Nimitz and Spaatz confirming their discussions, same date, both in Box 24, Spaatz Papers.

51. MacArthur's message to Marshall is in JCS 1388/1, "Details of the Campaign against Japan," 3, Xerox 1567, Marshall Library; his remark to Arnold is in the latter's *Global Mission*, 569.

52. On March 31, 1944, Stimson notified MacArthur that he was sending a Mr. Clarence Hall to discuss "certain natural resources in your theater." The secretary stressed that this mission was of an "especially secret nature." The "extensive exploration" of uranium was just getting underway in Australia at that time and it is unlikely that Hall was being sent out to discuss some other "natural resource." Folder 25, Microfilm reel 2, "Harrison-Bundy Files Relating to the Development of the Atomic Bomb," National Archives microfilm publication M1108. See Fred F. Langford, "Uranium Deposits in Australia," in M. M. Kimberley, *Short Course in Uranium Deposits, Their Mineralogy and Origin* (Toronto: University of Toronto Press, 1978), 205. Spaatz's account of this meeting with MacArthur is in Handy, Oral Interview, USAMHI, 42. For MacArthur's view on the invasion after Hiroshima, see Drea, *MacArthur's Ultra*, 223.

53. See Meeting of the Combined Chiefs of Staff with Truman and Churchill, July 24, 1945, and Report by the Combined Chiefs of Staff, Approved by the Heads of Government of the United States and the United Kingdom, both in *Potsdam Papers*, vol. 2, 339–44, 1462–73. Under "Plans and Operations in the Pacific," the report stated that the Joint Chiefs of Staff plan of operations was to continue air bombardment and blockade, and to launch an assault against Kyushu to further reduce Japanese capabilities and to "establish a tactical condition" favorable to "The decisive invasion of Honshu."

54. MAGIC Summary, no. 1224, part 2, August 1, 1945.

55. Charles S. Cheston, Acting Director, OSS, to Rose Conway, the White House, August 2, 1945, enclosing "Memorandum for the President," Conway File, Truman Papers. In a memorandum of August 9, the OSS reported that there was no direct evidence that the officials in Switzerland were acting on "instructions from Tokyo," OSS Reports to the White House, April–September 1945, William J. Donovan Papers, USAMHI.

56. The quotation about relative strength is from Drea, *MacArthur's Ultra,* 216; the comment about prisoners of war refers to their statements before the first atomic bomb was dropped, see report of August 10/11, G-2 Intelligence Summaries, MacArthur's Headquarters, Quentin S. Lander Papers, USAMHI.

57. For troop estimates, see Order of Battle Bulletin 74, August 4, 1945, SRH, War Military Intelligence Division, USAMHI. The bulletin also reported the appearance of three, possibly four, new tank brigades. See also "Preliminary Report to Pacific Order of Battle Conference, August 15, 1945," reprinted in Ronald H. Spector, ed., *Listening to the Enemy,* 249–73. The projection of 680,000 by X Day is in Walter Krueger, *From Down Under to Nippon: The Story of Sixth Army in World War II,* 333; the casualty estimate is from Lt. Col. D. B. Kendrick to Chief Surgeon, American Forces Western Pacific, July 31, cited in "Medical Service in the Asiatic-Pacific Theater," chap. 15, p. 18, an unpublished manuscript at the Center for Military History, Washington, D.C. The figure of 900,000 is from Drea, *MacArthur's Ultra,* 222.

Chapter 8

1. Spaatz to Marshall, July 31, and Marshall to Spaatz, July 31, 1945, both in Xerox 1482, Folder 207, Marshall Library.

2. Leahy, *I Was There,* 431, and Knebel and Bailey, *No High Ground,* 127–28.

3. Byrnes to Soong, July 28, 1945, *Potsdam Papers,* vol. 2, 1245.

4. Stimson diary entry, July 23, 1945.

5. Harriman to Byrnes, July 28, 1945, *Potsdam Papers,* vol. 2, 1243–44.

6. Hurley to Byrnes, July 29, 1945, Map Room Files, Truman Papers.

7. Harriman to Truman and Byrnes, July 31, 1945, *Potsdam Papers,* vol. 2, 1246–47.

8. Vincent memorandum to James C. Dunn, July 23, 1945, File 569 (2), Byrnes Papers.

9. Notes of Truman-Byrnes-Stalin-Molotov meeting, July 17, 1945, *Potsdam Papers,* vol. 2, 1582–87.

10. Byrnes to Harriman, August 5, 1945, Map Room Files, Truman Papers.

11. Knebel and Bailey, *No High Ground,* 228–29.

12. Martin J. Sherwin, *A World Destroyed: The Atomic Bomb and the Grand Alliance,* 221.

13. Knebel and Bailey, *No High Ground*, 229.

14. See Oppenheimer to General Thomas P. Farrell, July 23, 1945, as cited in Stanley Goldberg, "Note on Barton Bernstein's 'Seizing the Contested Terrain of Early Nuclear History,' " 5–7.

15. Rhodes, *Atomic Bomb*, 714, 733–34.

16. *Public Papers of the Presidents*, 200.

17. Lester Brooks, *Behind Japan's Surrender: The Secret Struggle that Ended an Empire*, 167; Butow, *Japan's Decision*, 245.

18. MAGIC Summary, no. 1231, August 8, 1945.

19. MAGIC Summary, no. 1232, August 9, 1945. And see Harriman's report of his talk with Stalin that evening, Harriman to Truman and Byrnes, August 9, 1945, Map Room Files, Truman Papers.

20. Herbert Feis, *The Atomic Bomb and the End of World War II*, 127.

21. Ferrell, ed., *Truman in the White House*, Eben Ayers diary entry for August 9, 1945, 62.

22. The material in these paragraphs is from a report prepared for the author by Colonel A. Orlov of the Russian Defense Ministry. It is based on published and unpublished (then) Soviet materials, and includes a copy of Vassilevsky's handwritten report to Stalin. See also "How Soviets Stole U.S. Atom Secrets," *Washington Post*, October 4, 1992. David Holloway, in *Stalin and the Bomb: The Soviet Union and Atomic Energy, 1939–1956*, 126, stresses the Japanese overture.

23. *New York Times*, August 9, 1945, and Ferrell, ed., *Truman in the White House*, Eben Ayers diary entry, August 8, 1945.

24. These paragraphs are based on Butow, *Japan's Decision*, 159–77.

25. FRUS, *1945*, vol. 6, *The British Commonwealth: The Far East*, 631–32.

26. Memorandum for the chief of staff from Colonel Frank McCarthy, August 10, 1945, Box 71, Folder 48, Marshall Papers. MAGIC Summary, no. 1233, August 10, 1945.

27. Stimson diary entry, August 10, 1945, Stimson Papers.

28. Walter Brown's notes, Folder 602, Byrnes Papers.

29. Stimson diary entry, August 10, 1945, Stimson Papers.

30. Byrnes's draft is reprinted in Feis, *The Atomic Bomb*, 134.

31. Barton Bernstein, "The Perils and Politics of Surrender: Ending the War with Japan and Avoiding the Third Atomic Bomb," 1–27; and Walter LaFeber, *The American Age*, vol. 2, 450.

32. Stimson diary entry, August 10, 1945, Stimson Papers.

33. Stimson, "Memorandum for the President: Proposed Program for Japan," July 2, 1945, *Potsdam Papers*, vol. 2, 888–92.

34. Truman diary entry, August 10, 1945, in Ferrell, ed., *Off the Record*, 61.

35. Byrnes's quotation is from a Walter Brown diary entry, August 10, 1945; Marshall's is from John Callan O'Laughlin to Herbert Hoover, August 11, PPI, Herbert Hoover Presidential Library. O'Laughlin's five-page, single-spaced letter is based on what must have been a lengthy talk with Marshall on August 9. The author is indebted to Professor Gary Clifford for providing a copy. Hereafter it will be referred to as "O'Laughlin letter."

36. Joint Chiefs of Staff to MacArthur and Nimitz, August 11, 1945, Operations and Plans Division, General Staff, Xerox 2800, Marshall Library.

37. Grew, "Memorandum for the Secretary," August 7, 1945, vol. 7, Folder 49, Grew Papers.

38. Marshall to MacArthur, August 7, 1945, Operations and Plans Division, General Staff, Xerox 2800, Marshall Library.

39. Joint War Plans Committee 397, August 4, 1945, CCS, Joint Chiefs of Staff RG 218, NARS. The Joint Intelligence Committee report is attached.

40. Drea, *MacArthur's Ultra*, 223.

41. Stimson diary entry, August 8, 1945, Stimson Papers.

42. Stimson diary entry, August 9, 1945, Stimson Papers.

43. "Military Use of the Atomic Bomb: Summary of Conclusions Based upon OPD Records," 31–32. This is a report prepared for the secretary of war sometime in 1946 by the Operations and Plans historian. See memorandum from George A. Lincoln, chief of the Plans and Policy Group, to the director of the War Department historical division, October 11, 1946. Both in Lincoln Papers. The report hereinafter will be cited as OPD, "Military Use." The Stimson quotation is from his diary entry, August 10, 1945, Stimson Papers.

44. Feis, *The Atomic Bomb*, 134–38; and Truman, *Year of Decisions*, 428–32. Byrnes's note as revised is in FRUS, *The British Commonwealth*, 631–32.

45. Marshall to Spaatz, August 11, 1945, and acting secretary, General Staff to Truman's military aide, same date, both in Microfilm roll no. 127, item 3342, Marshall Library. Spaatz's explanation about the weather is in Spaatz to Marshall, August 11, Box 21, Spaatz Papers.

46. See, for instance, Leon V. Sigal, *Fighting to a Finish: The Politics of War Termination in the United States and Japan, 1945*, 208–9. "There is no evidence in the public record to confirm that Admirals Leahy and King ever reversed their objections to the bomb," Sigal writes, "and if anything, General Arnold hardened his reluctance to use it." His sources for this statement consist entirely of memoirs, and he cites no evidence that even suggests these individuals made their "objections" known to the president. In these pages and elsewhere, Sigal wildly exaggerates General Groves's influence in depicting him as *the* master manipulator in successfully misleading, tricking, and circumventing various political and military officials—including Truman, Stimson, and Marshall—

thereby gaining almost complete power over use of the bombs. Again Sigal relies heavily on a personal account written after the war; this time Groves's boastful, often inaccurate version of events with himself in the starring role.

47. The Arnold quotation is in Knebel and Bailey, *No High Ground*, 221; Marshall to Spaatz, August 8, 1945, Box 85, Folder 25, Marshall Papers.

48. The LeMay quotation is in Alperovitz, *Atomic Diplomacy*, 17. For LeMay, Spaatz, and Nimitz recommendation, see Commanding General 313th Bomb Wing to Twining, August 9, and Twining to Nimitz and Spaatz, same date; Spaatz quotation is from Spaatz to General Lauris Norstad (Arnold's chief of staff), August 10, and Arnold's reply is in Norstad to Spaatz, same date, all in Box 24, Spaatz Papers.

49. Spaatz to Arnold, August 10 and 13, 1945, Box 24; Arnold to Spaatz, August 19, Box 21, Spaatz Papers. Arnold, in *Global Mission*, 598, wrote that "the abrupt surrender of Japan came more or less as a surprise, for we had figured we would probably have to drop about four atomic bombs, or increase the destructiveness of our B-29 missions by adding the heavy bombers from Europe."

50. O'Laughlin to Hoover, August 11, 1945.

51. Transcript of telephone conversation between General John E. Hull and Colonel L. E. Seaman, August 13, 1945, Atomic Bomb/Manhattan Project Folder, Marshall Library. And see Marc Gallicchio, "After Nagasaki: General Marshall's Plan for the Use of Tactical Nuclear Weapons," 396–404.

52. Gallicchio, "After Nagasaki," 403. Marshall, at least, knew about the test reports. He had said on August 9 that "the experiments conducted and the plans for invasion, called for the march by our troops upon a target a few hours after the bomb had struck [*sic*]." O'Laughlin letter.

53. Henry A. Wallace diary entry, August 10, printed in Stoff, Fanton, and Williams, *The Manhattan Project*, 245.

54. Groves to Marshall, August 10, 1945, Leslie Groves Collection, Box 1, Marshall Library.

55. Groves diary entry, August 11, 1945, Groves Papers.

56. Marshall to MacArthur and Spaatz, August 13, 1945, Operations and Plans Division, General Staff, Xerox 2800, Marshall Library, and Norstad to Spaatz, August 14, Box 24, Spaatz Papers.

57. Groves diary entries for August 13 and 14, 1945, Groves Papers.

58. Marshall's words are from O'Laughlin letter; Truman's are from Minister John Balfour to Ernest Bevin, August 14, 1945, Bevin private papers (FO 800), Public Record Office, Kew.

59. MAGIC Summary, no. 1237, August 14, 1945. American cryptographers would have had no reason to expedite such a communication through channels.

60. The Swiss message is reprinted in the *New York Times*, August 15, 1945. The Japanese cable is in MAGIC Summary, no. 1237, August 14, 1945.

61. Butow, *Japan's Decision*, 189–209.

62. *New York Times*, August 14, 1945.

63. MAGIC Summary, no. 1237, August 14, 1945, and Marshall to U.S. Military Mission in Russia, August 14, Operations and Plans Division, General Staff, Xerox 2800, Marshall Library.

Chapter 9

1. MAGIC Summary, no. 1238, August 15, 1945.

2. Zacharias, *Secret Missions*, 370–72. Under arrangement with the editors of the *Washington Post*, he published an "anonymous" letter the authorship of which he knew would be identified in the American press and be picked up by Japanese officials in neutral countries. It was. Martin J. Sherwin, in *A World Destroyed*, repeatedly confuses Japan's desire to obtain a negotiated peace with its willingness to surrender. On page 235, for instance, he cites a message from Togo to Sato on July 13: "Unconditional surrender is the only obstacle to peace," as though this were synonymous with saying that assurance about the emperor was the only obstacle to peace. On the contrary, Japanese militarists insisted on numerous conditions that would have undermined the goals set down in the Potsdam Declaration.

3. Sherwin, *A World Destroyed*, 233, 237.

4. As quoted in Lawrence Freedman and Saki Dockrill, "Hiroshima: A Strategy of Shock," in Saki Dockrill, ed., *From Pearl Harbor to Hiroshima: The Second World War in Asia and the Pacific*, 191–211.

5. "Statements of Japanese Officials on World War II (English Translations)," 7, Document Number 57692, The Center for Military History, Washington, D.C.

6. The "huge meteor" quotation is from a report sent to Groves on August 6 following a debriefing, attended by General Spaatz, of the airmen and observers who had witnessed the explosion. The report is contained in Groves's memorandum to Marshall, same date, Box 1, Leslie Groves Collection, Marshall Library. The presidential statement is reprinted in *Potsdam Papers*, vol. 2, 1376–78; and the last quotation is from OPD, "Military Use," 34.

7. U.S. Strategic Bombing Survey, *Japan's Struggle to End the War*, 13. See also Robert P. Newman's forthcoming *Truman and the Hiroshima Cult*. Newman's chapter 6 offers a persuasive argument that the survey was "cooked" to arrive at such a conclusion.

8. Gar Alperovitz and Kai Bird, "Was Hiroshima Needed to End the War?" 19. This report, which the authors breathlessly describe as "written in 1946 but

withheld from the American public for roughly four decades," actually was routinely declassified in 1975 and has been available at the National Archives and the Marshall Library. See "Memorandum for Chief, Strategic Policy Section, S & P Group, OPD," April 30, 1946, ABC File 471.6 Atomic, RG 165, NARS and the same document as Xerox 1482/213, Marshall Library. Aside from relying on information about Japanese defenses unavailable before V-J Day, it contains some very questionable assumptions. Referring to a June 20 statement by the emperor about having "a plan to close the war at once, as well as one to defend the home islands," for instance, the paper concludes that "Premier Suzuki decided to stop the war." That Suzuki had the power to "decide" such an issue shows little understanding of the power realities in Japan.

9. OPD, "Military Use," 35–36.

10. Major General Clayton Bissell to Marshall, August 11, 1945, Microfilm roll no. 109, item 2581, Marshall Library.

11. Publication of Pacific Strategic Intelligence Section, SRH 90, August 29, 1945, MAGIC collection, USAMHI; and "Summary of Ultra Traffic, July 1– August 31, 1945," SRMD–007 (part 4), The Center for Military History, Washington, D.C.

12. OPD, "Military Use," 26–27, 37.

13. Hirohito's remark is in Lester Brooks, *Behind Japan's Surrender*, 170; Togo's messages are in MAGIC Summary, no. 1237, August 14, 1945.

14. The Imperial Rescript is printed in Butow, *Japan's Decision*, 248; portions of Suzuki's speech can be found in the *New York Times*, August 15, 1945.

15. Sigal, *Fighting to a Finish*, 278–79.

16. Freedman and Dockrill, "Hiroshima," 208.

17. For estimates based on experiments made prior to the test explosion, see the summary of Target Committee meetings, May 10–11, 1945, and the minutes of the meeting on May 28, all in Microfilm roll 1, M1109, MED. And see documents cited in Gallicchio, "After Nagasaki," 404, endnotes 19 and 20. The Oppenheimer quotation is from his memorandum to the officers in charge of operations on Tinian, informing them about tentative fuse settings. As quoted in Stanley Goldberg, "Note," 6–7. The last quotation is from Wyden, *Day One*, 16.

18. Rhodes, *Atomic Bomb*, 632.

19. Telephone conversation with Oppenheimer, Groves diary, August 8, 1945; the press release is item 5-f-14, *Occupation of Japan;* and Marshall's comment is in O'Laughlin to Hoover, August 11, 1945, Hoover Library.

20. Groves to Nimitz, August 11, 1945, Microfilm roll 1, M1109, MED; Marshall to MacArthur, August 12, 1945, Box 1, Leslie R. Groves Collection, Marshall Library.

21. Groves memorandum to Chief of Staff, August 24, 1945, Microfilm roll 1, M1109, MED; transcripts of Groves telephone conversations are reprinted in Stoff, Fanton, and Williams, *The Manhattan Project*, 258–62.

22. Charles L. Mee Jr., *Meeting at Potsdam*, 234; the quotation about secret information is from Gar Alperovitz in a *New York Times* article, "U.S. Spied on Its World War II Allies," August 11, 1993. The "secret" document he alluded to is MAGIC intercept no. 1142, May 11, 1945.

23. See the *New York Times* article cited above, and "Giving Harry Hell," by Gar Alperovitz and Kai Bird, *The Nation*, May 10, 1993, 640–41.

24. See, for instance, J. Samuel Walker, "The Decision to Use the Bomb: A Historical Update," 97–114. In the *New York Times Book Review*, August 18, 1985, diplomatic historian Gaddis Smith reviewed the revised edition of Gar Alperovitz's *Atomic Diplomacy*. Despite a few "relatively minor" errors, Smith wrote, "the preponderance of new evidence since 1965 [date of the first edition] tends to sustain the original argument." This is a most remarkable conclusion, quite aside from the fact that Alperovitz's book is studded with errors that anyone familiar with the sources should recognize immediately. A revised edition of Smith's own *American Diplomacy during the Second World War, 1941–1945*, first published in 1965, also appeared in 1985. In his preface to the new edition, Smith wrote that it was based on the "vast amount of documentation" and the "outstanding works of scholarship" that had become available during the interim. Yet Smith's own work contradicts Alperovitz's most important themes and accepts only one "with a very qualified yes." How the "new evidence since 1965" could sustain *both* Alperovitz's work and his own opposite conclusions Smith did not reveal.

25. *Public Papers of the Presidents*, 2.

26. Stimson diary entry, July 19, 1945, Stimson Papers.

27. See Oppenheimer letter to Stimson, August 17, 1945, and George Harrison's "Memorandum for the Record," August 18, both printed in Stoff, Fanton, and Williams, *The Manhattan Project*, 254–56.

28. Stimson diary entries, "August 12 to September 3," 1945; entry for September 4, Stimson Papers.

29. September 28, 1945, Calendar Notes, Stettinius Papers.

30. Walter Brown diary entry, September 15, 1945, Folder 602, Byrnes Papers.

31. Clement Attlee to Truman, October 16, 1945, FRUS, *1945*, vol. 2, 58–59; Walter Brown diary entry, September 20, 1945, Folder 602, Byrnes Papers.

32. Messer, *End of an Alliance*, 132–33.

33. Walter Brown diary entry, September 20, 1945, Folder 602, Byrnes Papers.

34. Acheson to Byrnes, December 15, 1945, FRUS, *1945*, vol. 2, 609–10; Byrnes's remark about a "mistake" is on page 698.

35. The Kennan quotation is from his *Memoirs: 1925–1950*, 287–88; quotation about Conant's impression is from James G. Hershberg, *James B. Conant: Harvard to Hiroshima and the Making of the Nuclear Age*, 257; the Truman memorandum is reprinted in his *Year of Decisions*, 551–52. For the debate over whether he actually read this memorandum to Byrnes, as he claimed, see Messer, *End of an Alliance*, 156–65.

36. Truman diary entry, June 7, 1945, in Ferrell, ed., *Off the Record*, 44.

37. Stimson diary entries, September 5 and 12, 1945, Stimson Papers; his memorandum is printed in FRUS, *1945*, vol. 2, 40–44.

38. The Truman quotation is from Forrestal diary entry, September 18, 1945, vol. 3, Forrestal Papers; Truman's account of the meeting is in his *Year of Decisions*, 525–27, Forrestal's in his diary entry for September 21.

39. *New York Times*, September 21, 1945.

40. The Connally quotation is from the *New York Times*, September 22, 1945; the Gallup Poll is from Gaddis, *Origins of the Cold War*, 257.

41. *Public Papers of the Presidents*, 362–66.

42. Byrnes's quotation is from his *Speaking Frankly*, 265; Truman's is from his Navy Day speech of October 27, 1945, printed in *Public Papers of the Presidents*, 381–83.

43. McGeorge Bundy, *Danger and Survival: Choices about the Bomb in the First Fifty Years*, 92–93.

44. Mee, *Meeting at Potsdam*, 179.

45. Printed in Stoff, Fanton, and Williams, *The Manhattan Project*, 140–47.

46. Yuli Khariton and Yuri Smirnov, "The Khariton Version," 20–31. There are several articles in this issue pertaining to the debate between former KGB officials and Soviet scientists over the importance of espionage in constructing the first Russian bombs.

SELECTED BIBLIOGRAPHY

Manuscript Collections

Amherst College Archives: John J. McCloy Diary.

Center for Military History: "Medical Service in the Asiatic-Pacific Theater," unpublished manuscript; "Statements of Japanese Officials on World War II"; "Summary of ULTRA Traffic, July 1–August 31, 1945."

Clemson University: James F. Byrnes Papers.

Harvard University: Joseph C. Grew Papers.

Library of Congress: Henry H. Arnold Papers; Joseph E. Davies Papers; W. Averell Harriman Papers; Cordell Hull Papers; William D. Leahy Papers; John von Neumann Papers; J. Robert Oppenheimer Papers; William S. Parsons Papers; Carl A. Spaatz Papers.

George C. Marshall Library: Atomic Bomb/Manhattan Project Folder; Hanson Baldwin Collection; Leslie R. Groves Collection; Interim Committee Log; George C. Marshall Papers; records of the Joint Chiefs of Staff; records of the Operations and Plans Division; miscellaneous Xerox and Verifax files.

National Archives: Leslie R. Groves Papers; Harley Notter File, State Department Files, Record Group 59; Record Groups 77, 107, 165, 218, 319.

Princeton University: Bernard M. Baruch Papers; John Foster Dulles Oral History Project; John Foster Dulles Papers; James V. Forrestal Papers; George F. Kennan Papers; Harry Dexter White Papers.

Franklin D. Roosevelt Library: Harry L. Hopkins Papers; Henry Morgenthau Papers; Franklin D. Roosevelt Papers; Samuel I. Rosenman Papers; Map Room File; Official File; President's Secretary File; Soviet Protocol Committee File.

Harry S. Truman Library: Dean Acheson Papers; Eben E. Ayers Papers; William L. Clayton Papers; Clark M. Clifford Papers; Conway File; George Elsey Papers; Samuel I. Rosenman Papers; Charles Ross Papers; John M. Snyder Papers; Harry S. Truman Papers; Map Room File; Oral Histories; OSS Memoranda; President's Secretary File.

U.S. Army Military History Institute: William J. Donovan Papers; Thomas T. Handy Papers; John E. Hull Papers; Quentin S. Lander Papers; MAGIC collection.
U.S. Military Academy: George A. Lincoln Papers.
University of Virginia: Edward R. Stettinius Jr. Papers.
Yale University: Henry L. Stimson Papers.

Unpublished Material

Newman, Robert P. "Truman and the Hiroshima Cult." To be published by the Michigan State University Press.
Orlov, Col. A. (Russian Defense Ministry). Report on Stalin's decision to enter the war against Japan. With published material and unpublished documents from Soviet archives attached.

Microforms

"Correspondence (Top Secret) of the Manhattan Engineer District, 1942–1946." National Archives microfilm publication M1109. Washington, D.C.: 1980.
"Harrison-Bundy Files Relating to the Development of the Atomic Bomb." National Archives microfilm publication M1108. Washington, D.C.
Iokibe, Makoto, ed. "The Occupation of Japan: United States Planning Documents, 1945." Bethesda, Md.: Congressional Information Service, 1989.
Kesaris, Paul, ed. "Manhattan Project." Washington, D.C.: University Publications of America, 1977.
"The MAGIC Documents, Summaries and Transcripts of the Top Secret Diplomatic Communications of Japan, 1938–1945." Washington, D.C.: University Publications of America, 1980.
"O.S.S./State Department Intelligence and Research Reports." Washington, D.C.: University Publications of America, 1978.

Government Publications

Documents on British Policy Overseas. Ser. 1, vol. 1, 1945. London: Her Majesty's Stationery Office, 1984.

Ehrman, John. *Grand Strategy.* London: Her Majesty's Stationery Office, 1956.

Public Papers of the Presidents: Harry S. Truman, 1945–1946. Washington, D.C.: 1961–1962.

U.S. Department of State. *Department of State Bulletin.* Vols. 13 and 14. Washington, D.C.: 1945–1946.

———. *Foreign Relations of the United States. Annual Volumes, 1941–1946.* Washington, D.C.: Government Printing Office, 1958–1970.

———. *Foreign Relations of the United States: The Conference of Berlin (The Potsdam Conference), 1945.* 2 vols. Washington, D.C.: Government Printing Office, 1960.

———. *Foreign Relations of the United States: The Conferences at Cairo and Teheran, 1943.* Washington, D.C.: Government Printing Office, 1961.

———. *Foreign Relations of the United States: The Conferences at Malta and Yalta, 1945.* Washington, D.C.: Government Printing Office, 1955.

———. *Foreign Relations of the United States: The Conferences at Washington, 1941–1942, and Casablanca, 1943.* Washington, D.C.: Government Printing Office, 1988.

U.S. Senate. *Hearings on the Investigation of Far Eastern Policy.* 79th Cong., 1st sess. 1945.

U.S. Strategic Bombing Survey. *Japan's Struggle to End the War.* Washington, D.C.: 1946.

Woodward, E. L. *British Foreign Policy in the Second World War.* 5 vols. London: Her Majesty's Stationery Office. 1970–1976.

Articles

Alperovitz, Gar. "Why the United States Dropped the Bomb." *Technology Review* 93 (August 1990): 22–34.

Alperovitz, Gar, and Kai Bird. "Was Hiroshima Needed to End the War?" *Christian Science Monitor* (August 6, 1992): 19.

Bernstein, Barton J. "The Perils and Politics of Surrender: Ending the War with Japan and Avoiding the Third Atomic Bomb." *Pacific Historical Review* 46 (February 1977): 1–27.

———. "A Postwar Myth: 500,000 U.S. Lives Saved." *Bulletin of Atomic Scientists* 42 (June/July 1986): 38–40.

———. "Ike and Hiroshima: Did He Oppose It?" *Journal of Strategic Studies* 10 (September 1987): 377–89.

————. "Writing, Righting, or Wronging the Historical Record: President Truman's Letter on His Atomic-Bomb Decision." *Diplomatic History* 16 (winter 1992): 163–73.

Buhite, Russell D. "Soviet-American Relations and the Repatriation of Prisoners of War, 1945." *The Historian* 35 (May 1973): 384–97.

Gallicchio, Marc. "After Nagasaki: General Marshall's Plan for the Use of Tactical Nuclear Weapons." *Prologue: Quarterly of the National Archives* 24, no. 4 (winter 1991): 396–404.

Goldberg, Stanley. "Note on Barton Bernstein's 'Seizing the Contested Terrain of Early Nuclear History.'" *Society for Historians of American Foreign Relations Newsletter* (September 1993): 5–7.

Gormly, James L. "Secretary of State Byrnes: An Initial British Evaluation." *South Carolina Historical Magazine* 79 (July 1978): 198–205.

Khariton, Yuli, and Yuri Smirnov. "The Khariton Version." *Bulletin of Atomic Scientists* 49, no. 4 (May 1993): 140–47.

Maddox, Robert James. "Roosevelt and Stalin: The Final Days." *Continuity: A Journal of History* 6 (spring 1983): 113–22.

Miles, Rufus E. Jr. "Hiroshima: The Strange Myth of Half a Million Lives Saved." *International Security* 10 (fall 1985): 121–40.

Miscamble, Wilson D. "Anthony Eden and the Truman-Molotov Conversations, April 1945." *Diplomatic History* 2 (spring 1978): 167–80.

Orzell, Laurance J. "A Painful Problem: Poland in Allied Diplomacy, February–July, 1945." *Mid-America* 59 (October 1977): 147–69.

Sherwin, Martin J. "How Well They Meant." *Bulletin of Atomic Scientists* 41 (August 1985): 9–15.

Szilard, Leo. "A Personal History of the Atomic Bomb." *University of Chicago Roundtable* (September 25, 1949): 14–15.

Walker, J. Samuel "The Decision to Use the Bomb: A Historical Update." *Diplomatic History* 14, no. 1 (winter 1990): 97–114.

Books

Alperovitz, Gar. *Atomic Diplomacy: Hiroshima and Potsdam, the Use of the Atomic Bomb and the American Confrontation with Soviet Power.* New York: Simon and Schuster, 1965. Updated and expanded version by Elizabeth Sifton Books, 1985. 3d ed. Boulder, Colo.: Westview Press, 1995.

————. *Cold War Essays.* Garden City, N.Y.: Doubleday, 1970.

Ambrose, Stephen E. *The Supreme Commander: The War Years of General Dwight D. Eisenhower*. Garden City, N.Y.: Doubleday, 1970.

Armstrong, Anne. *Unconditional Surrender: The Impact of the Casablanca Policy upon World War II*. New Brunswick: Rutgers University Press, 1961.

Arnold, H. H. *Global Mission*. New York: Harper and Brothers, 1949.

Bailey, Thomas A. *A Diplomatic History of the American People*. 10th ed. Englewood Cliffs, N.J.: Prentice-Hall, 1980.

Baldwin, Hanson W. *Great Mistakes of the War*. New York: Harper and Brothers, 1949.

Bird, Kai. *The Chairman: John J. McCloy, the Making of the American Establishment*. New York: Simon and Schuster, 1992.

Bland, Larry I., ed. *George C. Marshall: Interviews and Reminiscences for Forrest C. Pogue*. Lexington, Va.: George C. Marshall Foundation, 1991.

Bohlen, Charles E. *Witness to History, 1929–1969*. New York: W. W. Norton, 1973.

Bradley, Omar, and Clay Blair. *A General's Life: An Autobiography by General of the Army Omar Bradley*. New York: Simon and Schuster, 1983.

Brooks, Lester. *Behind Japan's Surrender: The Secret Struggle that Ended an Empire*. New York: McGraw-Hill, 1968.

Buell, Thomas B. *Master of Seapower: A Biography of Fleet Admiral Ernest J. King*. Boston: Little, Brown, 1980.

Buhite, Russell D. *Decisions at Yalta: An Appraisal of Summit Diplomacy*. Wilmington, Del.: Scholarly Resources, 1986.

Bundy, McGeorge. *Danger and Survival: Choices about the Bomb in the First Fifty Years*. New York: Random House, 1988.

Butow, Robert Joseph Charles. *Japan's Decision to Surrender*. Stanford: Stanford University Press, 1954.

Byrnes, James F. *Speaking Frankly*. New York: Harper, 1947.

———. *All in One Lifetime*. New York: Harper, 1958.

Chase, John L. "Unconditional Surrender Reconsidered." In *Causes and Consequences of World War II*. Edited by Robert A. Divine. Chicago: Quadrangle, 1969.

Churchill, Winston S. *Triumph and Tragedy*. Boston: Houghton Mifflin, 1953.

Compton, Arthur Holly. *Atomic Quest*. New York: Oxford University Press, 1956.

Dallek, Robert. *Franklin D. Roosevelt and American Foreign Policy , 1932–1945*. New York: Oxford University Press, 1979.

Daniels, Jonathan. *Man of Independence*. Philadelphia: Lippincott, 1950.

Davis, Nuel Pharr. *Lawrence and Oppenheimer*. New York: Simon and Schuster, 1968.

Dilks, David, ed. *The Diaries of Sir Alexander Cadogan, 1938–1945*. New York: G. P. Putnam's Sons, 1972.

Divine, Robert A., ed. *Causes and Consequences of World War II*. Chicago: Quadrangle, 1969.

Dockrill, Saki, ed. *From Pearl Harbor to Hiroshima: The Second World War in Asia and the Pacific*. London: Macmillan, 1994.

Donovan, Robert J. *Conflict and Crisis: The Presidency of Harry S. Truman, 1945–1948*. New York: W. W. Norton, 1977.

Drea, Edward J. *MacArthur's Ultra: Codebreaking and the War against Japan*. Lawrence: University Press of Kansas, 1992.

Eisenhower, Dwight D. *Crusade in Europe*. Garden City, N.Y.: Doubleday, 1948.

———. *Mandate for Change*. Garden City, N.Y.: Doubleday, 1963.

Feis, Herbert. *The Atomic Bomb and the End of World War II*. Rev. ed. Princeton: Princeton University Press.

Ferrell, Robert H. *Harry S. Truman: A Life*. Columbia: University of Missouri Press, 1994.

Ferrell, Robert H., ed. *Dear Bess: The Letters from Harry to Bess Truman , 1910–1959*. New York: W. W. Norton, 1983.

———. *Off the Record: The Private Papers of Harry S. Truman*. New York: Harper, 1980.

———. *Truman in the White House: The Diaries of Eben A. Ayers*. Columbia: University of Missouri Press, 1991.

Fleming, D. F. *The Cold War and Its Origins*. Vol 1. Garden City, N.Y.: Doubleday, 1961.

Frisch, Otto. *What Little I Remember*. Cambridge: Cambridge University Press, 1979.

Gaddis, John Lewis. *The United States and the Origins of the Cold War, 1941–1947*. New York: Columbia University Press, 1972.

Gardner, Lloyd C. *Architects of Illusion*. Chicago: Quadrangle, 1970.

Gosling, F. G. *The Manhattan Project: Science in the Second World War*. Washington, D.C.: Department of Energy, 1990.

Grob, Gerald N., ed. *Statesman and Statecraft in the Modern West: Essays in Honor of Dwight E. Lee and H. Donaldson Jordon.* Barre, Mass.: Barre Publishers, 1967.

Groves, Leslie R. *Now It Can Be Told: The Story of the Manhattan Project.* New York: Harper, 1962.

Hankey, Maurice. *Politics, Trials, and Errors.* Chicago: Henry Regnery, 1950.

Harriman, W. Averell, and Ellie Abel. *Special Envoy to Churchill and Stalin, 1941–1946.* Garden City, N.Y.: Doubleday, 1971.

Hayes, Grace Person. *The History of the Joint Chiefs of Staff in World War II: The War against Japan.* Annapolis: Naval Institute Press, 1982.

Herken, Gregg. *The Winning Weapon: The Atomic Bomb in the Cold War, 1945–1950.* New York: Alfred A. Knopf, 1980.

Hershberg, James G. *James B. Conant: Harvard to Hiroshima and the Making of the Nuclear Age.* New York: Alfred A. Knopf, 1993.

Hewlett, Richard G., and Oscar E. Anderson Jr. *A History of the United States Atomic Energy Commission.* Vol. 1, *The New World, 1939–1946.* University Park: The Pennsylvania State University Press, 1962.

Holloway, David. *Stalin and the Bomb: The Soviet Union and Atomic Energy, 1939–1956.* New Haven: Yale University Press, 1994.

Hull, Cordell. *The Memoirs of Cordell Hull.* 2 vols. New York: Macmillan, 1948.

Irye, Akira. *The Cold War in Asia.* Englewood Cliffs, N.J.: Prentice-Hall, 1974.

Ismay, Hastings. *The Memoirs of General Lord Ismay.* New York: Viking Press, 1960.

Keckskemeti, Paul. *Strategic Surrender: The Politics of Victory and Defeat.* Stanford: Stanford University Press, 1958.

Kennan, George F. *Memoirs: 1925–1950.* Boston: Little, Brown, 1967.

Kimberley, M. M. *Short Course in Uranium Deposits, Their Mineralogy and Origin.* Toronto: University of Toronto Press, 1978.

Kirkendall, Richard S., ed. *The Harry S. Truman Encyclopedia.* Boston: G. K. Hall, 1989.

Knebel, Fletcher, and Charles W. Bailey II. *No High Ground.* New York: Harper and Brothers, 1960.

Krueger, Walter. *From Down Under to Nippon: The Story of Sixth Army in World War II.* Washington, D.C.: Combat Forces Press, 1953.

LaFeber, Walter. *The American Age: U.S. Foreign Policy at Home and Abroad.* 2d ed. New York: W. W. Norton, 1994.

Lanouette, William, and Bela Szilard. *Genius in the Shadows: A Biography of Leo Szilard, the Man behind the Bomb*. New York: Charles Scribner's Sons, 1992.

Leahy, William D. *I Was There: The Personal Story of the Chief of Staff to Presidents Roosevelt and Truman Based on His Notes and Diaries Made at the Time*. New York: Whittlesey House, 1950.

Lukacs, John. *1945: Year Zero*. Garden City, N.Y.: Doubleday, 1978.

McBride, Joseph. *Frank Capra: The Catastrophe of Success*. New York: Simon and Schuster, 1992.

McCloy, John J. *The Challenge to American Foreign Policy*. Cambridge: Cambridge University Press, 1953.

Maddox, Robert James. *The New Left and the Origins of the Cold War*. Princeton: Princeton University Press, 1973.

———. *From War to Cold War: The Education of Harry S. Truman*. Boulder, Colo.: Westview Press, 1988.

Mee, Charles L., Jr. *Meeting at Potsdam*. New York: M. Evans, 1975.

Messer, Robert L. *The End of an Alliance: James F. Byrnes, Roosevelt, Truman, and the Origins of the Cold War*. Chapel Hill: University of North Carolina Press, 1982.

Mets, David R. *Master of Airpower: General Carl A. Spaatz*. Novato, Calif.: Presidio Press, 1988.

Murphy, Robert. *Diplomat among Warriors*. New York: Pyramid, 1964.

Norton, Mary Beth, David M. Katzman, Paul D. Escott, Howard P. Chudacoff, Thomas G. Paterson, and William M. Tuttle Jr., *A People and a Nation: A History of the United States*. 3d ed. Boston: Houghton Mifflin, 1990.

O'Connor, Raymond G. *Diplomacy for Victory: FDR and Unconditional Surrender*. New York: W. W. Norton, 1971.

Pogue, Forrest C. *George C. Marshall: Organizer for Victory*. New York: Viking Press, 1973.

———. *George C. Marshall: Statesman*. New York: Viking Press, 1987.

Resis, Albert, ed. *Molotov Remembers: Inside Kremlin Politics*. Chicago: Ivan R. Dee, 1993.

Reston, James. *Deadline: Memoirs*. New York: Random House, 1991.

Rhodes, Richard. *The Making of the Atomic Bomb*. New York: Simon and Schuster, 1986.

Roosevelt, Elliott, ed. *FDR: His Personal Letters, 1928–1945*. 2 vols. New York: Duell, Sloan, and Pearce, 1950.

Rose, Lisle A. *After Yalta.* New York: Charles Scribner's Sons, 1973.

Rosenman, Samuel I., ed. *The Public Papers and Addresses of Franklin D. Roosevelt.* 13 vols. New York: Harper and Brothers, 1950.

Sherwin, Martin J. *A World Destroyed: The Atomic Bomb and the Grand Alliance.* New York: Alfred A. Knopf, 1975.

Sherwood, Robert E. *Roosevelt and Hopkins: An Intimate History.* New York: Harper, 1950.

Sigal, Leon V. *Fighting to a Finish: The Politics of War Termination in the United States and Japan, 1945.* Ithaca: Cornell University Press, 1988.

Skates, John R. *The Invasion of Japan: Alternative to the Bomb.* Columbia: University of South Carolina Press, 1994.

Smith, Alice K. *A Peril and a Hope: The Scientists' Movement in America, 1945–1950.* Chicago: University of Chicago Press, 1965.

Smith, Gaddis. *American Diplomacy during the Second World War, 1941–1945.* 2d ed. New York: Alfred A. Knopf, 1985.

Snell, John L. *Wartime Origins of the East-West Dilemma over Germany.* New Orleans: Houser, 1959.

Spector, Ronald H. *Eagle against the Sun: The American War with Japan.* New York: Vintage Books, 1985.

Spector, Ronald H., ed. *Listening to the Enemy.* Wilmington, Del.: Scholarly Resources, 1988.

Stimson, Henry L., and McGeorge Bundy. *On Active Service in Peace and War.* New York: Harper and Brothers, 1948.

Stoff, Michael B., Jonathan F. Fanton, and R. Hal Williams. *The Manhattan Project: A Documentary Introduction to the Atomic Age.* New York: McGraw-Hill, 1991.

Szasz, Ferenc Morton. *The Day the Sun Rose Twice: The Story of the Trinity Site Nuclear Explosion, July 16, 1945.* Albuquerque: University of New Mexico Press, 1984.

Truman, Harry S. *Year of Decisions.* Garden City, N.Y.: Doubleday, 1955.

Ward, Patricia. *The Threat of Peace: James F. Byrnes and the Council of Foreign Ministers, 1945–1946.* Kent: Kent State University Press, 1979.

Warner, Dennis, and Peggy Warner (with Commander Sadeo Seno, JMSDF [Ret.]). *The Sacred Warriors: Japan's Suicide Legions.* New York: Van Nostrand Reinhold, 1982.

Weart, Spencer R., and Gertrud Weiss Szilard. *Leo Szilard: His Version of the Facts; Selected Recollections and Correspondence.* Cambridge: MIT Press, 1978.

Williams, William Appleman, *The Tragedy of American Diplomacy*. Rev. and enl. ed. New York: Dell, 1962.

Wyden, Peter. *Day One: Before Hiroshima and After.* New York: Simon and Schuster, 1984.

Zacharias, Ellis M. *Secret Missions: The Story of an Intelligence Officer.* New York: G. P. Putnam's Sons, 1946.